Dancing in the Flames

Dancing

in the Flames

THE DARK GODDESS IN
THE TRANSFORMATION
OF CONSCIOUSNESS

Marion Woodman and Elinor Dickson

VINTAGE CANADA
A Division of Random House of Canada

VINTAGE CANADA EDITION, 1997

Chapter 5, "The Rose in the Fire," originally appeared in Human Medicine 6:2, Spring
1990, and is reprinted by permission of the publisher.

Chapter 6, "Chaos and Creativity," is based, with significant changes, on a recording of a
talk by Marion Woodman by the same title published by Oral Traditions Archives,
P.O. Box 51155, Pacific Grove, CA 93950.

Canadian Cataloguing in Publication Data

Woodman, Marion, 1928 –
        Dancing in the flames: the dark goddess in the transformation of consciousness

ISBN 0-676-97047-8

1. Women – Psychology. 2. Femininity (Psychology).
3. Goddesses. I. Dickson, Elinor J., 1939 –   .
II. Title.

HQ1206.W65 1997   155.6'33   C96-932148-1

Printed in the United States of America

⊖ This edition is printed on acid-free paper that meets
the American National Standards Institute Z39.48 Standard.

10 9 8 7 6 5 4 3 2 1

To Sophia

Integrity in love
is the only true guide
to the wisdom
that leads to freedom.

Contents

ACKNOWLEDGMENTS ix

INTRODUCTION 1

1. THE FIERCE AND LOVING GODDESS 13
From Great Mother to Goddess 14
The Eclipse of the Great Goddess 21
The Black Goddess 28
Rediscovering the Light in Matter 36

2. A HEART IN THE BALANCE 47
Beyond Duality 48
The Judgment of Maat 54
Building the Subtle Body 73

3. TELLING IT LIKE IT IS 87

4. AND A CRONE SHALL LEAD THEM 125

5. THE ROSE IN THE FIRE 163

6. CHAOS AND CREATIVITY 177

7. WHERE THREE DREAMS CROSS 201
The Eye of the Beholder 214

NOTES 231

CREDITS 239

Acknowledgments

Thank you

to our analysands and friends who courageously have shared their inner journeys;

to Joan Neville for her support and careful reading of the text;

to Ross;

to Michael Mendis, our typist;

to Emily Hilburn Sell and David O'Neal, our editors;

to ShaSha Island in Georgian Bay where this book was conceived where Sophia shines in the rose quartz of the Canadian Shield and dances in the fire of the Northern Lights.

—Elinor and Marion

Dancing in the Flames

Introduction

WHO IS THE GODDESS? Who is *she* who sometimes replaces *he* in our prayers? Is Goddess any different from God in our inner pantheon or have we merely changed the nouns and pronouns? What are the attributes of the Goddess? Who is she as Mother, Virgin, Crone? How does she relate to the masculine? If we throw ourselves into the flames of desire and then dance with her in the refining fire, how will our everyday lives be changed? If we really do believe she holds the whole world in the palm of her love, how do we live with that sacramental truth at our center?

This book explores these questions concerning the unknown feminine figure who is appearing in the dreams of so many contemporary men and women. Many people dismiss dreams as speculative and anecdotal. However, for those of us who have lived in close touch with our dreams all our lives, they offer truth far beyond facts. They bring new perspectives and new understandings to our experience. Fred Alan Wolf, a theoretical physicist, claims that "dreaming is vital to our survival as a species and a necessary 'learning laboratory' wherein the self and the universe evolve. In brief, matter evolves through dreams."[1]

This unknown figure whom so many people encounter in their sleep speaks to the psyche and to the very cells of the body. She seems to push through from the very depths of the collective unconscious like a universal force that speaks individually and culturally. Hopefully, this book will add to the pool of consciousness that is expanding around her.

Although she takes many different forms, this goddess—sometimes a Black Madonna or an Asian or Indian Madonna—

always carries authority. She guides and advises and acts with absolute clarity, often with a startling sense of humor that delights in play. These moments in dreams or active imagination are filled with her compassion for our human situation. She is blunt, neither indulgent nor sentimental. She demands embodiment. Living in the creative intercourse between chaos and order, she calls us to enter into the dance of creation, "her love in her living body."[2] She speaks to men as clearly as to women.

Both genders need a well-differentiated masculine and a well-differentiated feminine. The power structures of patriarchy have profoundly wounded both, making mature relationships almost impossible without hard psychic work. As a culture, we are presently stuck in the parental complexes. Many women have worked for years trying to find their own identity, freed from the mother and father complexes. Men, too, are working to find their own feeling values, values that are not dependent on pleasing or hating Mother and Father and all they represent. The archetype of the Black Madonna, or Lilith, or Mary Magdalene may be a way to freedom for both.

In writing this book, the authors have been very aware of the pitfalls of using the terms *masculine* and *feminine*. While these words are not synonymous with *male* and *female*, they unquestionably carry connotations that are so ingrained in our psyches that we consciously and unconsciously react to them with ancient gender prejudices. It would be a great relief to forget the words, but the fact remains that the balance of energies in the dream cannot be understood without a recognition of the interplay between the male and female figures. (The dream images are rooted in the instincts.) This interplay enacts the balance or lack of balance between the two complementary energies that are continually relating to each other within us and without, continually struggling to compensate for the one-sided world of consciousness. The Chinese yang and yin represent the two energies as two fish in a circle, each containing part of the other. The Hindus represent them as Shiva and Shakti, the universal lovers out of whose divine embrace everything is born. And in the Bible, the new paradigm is imaged as the New Jerusalem gradually taking shape throughout both the Old and New Testaments. In the final book, the New Jerusalem descends as a Bride to meet the Bridegroom in the divine marriage.

Part of the resistance to the words *masculine* and *feminine* lies in our inability to accept that each of us contains both masculine and feminine energy and that both energies are divine. We pay lip service to the concept consciously, but if we listen to ourselves, we hear the archaic, gendered, pigeon-holed thinking plop out of our mouths like an unexpected toad. For example, some men and women who accept the Goddess as equal to the God and proclaim her divinity in matter can still become angry if they hear femininity related to earth. At some unconscious level, they continue to relate femininity, to earth, snake, Satan, dark, evil—all these words that keep femininity in a subordinate position, or worse, a diabolical one.

If we expand our consciousness a bit, we begin to see that our attitude to the Earth, to nature, and to our own bodies is radically shifting. In the dire consequences arising from the well-documented abuse of Earth, nature, and our bodies, we begin to see that they will no longer tolerate the tyranny of our control. They will no longer submit to the slavery to which we try to subject them. The Goddess is the life force in matter. She has laws that have now to be learned and obeyed. Her indwelling presence is the sacred energy, energy on which our egos have no legitimate claim. Confronted with this reality—a reality that is a confrontation with our own threatened survival—we realize that like Earth, nature, our bodies, we too are the vessels of an energy far greater than anything that tries to contain it. We realize that we, like the rest of nature, are participating members in the vast community of life, whose sacredness we must embrace if we are to survive. If we are ever to arrive at this expanded consciousness, we will have to surrender our ego desires to the wisdom of the Self. Masculine and feminine will have to learn to cherish each other. (It is important to note here that Self with a capital S in Jung's terminology refers to the divine within that mirrors the divine without; self with a small s refers to the individual self.)

Many times throughout the book, we have chosen to use the word *transcendence* referring to the masculine spirit, and *immanence* referring to the indwelling feminine. Neither of us is a theologian, but both of us can believe in the unknowable mystery sometimes called God, and we can see that mystery manifesting its radiance through every living form in every moment. Transcendence uniting with Immanence. If you go into your garden, you may feel yourself present in the divine embrace right there in the presence of a golden sunflower with a mandala for its center—the Immanence of the Transcendent in the flower. (If not here, where?) Each has to be separated out from the other before the magnetic pull of the opposites brings them together.

While we are clarifying words, we need also to note that *patriarchy* and *masculinity* are not synonymous. Female patriarchs can be just as domineering as males. Like their male counterparts, they live in a patriarchal ethos that operates through control over others, over themselves, over nature. We need to recognize also that many men have a more finely honed femininity than many women. We all are the children of patriarchy and, therefore, we all have to take responsibility for a killer power shadow that would massacre the feminine and the masculine in whatever form they manifest. This book is not a defense of the feminine at the expense of the masculine. The one without the other leads to suicide or tyranny.

The historical data concerning the relationship of patriarchy to the feminine in Western culture has been well documented in other studies. The psychological implications of a few of the historical events of the past nine centuries have been included in chapter I in order to bring some added dimensions to the Black Madonna that lies buried in our depths. Psyche does not work on a basis of causality as history does. It does not respect temporal cause and effect patterns of everyday life. Sometimes historical facts illustrate psychological phenomena.

Historically, our Western concepts of feminine consciousness have been far too restricted to take in the Great Goddess as the majestic, empowered figure she once was. For most people today, femininity still has something to do with the social values that determine how a "lady" will act. That myopic vision makes it almost impossible for us to see the grandeur of the "thrones of wisdom" of the twelfth century. In Chartres Cathedral, for example, the great Goddess, Mary by name, sits on the *cathedra*, the throne of the cathedral. She is Wisdom, crowned with leaves. Enthroned on her knee is the young king, bearing in one hand the orb and raising two fingers of the other in blessing of her and the world. He is the Word made flesh, consciousness sitting on the lap of nature. Without the lap, consciousness is uprooted from its source, assuming a life of its own that can be self-devouring. It is as source that the lap is throne. The relationship between masculine and feminine is well balanced, if not on a physical scale, certainly on a psychic one.

Later, during the Renaissance, when the Christ figure became a suckling babe at the breast of the mother, the balance was dangerously upset in the direction of the tyranny of the feminine. The conventions of courtly love with its adoration of the feminine and the masculine putting itself in her service had intervened. Another aspect of the suckling babe is imaged in the pietas, in which the dead son lies in the lap of the Great Mother. History seldom, if ever, gets it right. The psyche, as a self-regulating system, yin and yang in perfect balance, is a vision that historically has yet to be realized. Even now, in the patriarchal excesses of militant feminism, we see in yet another swing of the pendulum, the failure to find the balance. In history, as in marriage, or within the individual, when a balance becomes stagnant, one or other of the energies moves out to new adventures. The spurt forces the complementary energy to move also, until a new balance is found. So the spiral moves.

In this book, we look at some of the history of the Goddess in order to orient ourselves in relation to the past. We look at contemporary dreams in an attempt to discern the quality of her energy, as it manifests today. We look at some of the recent scientific discoveries concerning the "light in matter." Because the Goddess in her virgin aspect carries the transformative energy, some of the recent findings of psychoneuroimmunology related to the transformation of energy bring new meaning to metaphors. Hopefully, new thoughts and new connections will open new eyes and new ears to what it means to worship the Goddess. Perhaps, too, by recognizing the dawning of feminine energy that is moving in the collective psyche, we may catch more of our own personal dreams and ask ourselves again, "What is conscious femininity?" What does the balance of masculine and feminine as a self-regulating system operating in both men and women look like?

THE GODDESS

It might be of value to you, the reader, to meditate on the Goddess for a few moments and then to write down a list of words that you associate with her. Afterwards, you might compare it with a list that came out of a recent workshop. The first associations, for the participants, were to the Goddess in her motherly aspects: Creator, nurturing, cherishing, large breasts, child-bearing, mandala, earth opening to sky, earth itself, solid like a rock, reality of the body. The other side of the mother archetype came out in words like untamed, volcanic, terrible, ferocious, voracious, Goddess of Death, Devourer of the Dark, inertia, crocodile, mud.

In working with these attributes, we have to recognize the difference between archetypal and personal energy. Archetypal energy carries a much higher charge than personal energy—the difference between a thunderbolt and a duckling's quack. Jung understood the archetype as a magnetic energy field at the core of a personal complex. For example, around our personal mother or loss of our personal mother, we build up powerful responses, psychologically and physically. These responses are laden with uterine, preverbal, and early childhood feelings. They reverberate in our responses to women in general.

At the core of the mother complex is the archetypal mother, the Goddess. The archetype itself cannot be seen. It is a potentially magnetic energy field onto which we fasten an image that is eventually projected out. That energy attracts or repels other creatures that come within its orbit. More important, it attracts or repels the ego so intensely that it can wipe out consciousness to the point where the ego is no longer present to make choices, yes or no or maybe.

Now, mud and crocodiles hold immense creative energy so long as you are not being sucked into them. But watch addicts steadily sink into the mud of mother crocodile if they take one bite out of the second muffin, or two swigs from a bottle of Scotch, or one lusty kiss too many, or too much of whatever their mud is. You can see in their glazed eye the moment the archetypal energy vanquishes the ego. No one is home. So long as the ego container is not strong enough to relate to that numinous power without identifying with it, destruction lies ahead. *To identify* is "to become" the God or Goddess without the feminine ground to reestablish the boundaries that return us to our humanity. *To relate* is to know that the ego is the instrument through which the divine energy flows. Pavarotti both relates when he honors the divine for his gift, and when he steps off the stage and becomes just plain Luciano enjoying his pasta.

In the early phases of learning to relate to archetypal energy, we usually think of the archetypal as having two opposing sides. Associating with the Mother, for example, we think of the positive mother as the nurturing, cherishing, protective feminine. We in the West split those characteristics off from the voracious, devouring, terrible Death Goddess. At the same time, we know that if we fail to break out of the feathered nest in our adolescence, we may find ourselves incapable of standing free. We may then be compelled to find another mother who will tenderly take away our strength.

If, on the other hand, we were raised by a judgmental, even rejecting, mother, we may have assimilated her strength in order to survive. Simply by contending with her every day, we finally stood on our own feet—liberated. And free to find a liberated partner, free to create a mature partnership.

With the broader perspective, we can see that the words *positive* and *negative* do not ultimately apply. They become judgmental words. The fact is the Goddess who gives life is the Goddess who takes life away. That fact allows for no sentimentality. In feminine thinking, we hold the paradox beyond the contradictions. She is the flux of life in which creation gives place to destruction, destruction in service to life gives place to creation. .

Relationships in our culture are in crises around mothering. For centuries, mothering has been synonymous with femininity, and many of us still think our femininity is well developed if we are manifesting the nurturing, solid-like-a-rock aspects of the mother. If we look again, however, with a new pair of glasses, we may ask ourselves some new questions: Have I established manageable boundaries for my children? Do I mirror them, reflect back to them their own feelings and values, or do I expect them to mirror me? Am I dependent on their dependence on me? Am I coming from power or love? Am I identified with mothering? Am I a conscious mother?

Many men (including male therapists) are doing as much mothering as females. They, too, need to ask themselves these questions. In homosexual and lesbian relationships, these questions are equally relevant, because mothering is a part of every relationship.

Men are also looking at their own wounding from the patriarchs (both male and female). If they have been raised as son heroes, they may be fearful of their own femininity. They may know that their fathers cannot accept the reality of their sons. As sun heroes of their mother, they may have to deal with shattered idealism. "Who am I when the ideals crumble? What aspects of myself can I not face? Greed, lust, violence? Who am I without my inflated fantasies?" To pass from son to mature man, they need the strength to hold onto the totality of themselves—their full humanity, shadow included. That humanity is grounded in the love that holds the cells of the body together. The life force is another aspect of the Goddess. Men's bodies, like women's bodies, carry both the masculine and feminine energies.

All of us need to remind ourselves that mothering is only one aspect of femininity. Otherwise, in our self-satisfaction in being conscious mothers, we are going to be shocked out of our complacency when our partner one day responds from a place that is not mother. The feminine that is striving to find its own voice comes from the Virgin archetype. This is not the voice that comes from the constricted throat and military shoulders of the patriarchal complex saying, "This is who I am and this is what I want."

The real work in many relationship problems for both men and women is separating their new femininity, their own virgin, from the mother complex. Thus, instead of acting from introjected, automatic responses, the virgin learns to live spontaneously from the emotions and values that are grounded in her own musculature. The initiated virgin is the feminine who is who she is because that's who she is. Like the virgin forest, she is full of her own life force, full of potential, pregnant. Her characteristics cannot be totally separated from mother and crone. One day, hopefully, mother, virgin, crone become an integrated whole.

For purposes of differentiating the Virgin, let us look once again at the workshop associations: resonating, veiled, embodied, connected, erotic, natural rhythms, fearless, fecundity, living in the Now, poetry, light in the darkness, consciousness in the darkness, complete within herself, black.

As soon as we put the word "black" with the Black Virgin or Black Madonna, we hear deeper resonances. According to Robert Graves in his exquisite version of *The Song of Songs*, "[t]he words black and wise [are] almost indistinguishable in Semitic script."[3] Further explaining the connection between *black* and *wise* he writes, "The many black Virgins in Spain and Southern France . . . are black because the Saracen occupation during the Middle Ages taught the local Christians to equate 'black' with 'wise'—hence the 'Black Arts' were originally the Wise Arts."[4]

This connection between blackness and wisdom may also have

something to do with the Black Madonnas that were brought back to Europe by the Crusaders from the Islamic world. Their love for these figures was sometimes connected to their belief that they had survived a fire and, therefore, understood their suffering. It was love forged in fire. Within a century, the Black Death was ravaging Europe. People began to fear that they were being punished by God for heretical practices. The order of the universe (wisdom), which they connected with the Goddess, was collapsing into chaos, the Black Arts, and everything associated with their own shadow side. Their love for the Black Madonna was not diminished but became tinged with fear.

Today her darkness is associated with the unknown, repressed side of our femininity. She is intimately tied to the integration of shadow materials as compensation for the one-sidedness of logocentric thinking, even, as we shall see, as the acausal behavior of atoms at a subatomic level compensates for an overdetermined perception of their classically conceived rational behavior. Experiencing her in our body is a startling step toward experiencing ourselves whole. That sense of wholeness is essential to healing. It cannot, we shall suggest, be achieved until we are able to surrender in trust to a reality that cannot be contained in a rational system of causality, a system that the new physics has now, if not abandoned, at least corrected by making it answerable to a larger indeterminacy.

The Black Madonna somehow carries the energy of the Black spirituals as sung by Blacks—passionate, rooted in suffering, lusty, singing the tragedy in the ordinary, imponderable, subatomic depths.

The connection between Virgin, Wisdom, and Sophia is significant. In their book entitled *Sophia*, Cady, Ronan, and Taussig explain their "use of the name 'Sophia' . . . when the biblical translators invariably prefer 'Wisdom.' Sophia is, in fact, the Greek word for wisdom, or rather, a transliteration of that word. Sophia immediately suggests a person rather than a concept. . . . Use of the title 'Wisdom' rather than the name 'Sophia' contributes to further avoidance and repression of this unique biblical person."[5] Since the unknown feminine figure that appears in contemporary dreams carries so many of Sophia's attributes, and since these attributes span feminine qualities from primal goddess to immanent radiance, we will sometimes refer to her as Sophia.

The Virgin is not to be identified with Mother. She is born

from the womb of the conscious mother within us. She is matter in the process of being refined—dancing in the flames. Within her, the metamorphoses are slowly taking place. The Virgin carries the new consciousness—the consciousness that may radically shift the consciousness of the planet, and in the new physics *is* shifting it. We will focus on this process in depth in chapters 6 and 7.

The Crone is the third in the feminine trinity. Words associated with her begin to take on a different dimension: timeless, spaceless, detached, fearless, free, beauty, guide, Wisdom, surrender, spontaneity, paradox.

While age does not necessarily create a crone, certainly "the slings and arrows of outrageous fortune" do have something to do with her maturing. She evolves out of the conscious Mother and conscious Virgin. As we, men and women, respond to what life brings, the Crone very gradually presents herself. She can shock us when we hear what comes out of her mouth. She speaks her blunt truth and lets the chips fall where they will. Not that she is without feeling, certainly not without sensitivity. But she has seen enough to be able to separate the irrelevant from the essence. And she has neither the time nor the energy to waste on superficialities.

Having passed through her crossroads, the divine intersecting the human, the Crone will have learned to accept the surrender of her ego desires and, having accepted her own destiny, she is free and fearless. She no longer has to justify her existence, nor fear the judgment of others. This deep acceptance of herself unites her with the Virgin—the Virgin forever transforming into the maturity of the Crone. The new sense of freedom brings with it a childlike energy—spontaneity, play, creative ideas. With her well-developed masculinity, she may put her ideas into action in the world, ideas that confront causality with what Jung calls *synchronicity*.

In a well-honed crone, we may feel the transparency of her body that is open to another reality. Being with her, we feel the presence of a timeless, spaceless world. We begin to see everything from two sides—the side that is totally in life and the side that is already dwelling in disembodied soul. The Crone helps us hold the paradox.

Because she has learned to love without any personal agenda, she makes an excellent guide. She knows how tough and how gentle we have to be to enter into this life and to leave it. She holds an unspeakable wisdom in the very cells of her body. The beauty and the horror of the whole of life are held together in love.

The Crone energy is strong enough to guide men into the feminine. She can hold the container in which they can experience their own shadow rage without destroying themselves or others.

As we move into the new millennium, we are dancing deep in the flames—physical and psychic. Sophia calls to us as she has called throughout the centuries.

> O people: I am calling you;
> my cry goes out to the children of humanity.
> You ignorant ones, study discretion;
> and you fools, come to your senses.
> Listen, I have serious things to tell you,
> and from my lips come honest words.
> My mouth proclaims the truth . . .
> All the words I say are right,
> Nothing twisted in them, nothing false,
> all straightforward to the one who understands,
> honest to those who know what knowledge means.
> Accept my discipline rather than silver,
> knowledge in preference to gold.
> For wisdom is more precious than pearls,
> and nothing else is so worthy of desire.[6]

The Fierce and Loving Goddess   I

THE INVOCATION TO KALI

... The Black Goddess Kali, the terrible one of many names, "difficult of approach," whose stomach is a void and so can never be filled, and whose womb is giving birth forever to all things ...

—JOSEPH CAMPBELL

It is time for the invocation:
Kali, be with us.
Violence, destruction, receive our homage.
Help us to bring darkness into the light,
To lift out the pain, the anger,
Where it can be seen for what it is—
The balance-wheel for our vulnerable, aching love.
Put the wild hunger where it belongs,
Within the act of creation,
Crude power that forges a balance
Between hate and love.
Help us to be the always hopeful
Gardeners of the spirit
Who know that without darkness
Nothing comes to birth
As without light
Nothing flowers.
Bear the roots in mind,
You, the dark one, Kali,
Awesome power.

—MAY SARTON

FROM GREAT MOTHER TO GODDESS

ABOUT FIVE YEARS AGO I was sitting in my sun room reading the morning paper. A sense of excitement grew as I read an article on the dedication of a temple to the black goddess, Kali, right here in Toronto, Canada. Although I knew very little about her, I had become fascinated by her image. I saw her dancing, a bloodied sword in one hand and a severed, bearded head in the other. Her lolling tongue hung out of her gaping mouth, and around her neck dangled a necklace of skulls. Why was I fascinated by such a fierce image? Was I harboring some unconscious rage that wanted to burst out? Much as the patriarchal systems that dominate our culture irritate me, even enrage me, I sensed that that wasn't the explanation. I felt Kali herself crying out to me.

At first glance, Kali comes across as a fierce embodiment of the devouring mother, who gobbles up everything, even her own children. A closer look, however, reveals a great halo around her head, a halo not seen in early depictions of the Great Mother. The halo attests to Kali's status as Goddess, to her need to be understood not only as devourer, but also as transformer. She is black, dark as the matrix, dark as the vortex, from which all creation comes and to which it returns. To her devotees, she is like a black sapphire; radiance shines through her blackness. She dances and laughs with abandon, intoxicated with the mystery she is.

Kali's dual role as devouring mother and enlightened goddess is highlighted in a poem written by Vivekananda, a Hindu sage of the twentieth century.

> "I am not one of those," he chanted,
> "Who put the garland of skulls round
> Thy neck,

The Great Goddess Kali, India. Kali, when viewed in her highest form as wife of Shiva, is a perfect example of the assimiliation of the old Great Mother image into a new and higher corpus of Great Goddess mythology.

"And then look back in terror
"And call Thee 'The Merciful.'"
"The heart must become
   a burial ground,
"Pride, selfishness, and desire all
   broken into dust,
"Then and then alone will the Mother
   dance there!"[1]

In this poem, Vivekananda dissociates himself from those who project their own fear onto Kali and then tremble before her, seeking to appease her wrath. In these few opening lines, the poet captures the essence of genuine Great Goddess worship: there must be a death to the ego self; there must be a transformation in which there is a letting go of all false values, of all the things that the egotistical nature mistakenly clings to. In the burial ground of the heart, Kali's enlightened devotees see beyond literal death to the death of values rooted in fear. When they come to accept death as a necessary step in their transformation, then Kali can dance her dance of perpetual becoming. Once her cycles are accepted, those who love her are free of the fear of death, free of their own vulnerability, free to live her mystery.

The mystery of Kali is that she is perpetually destroying and, at the same time, creating—destroying in order to create, creating in order to destroy, death in the service of life, life in the service of death. Kali is time, immanence, ceaseless becoming, nature as process. As ceaseless motion that has no purpose other than its own activity, Kali is as indifferent to the demands of the ego as she is to the instinct to survive. The opposites of life and death, love and hate, humility and pride, poverty and riches, mercy and revenge, justice and tyranny, mean nothing to her, because with her there is no polarity. For Kali, all experience is one—life as well as death.

In the Indian villages where Kali is celebrated in her own festival, the villagers spend weeks shaping a clay statue of their beloved Goddess, she who is the feminine wisdom deep in the body, who makes no sense in the light of rationality. When her day arrives, they sing and dance from their primordial roots, carry her through the streets, and at the close of day throw her into the river. Instantly, she goes back to mud. All the love and care that have gone into her creation are dissolved in the waters. Kali's creation and dissolution symbolize what the world of appearances looks like to those who recognize it as part of a larger totality. Those who can accept her cycle—life and death—are no longer vulnerable. They are fearless.

Along with Krishna, Kali became one of the most popular deities in the Hindu pantheon. As David Kingsley points out, "In many Tantric texts Kali's position is unambiguously declared to be that of a great deity; indeed, in many texts she is declared the supreme deity, triumphant over all others, equivalent, in fact, to Brahman."[2] This rise in the worship of Kali and her subsequent elevation to supremacy represented a significant step in the evolution of matriarchal mythology.

Drawing on the works of Bachofen, Neumann, Campbell, and others, Ken Wilber outlines three stages in this evolution. The first stage, the typhon, refers generally to the period of earliest *Homo sapiens* (Neanderthal and Cro-Magnon), and is itself a structure of consciousness dominated by body-bound mentality and instincts.[3] "In the earliest typhonic times," Wilber writes, "the Great Mother was probably not much more than an impact, a non-verbal shock at separate-self existence, and an expression of simple biological dependence."[4] In this period, the Mother was the one who fed, who provided the necessities of life through plants, seeds, and animals. Caves afforded the protection of her womb, which eventually became the tomb in the cycle of life and death. She was both the nourisher of life and the destroyer. Life and death, joy and pain, were a seamless reality. "And death," declares the Earth Mother, in Shelley's *Prometheus Unbound,*

> shall be the last embrace of her
> Who takes the life she gave, even as a mother,
> Folding her child, says, "Leave me not again."[5]

Life, in this first phase, was closely associated with blood. The monthly bleeding of women was thought to be the source of creation: when a baby was being formed in the womb, the bleeding stopped. New life was, therefore, assumed to come from the blood of the mother. Likewise, the Great Mother created out of her blood. She was the womb/tomb of existence. All physical existence and the Earth's abundant provision for the sustenance of life flowed from that essential source—the Mother's fertility.

The second stage of Great Mother mythology, as Wilber describes it, grew out of the earliest awareness of separation from the mother. As humans slowly separated out from nature, the primitive emotions of life and joy became differentiated from those of death and pain. In this phase, "the self sense [was] more structured, more articulate, and so likewise the Great Mother. Men and women were more conscious of their own tenuous existence, and thus more conscious of the Great Mother—what she was, and what she demanded."[6] As life and death became polarized, humans began to contemplate the possibility of nonbeing—a terrifying prospect for a fledgling consciousness. Death came to be invested with starkness and terror, and the question then became, "How do I please Mother so that she will give me life rather than death?"

> [W]hat was the way to appease the Great Mother, to keep her as protectress and prevent her wrathful Vengeance? Give her what she demands—blood! And likewise, invent a precise way to do it—ritual! Thus, the first great ritual was a ritual of blood sacrifice, offered to the Great Mother—to Mother Nature—in a bartered attempt to quench her desire for blood. . . . Blood is indeed bodily life, and if you want to purchase life, you buy it with blood. So goes paleologic; like magic it works with partial truths; and like magic, since it is unable to grasp higher perspectives or wider contexts, it arrives at barbaric conclusions.[7]

Just prior to and during the early part of the pre-Iron Age, a third form of matriarchal mythology began to emerge. Those with a more highly evolved consciousness began to see beyond the concrete reality of nature and saw into the underlying essence that pervaded and unified all things. With this insight came the first glimmerings of an awareness of the subtle or archetypal realm. The unifying light in nature came to be worshiped as the Goddess, the mediator of transformation.

The Great Mother was seen as the "One," the creatrix of all things and the ultimate source of life and death. Her Oneness was bound to the realm of nature as the unconscious personification of it. The Goddess, as distinct from the Mother, while remaining immanent in nature, and while demanding sacrifice, did not require blood sacrifice. Worship of the Goddess required a movement from the literal and concrete to the symbolic, a movement that launched a radical mutation in consciousness. This mutation effected a release from the mother-bound limitations of nature not unlike that which occurred when Abraham was released from the blood sacrifice of his son, Isaac, a release that launched the ethical consciousness identified with the Semitic tradition.

The Goddess reached a high level of conscious articulation in many of her numerous forms. Perhaps the best known are the Egyptian goddess Isis and Sophia, the wisdom figure of the Old Testament. The sense of oneness, the sense of absolute authority that each carried in her respective milieu is evident from the following descriptions. In the Book of Wisdom, Sophia "reaches mightily from end to end of the earth (8.1) and . . . is praised because 'Though she is but one, she can do all things' (7.27)."[8] In the aretalogies of Isis we read, "I am Isis, sole ruler forever, and I oversee the ends of the sea and the earth. I have authority, and though I am but one I oversee them (Cyrene 4)."[9]

Isis was recognized as "the creator of the universe and as such preside[d] over all its elements: 'I divided earth from heaven. I set forth the paths of the stars. I established the course of the sun and moon. . . .' (Cyme 12–14) . . . 'Whatever I determine, this too will be performed for me: all things obey me' (Cyme 46)."[10]

The goddess, Sophia, whom we are called to enthrone in our

The Black Virgin of Rocamadour, France.

Isis suckling Horus. The Earth, the lap of the Great Mother, is the seat of power. The Egyptian goddess Isis and the Virgin Mary are both often represented as the Throne of Wisdom.

being, is our life, "and no choice possession can compare with her."[11] Continually, she prepares a banquet that is food for the soul.

> Wisdom has built her house, she has set up her seven columns; she has dressed her meal, mixed her wine, yes, she has spread her table. She has sent out her maidens; she calls from the heights out over the city: "Let whoever is simple turn in here; to him who lack understanding, I say, 'Come, eat of my food and drink of the wine I have mixed!' Forsake foolishness that you may live; advance in the way of understanding."[12]

The most important factor in the evolution of consciousness is that in reaching this level of archetypal Oneness the individual dies to the sense of a separate self. As stated by Wilber,

> That simple yet crucial insight—"the sacrifice of self discloses the Eternal"—was the esoteric insight empowering the mythology of self-sacrifice to the Great Goddess, sacrifice carried out in prayer, in contemplation, in meditative ritual and ceremony, in symbolic Mass.[13]

Worshiping the Great Mother meant identifying with her and trying to appease her great power over one's life by offering a sacrifice outside of oneself. The worship of the Goddess, on the other hand, involved entering into a process of self-transformation. In order to reach the desired level of archetypal oneness, one had to transcend the ego boundaries. At this early stage in ego development, transcendence could be very threatening. It was safer merely to maintain *participation mystique* with the Mother. Penetration to the level of archetypal Oneness involved moving beyond the body-self, beyond the ego-self, to a realization of soul consciousness.

THE ECLIPSE OF THE GREAT GODDESS

With the onset of the Iron Age, worship of the Sun God, albeit a Sun God bound to the Mother, began to emerge. As consciousness developed, a sense of self began to emerge from the body-self. This is the natural course of human development. As the self developed even further, human beings began to take their projections of divinity off the Great Mother and the Goddess and to identify with the ascendant symbol of the Sun God. Whereas they had once taken power from nature through bone, feathers, and blood, now they sought to exert power over nature. All the powers of nature that had been an expression of the Great Mother were transferred to the Sun. Humanity moved from polytheism to monotheism. No longer did the king serve as the phallic consort of the Great Mother, but, in keeping with the shift to monotheism, he assumed supremacy as the representative of the Sun God.

Nature, in this patriarchal paradigm, was seen as something to be controlled and dominated. In an odd reversal of roles, nature was now pressed into the service of man. Power came to be perceived as deriving from strength. Virtually unchanged since its inception, this paradigm has dominated Western civilization down to the present.

The new state of ego consciousness that emerged gave rise to the Hero Myth, which achieved dominance by 1500 BCE.

> Now there are several fascinating aspects to this historical emergence of the Hero Myth—the myth of the individual Hero triumphing over the Great Mother or one of her consorts, such as the old serpent-dragon-uroboros, or over a Great Mother derivative, such as the Medusa with serpent-monster hair, or over a Great Mother offspring, such as Typhon. The first aspect is that *the Hero is simply the new egoic structure of consciousness,* which, coming into existence at this time (the low egoic period), is naturally given living expression in the mythology of the period.[14]

Since she was rooted in the chaos of nature, the Great Mother was defeated by the Hero. Her cyclical realm allowed only for repetition, not for the linear sense of progression that the Hero desires. Instead of integrating the mother mythology, the Hero dissociated from it. So complete was that dissociation that generations of children have grown up and come through the educational system without ever having heard of the Great Mother. At best, it is an historical footnote of little significance.

Tragically, with the rise of ego consciousness, repression of the Great Goddess as well as the Great Mother occurred. The result was a gradual eclipse of the understanding of the unifying light in creation, the subtle Oneness of the Goddess that had begun to break through into human awareness.

With the loss of this burgeoning consciousness as a container for the process of transformation, an enormous split took place in the psyche, both culturally and individually. *The Encyclopedia of Human Behavior* describes a dissociative reaction as "a psychoneurotic reaction in which a portion of experience is split off, or isolated, from conscious awareness."[15] This dissociation not only protects us from threatening impulses, it also allows us to act them out without having to bear any conscious responsibility for our actions. We thereby avoid both anxiety and guilt.

When the dissociation takes place at a cultural level, it forms a basis for the neurosis of the whole culture. Patriarchy dissociated from its maternal ground reconstructed that ground in the guise of a phallic mother that appears, for example, as Mother Church, Motherland, Alma Mater. Ironically, the very fear that led patriarchy to repress matriarchy has kept patriarchy neurotically bound in a struggle for power to what it did and does repress. What is repressed out of fear reemerges in the form of its repression. It is not therefore the absence of the feminine that should be lamented (both feminine and masculine are always already present in some form); it is the distorted forms of their presence that exaggerate the tragic imbalance between them. That imbalance undermines an entire civilization, contributing to its collapse.

With characteristic insight and wit, Gloria Steinem invents Phyllis Freud, who, unlike her more celebrated male namesake, does not come to the conclusion that women are obsessed with penis envy. "Female psychiatrists and psychoanalysts were imbued with the philosophy of this female Freud, the founding genius who had proved that men's lack of wombs made them anatomically inferior and terminally envious; men who dared protest were doubly pathologized by a diagnosis of womb envy, thus it was a belief system with *no way out. . . .*"[16] This notion of "womb envy" does, in fact, have historical support, namely, in patriarchy's ongoing attempts to reinvent and control the womb through its assumptions, institutions, and legislation.

If we look at the English Romantic poets of the early nineteenth century, we see something very different going on. Essentially, their gifts made them outcasts from patriarchal society. Their genius opened them to the collective unconscious, and their poetry is an articulation not only of their personal unconscious, but of the cultural unconscious as well. Great poetry may be compared to big dreams in that both come directly from the unconscious and are then amplified in the waking state in order to understand them more fully. When Blake, Shelley, and Keats were writing, they did not understand, nor did they have the means to understand, the unconscious as it was unveiled by Freud and Jung in our century. The unifying light in creation, the Feminine that had been eclipsed particularly during the seventeenth century, began her return and made her presence known in the unconscious of these male poets.

Although the patriarchal ego prides itself on being reasonable, the twentieth century has been anything but the Age of Reason. In our collective neurosis, we have raped the earth, disrupted the delicate balance of nature, and created phallic missiles of mass destruction. Ironically, in our desperate attempt to keep death at bay (or prevent dissolution, from the point of view of the ego) we have brought ourselves to the brink of extinction. So long as we deny the Great Mother and refuse to integrate her as Goddess in our psychic development, we will continue to act out neurotic fantasies and endanger our very survival as a species.

In spite of the rising sun, the Great Mother is still very much alive in the murky depths of our unconscious. Her presence is often demonstrated in our dreams. In one dream, for example, a man sees his mother in the kitchen. Blocking the kitchen door is a large crocodile. The man goes into the living room with his cat and dog. The crocodile comes toward him and swallows the dog. He manages to save the cat.

In our homes, as in fairy tales, the kitchen is one of the most important rooms. There we prepare food, and, through the miracle of fire, we transform the energies of nature into energies we are able to assimilate. This dreamer's mother is in the kitchen, but his way to her is blocked by a crocodile. He later recalled that when he was ten or eleven, his mother was very depressed. In this image, he is cut off from her by this immense animal that sleeps in the mud, the epitome of inertia. The crocodile is near the beginning of the evolutionary scale. Symbolically, it brings up images not only of the personal mother but also of the collective mother, that huge mother half asleep in the unconscious, who can either suck us to our doom or fill us with creative energy. The transformative potential lies in her massive energy.

This dreamer's personal mother was depressed and needed her son to mirror her. She became overprotective and constantly forbade him to go swimming with the boys, climb trees, or do anything that might hurt him. His burgeoning masculinity and his yearning for action were thus swallowed up. He lost his dog but he did manage to save his cat (feminine instinct). He explored the realms of art, and eventually achieved success in film, art, and music. In his marriage, however, he was insecure and jealous, fearing that other men, because he perceived them as more potent, would steal what he had. His energy, erratic at best, tended to flow toward depression and inertia in anything he did. The energy of his personal mother and the energy of the collective unconscious, which prefers sleeping in the mud to transforming in the fire, was in the Great Mother crocodile. Her energies were not available to him, and he was therefore unable to transform them into higher levels of integration.

The word *mother* sometimes elicits a negative response—a fact that displeases many women. It must be remembered, however, that like fairy tales and fantasies, dreams use metaphorical language. The image "mother" is a tuning fork that sets off vibrations far beyond the realm of the personal mother. It resonates in the creative matrix at the core of the psyche—the matrix that contains both the devouring mother and the cherishing mother. It is the ego's fear of being sucked into an earlier unconscious state that makes it regard the Great Mother as negative. When the ego is strong enough to relate to the Mother without losing its own identity, then Mother becomes the source of all creativity. Paradoxically, so long as the ego fears the unconscious, it is at the same time magnetized by it. Driven by fear, it moves into Mother in destructive ways—drugs, food, sex, alcohol, spending money, whatever. These destructive ways indicate the hostility that, quickened by fear, inevitably lashes out against the mother and/or against oneself.

Falling into the maternal unconscious is a repeated theme in the consulting room. A woman has a dream in which a young man is riding toward her on a bicycle. He falls into the ditch and ends up in the mud (primeval matter). His mother appears behind him and says, "Now come on home. Everything will be all right." This seemingly simple dream reenacts the classical myths and summarizes whole periods of history, both personal and cultural.

In this dream the woman's new masculinity is seeking to break out of the unconscious depths, but instead he is thrown into the primal mud. Matter, mater, mother, and Mother are pulling his ego into the mud of oblivion. "Be safe here. I will look after you. Why do you want to leave home? Stay here and be a good boy." This is Oedipus, who "rebels against the solar-father principle of a higher and more demanding mode of awareness, and seeks instead a union with the old comfort of the chthonic earth, an emotional-sexual incest with the Mother, an immersion in her domain."[17]

When a young boy begins to separate out from his mother, he may suddenly start imitating his father—walking like him, sitting like him, dressing like him. As soon as he is tired or hurt, however, he runs to Mother for comfort. This pre-Oedipal stage soon gives way to confrontations with Father, and an increased turning to Mother for support. Thus, the process of separating out from Mother can often be waylaid. A man may remain locked into Mother all his life, with varying amounts of resentment occasioned by a deep psychic fear of being cut adrift, of being alone physically or psychologically. Because his own inner feminine has not separated out from his mother, he is unable to express his real needs or stand up for his own values. He probably does not know what they are at a mature level. Ironically, he may be married to a woman who finds her strength in mothering her boy.

Girls can identify with Mother for a much longer period of time, since there is no biological or social imperative for them to separate from her. Yet even with the most loving and caring of mothers, a girl needs to separate out and become her own person. Failure to sever the unconscious bond eventually constellates a negative relationship. The need to separate is captured in a young girl's poem, which was written for a high school yearbook.

> Who am I?
> I see the answer
> half at least
> in your eyes
> when you smile at me
> just me
> focusing and defining me
> in time and space
> I feel
> the fine ground lenses
> of love
> pulling me together
> oh how beautiful
> you make me seem
> you love me
> and give me life
> and courage
> and a way to be
> you surround me with
> yourself
> and I never notice
> that I don't exist
> apart from you.
> You are always here
> standing between me
> and the emptiness
> between me
> and myself.[18]

It is this fear of emptiness that blocks most people from coming to at-one-ment. To reach the place where we belong to ourselves, we have to sever the umbilical cord that binds us to archaic dependencies. If we have never known a loving mother, that severing can be even more difficult, because we continue to long for what we have never had. We continue to seek Mother in our relationships. Often in analysis, the analyst must hold the role of loving mother until the Great and Loving Goddess has become a reality in the analysand's psyche. Out of this reality comes a love affair with life and sheer delight in creativity.

When the differentiation between mother and the young feminine is about to begin, the young masculine usually asserts himself. The following dream focuses on the ego's decision to encourage the young boy to act:

> I am on a ship. We are whale-watching. The whales are gracefully riding the waves. On the other side of the boat there are two whales, one practically on the back of the other. A little girl falls overboard and is swallowed whole by the whale. I encourage a young boy to open the whale's mouth and take out the little girl. It's incredible how this happens. The whale seems to be in a playful mood, and it is no trouble for the boy to release the tiny girl. Then there is a party to celebrate the girl's safe return. Everyone is in colorful costumes and there is dancing and lively music.

This is not the patriarchal masculine, which makes the rules that keep people in their place. This is a new masculine consciousness that can pull the feminine out of the inertia of the mother, bringing a new assertiveness, a new perspective on life.

Most men and women are appalled when they look at the condition of their femininity in their dreams. They are more deeply appalled when they talk to those female figures. Those female figures have stories to tell, and they will tell them if they are listened to. Our culture has made us deaf and blind to feminine anguish. The media is making us increasingly aware of marital batterings, assaults, harassments, rape. As a culture, however, we are still blind to the false assumptions underlying many relationships, still deaf to the snide remarks some women make to undercut other women, still unable to pull the feminine out of the mud.

Why has that energy become so mired? Working with dreams is like working on an excavation. We have to dig through layer upon layer of facades that cover the feminine before we can reach it. The individual psyche is a microcosm of the cultural macrocosm. Centuries of abuse have brought us to a crisis in which we look the Death Goddess straight in the eye. That look can change our lives. It may not, in which case, we may obliterate ourselves. Even a very brief look at a few of the critical turning points in Western culture over the last eight centuries will give us some insight into the Goddess that lies buried in our depths.

Anyone who has labored to release the Goddess from the darkness of centuries of abuse has returned from the excavation with a paradox. She who is dead is alive. All we have to do is open our eyes an extra sixteenth of an inch, and there she is, dancing in every apple blossom, in the song of every purple finch, as well as in the flames of passion that we call life.

THE BLACK GODDESS

Beginning in the eleventh century, the Crusades unleashed immense slaughter and plunder across the ancient world. Something of Kali's energy was manifested in the passion and excess that accompanied this well-intentioned but ill-fated campaign. The goal was to release Jerusalem (biblically imaged as the Bride)—and indeed the entire Holy Land—from the captivity of the Muslim hordes. Although this goal was, in the long term, not achieved, the Crusades were to have far-reaching consequences, both for Europe and for the rest of the world.

Along with a vastly expanded vision of life, the Crusaders brought back to Europe many treasures of the East. Among them were exquisite statues of the Black Goddess, Isis. These were enshrined as the Black Virgin. Devotion to her spread from cathedrals to small shrines dotted over the countryside in settings natural to the goddess of fertility. Literally hundreds of shrines to the Black Virgin sprang up throughout Europe in the twelfth and thirteenth centuries.

One reason for the Black Virgin's great popularity during this period was the growing adoration of the chaste Virgin Mary. Courtly love, the legend of the Holy Grail, the veneration of the Virgin, the ascendancy of the idealized woman, were balanced by the compensating adoration of the Black Virgin. She was an underground figure; much of her so-called paganism still adhered to her (fertility, nature, earth). She was revered in an underground way—the blessing of the crops in the field, the blessing of pregnancy and childbirth, the dark excesses of sexuality and delight in the mysteries of the body, and the wisdom that can be experienced in lovemaking. She it was who in the most intimate experience possible to the soul, opened herself to the Holy Spirit, was impregnated, and bore God a son. In her aloneness she was independent—a liberated image of the feminine.

In the thirteenth century, the magnificent "thrones of Wisdom" were beloved icons in the cathedrals. A stately, royal mother figure sits on her throne, her skirt sweeping in majestic folds. Her throne is the *cathedra*, the chair that makes the cathedral her palace. (In dreams, a large chair or a large lap often symbolizes a mother complex.) Standing on her knee is the Child King, with his ancient face, holding the scepter and the orb. He stands like a king; his standpoint is secure on the lap of Wisdom.

This image of the Madonna and her son shifted into mother and young child. By the Renaissance, the icon had come to carry a totally different meaning. Leonardo da Vinci, however, maintains the concept of Sophia (Wisdom as Nature) in his cartoon of Mary and her son sitting on the lap of her mother. Mary appears as a finely honed feminine, totally integrated with the powerful nature goddess. Her son echoes the Little King of the "thrones of Wisdom." In the *Virgin of the Rocks*, the nature goddess appears as the grotto and the rocks, the womb in which Mary and her child and John are located.

The Age of the Black Virgin, the twelfth and thirteenth centuries, was followed by the Black Death of the fourteenth century. In 1347 the Black Death devastated Europe and by 1361 had killed up to one-half of the population. In 1349 alone, it killed at least a third of the population of England. In today's terms, this would be the equivalent of a nuclear holocaust. It had an enormous effect on the psyche and the future development of the Western world. Historian Barbara Tuchman, writing about this period, concludes:

> Survivors of the plague, finding themselves neither destroyed nor improved, could discover no Divine purpose in the pain they suffered. God's purposes were usually mysterious, but this scourge had been too terrible to be accepted without questioning. If a disaster of such magnitude, the most lethal ever known, was a mere wanton act of God or perhaps not God's work at all, then the absolutes of a fixed order were loosed from their moorings. Minds that opened to admit

these questions could never again be shut. Once people envisioned the possibility of change in a fixed order, the end of an age of submission came in sight; the turn to individual conscience lay ahead. To that extent the Black Death may have been the unrecognized beginning of modern man.[19]

The fixed order Tuchman refers to is the hierarchical order of the feudal system: king, prince, dukes, all the way down to the serfs. Equally rigid was the hierarchy of the Church: pope, bishops, clerics, laity, all fixed in their place by divine decree. Not only was the divine purpose of the rigidly controlled patriarchal order questioned, but so was the Divine purpose of death, which had hitherto been seen as part of the natural order.

The plague was a catalyst for a major shift in human perception in many areas—in cosmology, in science and medicine, in attitudes toward women, and in philosophy and religion itself. Unexplained and irrational, death was an insult—an aberration thrown in the face of man's newly acquired image as the "controller." Man turned increasingly to his own rational power, and began to look upon death, nature, woman, his own body and sexuality as being irrational, and therefore as something to be subdued and brought under more rigorous control. Man began to be more resolute in his confrontation with the created universe. His dominance over nature became one expression of his power. As E. F. Schumacher succinctly puts it, "The old science looked upon nature as God's handiwork and man's mother; the new science tends to look upon nature as an adversary to be conquered or a resource to be quarried and exploited."[20]

Man began to put distance between himself and the forces of death. The new order would create a more habitable world built on a more precise knowledge of the universe, including man himself. All elements of chance were to be systematically eliminated.

The irrational elements that man so rigorously attempted to subdue after the fourteenth century, and well into our century, are the very elements that we are now finally learning to creatively embrace in, for example, contemporary science, depth psychology, and the arts. The underground Black Goddess is surfacing again to become the *cathedra* of the creative mind. This surfacing, first seen in its modern form in the visionary world of Romanticism in the first quarter of the nineteenth century, is now finding its way into actual life, a life now experienced by most inhabitants of the planet as far more acausal than causal, far more inexplicable than explicable. Before we could arrive at this apparently chaotic state, however, rationalism had to bring us to the brink of extinction as a result of the mind's determination to enslave the body.

Man's focus on the mind was to find its fullest expression in the writings of Descartes in the seventeenth century. Descartes introduced a view of mind as an incorporeal thinking substance, radically distinct from body. As entirely mindless, matter or body had to be controlled by mind, mind not being *in* matter but *over* matter as a master ruling a slave.

The mind as the enslaver of matter became, in the seventeenth century, a metaphor of the operation of the mind of God in its creation of a material world. For Sir Isaac Newton, the cosmos itself was the enslaved body of an omnipotent mind which, having created the cosmos by an act of divine will, withdrew into the contemplation of itself, leaving the cosmos as an autonomous self-regulating mechanism. In this image of a vast self-regulating mechanism lay for Newton what Thomas Berry has called "a model for human activity"[21] behind which lay mind itself contemplating, like Descartes' *cogito ergo sum* ("I think therefore I am"), its own detached divinity.

The goal of science as initiated by Descartes and achieved by Newton lay in the total submission of matter to mind, of slave to master. As "a model for human activity" it affirmed man's rational submission to the immutable laws of nature. That matter had a mind of its own that would eventually rebel against its enslavement belonged to the realm of fantasy rather than reality.

Not surprisingly, therefore, considering the long-standing patriarchal association of matter (*mater*) with the feminine, the feminist revolt in this century against what many feminists considered patriarchal subjugation, belonged for many men (and women) not to the realm of reality as masculine science defined it, but to the realm of myth as women by their "inferior rational nature" continued to inhabit it.

The dualism of mind and matter epitomized by Descartes began, however, long before Descartes. Immediately following the Black Plague, nature was more and more perceived as a chaotic realm unrelated to the thinking principle. Prior to the plague, the body had been studied not just by those wishing to become doctors, but also by those desiring a more intimate knowledge of God. During the plague, however, the need to control disease and death gave the practical applications of the study of anatomy greater impetus. The interaction between self-knowledge and medical practice disappeared in a system that was becoming more and more materialistic the further away man moved from seeing himself as a part of the created order. The link between consciousness and body no longer applied. The body became a fascinating system to be studied in the same way as the stars and planets. With the nineteenth-century formulation of the Doctrine of Specific Etiology (namely, that a single agent such as a microbe can be the cause of disease), the door was opened for the control of the spread of infectious diseases. Man began to develop a new sense of power over his own body.[22]

These advances in science were accompanied by a profound alteration in man's perception of woman and death. As Philippe Aries has observed, it was during this period that death began to take on an erotic meaning in art and literature. Death and the sex act were "henceforth increasingly thought of as a transgression which tears man from his daily life, from rational society, from his monotonous work, in order to make him undergo a paroxysm, plunging him into an irrational, violent, and beautiful world."[23]

The intensified association of woman with death and erotic love increased greatly the anxiety that man experienced. He began to project his own guilt about his sexual impulses onto woman. An example of this re-enactment of Adam's blaming Eve can be found in a 1486 report by the Dominican inquisitors, Heinrich Kramer and James Sprenger.

> But the natural reason is that she [woman] is more carnal than a man, as is clear from her many carnal abominations. And it should be noted that there was a defect in the formation of the first woman, since she was formed from a bent rib, that is, a rib of the breast, which is bent as it were in a contrary direction to a man. And since through this defect she is an imperfect animal, she always deceives. . . .[24]

While guilt and carnality were projected onto women in general, there occurred a compensating idealization through the cult of virginity, both within and without the Church. Within the Church, the emphasis was placed on chastity, since death and sexual coupling were regarded as synonymous. Thus St. John Chrysostom wrote in *Della Verginita:* "For where there is death, there too is sexual coupling; and where there is no death, there is no sexual coupling either. But virginity is not accompanied by such things."[25]

Rosemary Ruether sees the disjunction that occurred in man's perception of woman as a split between spiritualized femininity and carnal femaleness. She points out that this split is analogous to the one between mind and body:

> This split continued to grow more and more intense during the Middle Ages until it erupted in a veritable orgy of paranoia in the late medieval period [1300s–1600s]. It can hardly be a coincidence that the same period that saw Mariology reach the greatest heights of theological definition and refinement with the triumph of the doctrine of the Immaculate Conception in nominalist theology also saw the outbreak of witch hunts that took the lives of upwards of one million women between the 14th and 17th centuries.[26]

Man's split perception of woman manifested itself most clearly in the witch hunts. Not only did woman carry the burden of man's guilt and response to death, but she also became the scapegoat for the economic instability that came in the wake of the plague. In *Gesta Trevirorum* we read: "Inasmuch as it was popularly believed that the continued sterility of many years was caused by witches through the malice of the Devil, the whole country rose to exterminate the witches."[27] In town after town, the Inquisitors ordered countless women stripped and shaved and subjected them to vaginal and rectal searches. Those found to have the devil's mark were hanged or burned at the stake. Women became the scapegoat, for, as the Inquisitor concluded, "all witchcraft comes from carnal lust, which is in women insatiable."[28]

About this time, devotion to Mary as Universal Mother began to spread, as man started looking for a new source of security. Mary became the disembodied Mother. As Queen of Heaven, she became part of the Church's redemptive theology—not as the Black Madonna, bridging sexuality and spirituality, but rather, as the obedient, chaste, *Virgin* Mother.

With consciousness focused on the perfection of the Virgin

Mary, the dark shadow of lust constellated in the unconscious. A reflection of the mind/body dichotomy, this virgin/whore split drove the feminine soul, the receptive, unifying principle that had begun to emerge, deeper into exile. The soul became an isolated entity, the immortal and immaterial part of oneself that needed to be "saved" out of the corrupting influence of the material world.

Although it was woman who suffered the most through this period, man also became painfully alienated from himself, torn as he was between the need to idealize woman (reflected in the disembodied mother/virgin) and the simultaneous need to dominate and control her. There can be no real wholeness in heterosexual relationships until this split is healed in both man and woman. In their dreams, men often encounter the good little girl or docile mother along with the seductive snake woman or beckoning whore. The virgin soul, meanwhile, lies buried in the basement or is dumped into a trash can. Such dreams of the exiled soul are among the most common initiatory dreams.

The virgin/whore split manifests in women's dreams as well. A woman dreams, for example, that she is visiting a construction site, where a house is being built. The dream ego, white and properly dressed, is supervising. A dark shadow woman is also present, fornicating with the workmen. The dream ego wants to make a hasty retreat, but is fascinated by the energy of the shadowy whore. The shadow is distracting the workmen (the constructive energies of the unconscious), and it is she who will have to be integrated if the construction of the inner house is to go ahead.

Given this split and the repression of the feminine, it is not difficult to see why Freud mistakenly placed sexuality at the root of the underlying anxiety in the psyche. Only very recently has it become clear that patriarchal pathology is rooted in the dread of death, the fear of dissolution. Not since the plague of the fourteenth century have human beings been so traumatized by the sudden loss of the boundaries that established their security. The holocaust in Europe, the bombings of Hiroshima and Nagasaki, were a nightmare that everyone has had to contend with ever since. Here was mass death on an unprecedented scale. Now the terror was not the unknown forces of nature rebelling against man, or God punishing man for his sins; now it was "man's inhumanity to man" that was to be feared. Inasmuch as the plague had forced man to relate differently to nature, so the Second World War placed man in a new relation-ship to himself. Not only did men begin to fear each other, but man also began to fear himself, his own overwhelming capacity for destruction.

The suppression of death, or "forbidden death," to use Aries's term, has had a profound effect on the organization of the self. In Freud's day, the suppression of sexuality took the form of hysterical neuroses and obsessions, which characterize the deterioration of the ego from internalized pressures. In our own day, particularly follow-ing the Second World War, the breakdown of the self has become evident in the predominance of the narcissistic personality. Power-lessness, emptiness, and paranoia characterized the neuroses of the eighties and continue to make their presence felt in the present dec-ade. As Peter Giovacchini writes, "The growing prominence of 'char-acter disorders' seems to signify an underlying change in the organization of personality, from what has been called inner-direc-tion to narcissism."[29] Michael Beldoch has this to say: "Today's pa-tients by and large do not suffer from hysterical paralyses of the legs or handwashing compulsions; instead it is their very psychic selves that have gone numb or that they must scrub and rescrub in an exhausting and unending effort to come clean." These patients suffer from "pervasive feelings of emptiness and a deep disturbance of self-esteem."[30]

The characteristic feature of borderline patients is an obsessive need to re-create a womb, which will rescue them from their sense of emptiness. Addictive or dependent relationships are often sought as an antidote to a traumatized ego. While the regression to the womb is predominant in the borderline personality, many people in our crumbling society seek to establish relationships based on *partici-pation mystique* through sharing drugs, alcohol, sex, or other addictive behaviors.

We have become alienated from the earth, from others, and from our own deepest feelings. In such a condition we become nar-cissistic. In all the mirrors that reflect reality we see only ourselves. We have become highly self-conscious, but this state is a mere par-ody of true self-knowledge. Self-knowledge comes through a rela-tionship with and a commitment to something or someone beyond one's self, beyond the gratification of one's personal needs. Sexual repression has given way to sexual liberation, but neither has anything to do with true passion or true self-knowledge. In the eighteenth and nineteenth centuries, we denied, through the practice of puritanism, the guilt we felt toward our bodies; in the twentieth century, the discomfort of repressed guilt became too much to bear, so we abandoned it in favor of bodily gratification. We may now be a little more comfortable with the fact that we have bodies, but we have no context to give meaning to our new-found awareness.

Existential guilt requires forgiveness, something we cannot give ourselves. Instead we remain trapped in a hedonism that is at best a manipulation of our own bodies.

> It is commonly thought that contemporary man has swung from Puritanism to hedonism—to the pursuit of pleasure rather than the denial of pleasure. But these are two sides of one coin. Both these are two sides of one coin. Both the hedonist and the puritan face the body in the condition of fear; the puritan fears gratification while the hedonist fears the absence of gratification. Both derive their sense of identity through conflict with the natural rhythms of the organism; both are manipulators, at war with what is.[31]

REDISCOVERING THE LIGHT IN MATTER

Not until we recognize the Divine Immanence, the light of the Goddess in matter, can we hope to establish a balance, a reconnection with our own deepest nature that can root us in a world of meaning and imagination. Perhaps, we will have to face the darkness, walk out on the moor alone at nightfall, or dive to the bottom of the sea before the old ossified ego boundaries can be shattered to make room for the dance.

In dreams, the Goddess often leads the dreamer into a deep cave or a dark place. In the following dream, the dreamer, a woman, was led down into the basement, where everything was pitch black.

> I am at a large celebration. I go down into the wine cellar to get some wine. As I go down, it is extremely black. I lose my direction walking down the corridors. I feel an opening and I get down and start feeling around the walls and then I touch the floor. As I do this, little clumps of golden light spark up in every spot I touch, and soon I begin to see where I am—a large empty room. Next, the golden light becomes

women—young, middle-aged, and very old, on crutches, in wheelchairs. What is peculiar is that their faces are radiant—glowing eyes, clear and sparkling. I distinctly hear the words: "I will give you treasures out of the darkness, and riches that have been hidden away."

In search of wine (spirit), the dreamer goes down into the blackness of the basement (the unconscious). In her searching, she finds the light (spirit), but it is light embodied in matter—the gold sparks that appear where she touches the black walls. This is the light, the consciousness within our own bodies as well as within all creation, that will be recognized and released as we continue to evolve. The embodied light reveals itself in the feminine threesome (mother, maiden, crone). The crones are crippled, but their eyes are shining. The voice knows where the treasure is hidden. Out of the darkness will come the treasures, and the hidden riches.

This is the darkness we have always feared. Beneath the mature persona of the ego lies the child's imagination, which fears being devoured by the wolf or the wicked witch. If we remain trapped in fear, we will never know the treasures of the dark. Being catapulted into the underworld is a common mythological theme, found in almost all cultures. The descent is undertaken either voluntarily, in search of a deeper goal, or involuntarily, when the abyss unexpectedly opens. The potential in either case comes from the fact that ordinary ego perceptions are shattered; cracks occur in the well-crafted persona. Through these cracks emerges the possibility of something new.

In tribal cultures, the shaman had to go into the underworld and sometimes wander there for three years. Usually, he had to undergo dismemberment—a death and resurrection—before he could assume his true vocation. Often, crystals were placed in the orifices of his body during this period to signify the light in matter.

Descent into the underworld can happen at different stages in life. The midlife descent often requires a whole reorientation of identity. In the first half of life we live mainly in terms of doing. We find out who we are through going to school, pursuing a career, marrying, having children and raising them. In the second half of life, we are pushed toward a deeper consciousness of who we are, an identity in terms of being, an identity based not on the ego but on the soul. The gap we pass through, sometimes lasting several years, is what is commonly known as the midlife crisis.

Tibetan Buddhism has a tradition of *delog*—stories of people who are catapulted into the underworld, often through grave illness. Depression can also lead us into the black hole that exists at the center of our being. Perhaps, if we are "lucky" enough, we fall into that hole—the confusion, the lethargy, the hollowness of old enthusiasms, old addictions that don't work any more. Until the ego feels its own despair, there is little motivation toward change.

If all we have known of the feminine is the old devouring Mother, we may become stuck in the black hole. If, however, we are able to recognize the Great Goddess in her role as the *transformer* of energy, then we can trust, even if we don't know where we are going. The blackness will reveal its gold. Sometimes with humor, sometimes with bluntness and even harshness, sometimes with tenderness, she will both challenge and guide.

In writing about the dakini in the Buddhist tradition, Tsultrim Allione speaks of the possibility that "[w]e could have little gaps in the claustrophobic game of dualism, and clarity could shine through. . . . The world is not as solid as we think it is, and the more we are open to the gaps, the more wisdom can shine through and the more the play of the dakini energy can be experienced."[32]

These "gaps" in the "solidified fantasies of dualistic fixation"[33] have become the subject of present-day physics. Chaos theory puts a scientific spin on the myth of Tiamat, the early Babylonian goddess of chaos out of which everything was created. Until recently, the problem was that chaos has been seen as "bad." In fact, up until this century it was widely believed that we would, sooner or later, find an explanation for chaos, and then order would prevail. "Chaos was merely complexity so great that in practice scientists couldn't track it, but they were sure that in principle they might one day be able to do so. When that day came there would be no chaos, so to speak, only Newton's laws."[34] Reductionism lasted until the 1970s, or until high-powered computers made it possible for us to solve nonlinear equations more rapidly. It was found that the most minute variation in any system, when amplified, would lead to random behavior—that is, to chaos.

Science has very nearly grasped the paradox at the heart of reality—the paradox that mythology calls "Goddess"—creating a momentum that has never existed at any other time in history. As we begin to look at the quantum reality of nature and of our own bodies, we are called to a new level of consciousness. In many ways, we are discovering what we have intuitively known for centuries. In psychological terms this is the yin/yang reality, separate but indivisible. While the new metaphors—"chaos theory," "quantum reality"— speak more directly to contemporary culture, the ancient yin/yang and Shakti/Shiva realities still hold true.

Gaps in nonlinear systems make most naturally occurring processes impossible to predict with certainty. With nonlinearity, reductionism and the great illusion of ultimate control go out the window. Ancient wisdom, in which chaos was recognized and preserved (particularly in gnosticism and alchemy) as the necessary element of transformation, has finally been restored.

It is within this chaos that a deeper, intrinsic order reveals itself. This is not the imposed order that we have become so accustomed to in a patriarchal, conceptualized world, an order that is not connected to the creative matrix. Rather, it is an order that emerges instead of being imposed. When we are connected to this emerging order we are psychically living from the incarnate feminine energy that has within it the possibility of transformation. We are in touch with the rhythms of matter and its deepest wisdom.

The oldest mythologies of the Great Mother saw life essentially as an unending cycle of life-death-rebirth, a process that did not allow for transformation into new levels of consciousness. Patriarchy rejected this cycle as something that was "stuck" because it did not allow for linear progression. In a linear concept of progression, death is seen as something that can only be denied or projected.

While the manipulation of material things may give the impression of progress, consciousness and the movement upward from an animal existence to a more humane human existence are less obvious. We need only watch television news to realize that the evolution of human beings has, in fact, been "stuck" for a very long time. Animals, being closer to the rhythms of nature, have a more intrinsic morality. Sometimes, the only sign of "progression" seems to be our more precise technologies, which perform blood sacrifices with greater depravity.

The energy that is now emerging from the unconscious of so many contemporary dreamers is not the energy of the old matriarchal consciousness. One woman, for example, recently had a dream in which she was a little girl; she had moved into a huge new house and was wandering around, amazed at the size of the rooms. In the second part of the dream, she shifts locales:

> I am standing on a dock beside a lakeside house. It's a sunny, warm day. Looking down into the brown water of the lake, I see the long backbone of a whale. As I move closer to look at the whale, suddenly a huge woman rises from the water. She has light-brown skin and thick black hair that falls to her shoulders. She is draped in cloth of dark brown and blue and her huge breasts are bare. She stands hip-deep in the water. She laughs, and her teeth look very white against her brown skin. "What are you gawking at?" she says to me. "Go inside."

In the first segment of this dream, the young feminine has moved into an enormous new house and she is exploring this large space with wonderment. In daily life, the dreamer had entered a new understanding of the feminine, which had led her into an entirely new concept of the Self, the God/Goddess image within. It is these large, new spaces within herself that amaze her.

With the feminine having moved to a new place, the second part of the dream introduces the dream ego to a sun-filled space that includes both conscious and unconscious energies (the lake). The dreamer sees what appears to be a whale (an old mother symbol). Suddenly, it is not a whale, but a huge brown-skinned woman. Figures that appear larger than life are archetypal energies from the collective unconscious, in this case, a Goddess. She is laughing and merely asks the dreamer what she is gawking at, or why she is so surprised at her appearance. Then, in her customary fashion, she gives the dreamer a very cryptic message: "Go inside." With this transformation in her interior landscape, the dreamer may be on the way to genuine change.

In another dream, a multi-bodied snake slides out from the hair of a large, black, African woman. The dreamer recalls: "It looks gross and disgusting to me, but she cheerfully shows me how it unfolds into a complete circle, which she puts on top of her head. She says she uses it as a basket to carry things in, and it protects her head from the rain, like an umbrella."

On hearing the dream, one is immediately reminded of the

snake hair of the Medusa, the Gorgon who was so ugly that anyone who looked at her turned into stone. As the dream continues, it becomes clear that this energy is not that of the Devouring Mother. The unconscious deftly presents it as a beneficent Goddess figure. The dreamer later drew the "halo" formed by the snake. Her sketch called to mind the image of the enlightened Buddha with the halo of seven snakes (representing the seven chakras) that appears above the head to signify an enlightened consciousness.

The Buddha is depicted with seven heads emerging from one body. In the dream, the Goddess is shown with seven bodies uniting in one head. Could this be an indication of the difference in the processing of masculine and feminine energies?

In dreams, the position of the serpent is very important. If it is crawling on the earth it is usually representing an old, chthonic life force, regressive and possibly treacherous. When it is upright or beyond the head, it represents ascendance of energy through the energy centers of the body to a place of enlightenment. This is the kundalini energy that has risen from its coiled position in the lowest chakra, the biological energy, that has become the spiritual consciousness.

The reemergence of the Goddess as distinct from the Great Mother is also apparent in men's dreams. One man had a dream in which he was approaching what looked like a mountain. This turned out to be the pubic mound of the Great Mother. He stood between her massive legs and then approached her vagina, realizing he was supposed to walk into it. Atop the pubic mound were three witches straight out of Macbeth. In his fear of being devoured—a deep-seated masculine fear—he attached a feather to the foot of the Great Mother. To the feather he fastened one end of a rope; the other end he held in his hand. The idea was that, if he became trapped inside, he would pull on the rope, which would tickle the foot of the Great Mother and he could escape. Once in-

side the Great Mother, however, he saw a haloed object, which turned toward him, revealing the Goddess buried within the womb of the Mother.

In this dream as well, the unconscious seems to be differentiating between the old Mother mythology and her more conscious form, the Goddess. This image is reminiscent of the Tantric dakini, Vajra Varahi. "She springs out of the cosmic cervix, the triangular source of dharmas, burning with unbearable bliss, energy in an unconditional state. She has the three-dimensional triangular source of dharmas just below her navel and she is standing on one. This form acts on the being of the tantrika when he or she visualizes Vajra Varahi, and the effect is the activation of internal energies which dissolve the sense of inner and outer and plug in to a sense of all-pervading energized space which is primordial wisdom and a kind of burning transcendental lust and bliss."[35]

This dakini energy that emerges from the womb of the Great Mother is similar, in many respects to Kali's. The three main objects that accompany the dakini are the hooked knife or sword, the skull cup of blood, and the trident staff. According to Allione, the hook in Tibetan Buddhist imagery is the hook or knife of compassion, "the hook which pulls beings out of the cycles of transmigration. . . . [It] pulls one forth from suffering, chops up the ego-centered self

and is guided by the diamond clarity of the vajra."[36] The skull cup is likened to the cauldron, the container which holds the primordial passion of blood. "The red blood suggests the burning interior power of women, primal matrix which can become babies, milk, passion and fierceness, primal lava of life."[37]

The third accouterment is the staff "with a trident at the top, and underneath the trident, tied to the staff, is a double vajra with three severed heads. The top head is a dry skull, under the skull is a head that has been severed several days, and below that is a freshly severed head. The staff is held in the crook of the elbow of the left arm and extends from her head to her foot. Usually she is dancing, so one foot is raised and the other is standing on a corpse, which represents the negativity which has been overcome."[38] By her staff, the death that the Goddess brings is the transformation of the three poisons: lust, anger, and ignorance.

The three skulls symbolize not the concrete blood sacrifice of an earlier time but the death (transformation) of the three highest levels of consciousness: the Nirmanakaya body (physical body), the Sambogakaya body (subtle body), and the Dharmakaya, the latter represented by the dry skull, "a level of being which has no form, but contains the potential for everything."[39]

The staff also carries the symbolism of a deeper integration. "The overall significance of the Khatvanga staff is that of the 'hidden consort'. . . . By holding the Khatvanga she shows us that she has incorporated the masculine into herself. This energy is at her service. With this staff she has the power to stand alone. . . . The same is true for male figures who hold the Khatvanga as their 'secret consort.' The Tantric practitioners who visualize themselves as these deities understand that in order to be whole we must embody and appreciate *both* the masculine and the feminine in ourselves."[40]

The stake, or staff, as analyzed by Sylvia Perera in *Descent to the Goddess*, is the peg of Erishkiqal, the peg on which she hangs her bright sister, Inanna. It "fills the all-receptive emptiness of the feminine with feminine yang strength. It fills the eternally empty womb mouth, and gives a woman her own wholeness, so that the woman is not merely dependent on man or child, but can be unto herself as a full and separate individual."[41]

Given this potential to grasp our own uniqueness, our own wholeness through an ability to stand alone, we can begin to manifest the interaction of positive masculine and feminine energies within us. These are not the old devouring matriarchal energy or the tyrannical, one-sided patriarchal energy. The evolutionary imperative within the collective unconscious is pushing us toward a new level of consciousness.

An alienated ego can think of wholeness only as the accumulation of more and more matter under its control. It stands in relationship to people and things as outside of itself, no matter how it may

Dakini by Mayumi Oda

secretly long to incorporate or devour whatever is around it. In probing the deeper symbolism of the Goddess, we are challenged to go "inside." Evolution at this point is no longer in terms of the material body; it seems to be moving toward a greater interiority, and, paradoxically, a greater sense of all.

In terms of our mythology, a new image of God/Goddess yearns to be found within ourselves. The kingdom is first within. It is manifested through body and mind. We are moving beyond an ego consciousness not only to an integration of body and mind but to a transcendence of the body/mind split, to a new level of consciousness based on the dance between soul and spirit.

The soul embodied in matter, manifested in the Goddess as container and transformer, will take us beyond dualism, beyond the defensive splits within our psyche if we open up to her energy within us. She faces us with our greatest fear and by showing us the treasure hidden away within it, she takes us to a place where love is born. Love is the true antithesis of fear. It expands where fear constricts. It embraces where fear repels.

In "The Tablet of the Holy Mariner" of Baha'u'llah, the prophet of the Bahai faith, Wisdom as the Maid of Heaven descends to earth seeking one who is able to embrace her. Unable to find anyone worthy of her love, she returns to her own lofty mansion, shares her grief with her handmaidens, and falls prostrate upon the dust.[42] In the Book of Enoch we are also told of the flight of Wisdom:

> Wisdom went forth to make her dwelling
> Among the children of men,
> And found no dwelling place;
> Wisdom returned to her place
> And took her seat among the angels.[43]

The Black Goddess, who emerged in history centuries ago, was exiled into the unconscious. Will it be any different this time? Perhaps not by choice but by necessity, we will recognize and honor her. Without the recognition of the cycle of life-death-rebirth there can be no transformation, no true progression grounded in nature for the human species. In the transition from Great Mother to Great Goddess, the possibility of transformation in rebirth began to dawn. The chaos that she embodies is a shattering of rigid categories. If we enter into it, that chaos can resurrect us into a higher wisdom, rooted in the wisdom of the creative process. The chaos that we fear is the very thing that can free us. To refuse to enter into Kali's dance of creation and destruction is to get stuck in a one-sided view of reality that can bring anarchy—destruction without creation. Armed with a new understanding of the very nature of reality itself, we may now be able to embrace the Goddess energy that is necessary if we are to move forward in our evolution.

In examining the Goddess as she has functioned in her role as the One of creation, the chapters that follow will attempt to make her energy and her challenge more visible. Hopefully, we will recognize her when we see her and welcome her among us.

LEPIDUS: Y'have strange serpents there.

ANTONY: Ay, Lepidus.

LEPIDUS: Your serpent of Egypt is bred now of your mud by the operation of your sun; so is your crocodile.

—SHAKESPEARE, *Antony and Cleopatra*, II, vii.

Split the Lark—and you'll find the Music—
Bulb after Bulb, in Silver rolled—
Scantily dealt to the Summer Morning
Saved for your Ear when Lutes be old.

Loose the Flood—you shall find it patent—
Gush after Gush, reserved for you—
Scarlet Experiment! Sceptic Thomas!
Now, do you doubt that your Bird was true?

—EMILY DICKINSON

The tree that would grow to heaven must send its roots to hell.

—NIETZSCHE

BEYOND DUALITY

WHETHER YOU'RE A KNIGHT looking for a horse, a maiden looking for fire, or a youth looking for a bride, in Russian folk tales you usually end up deep in the forest. On your journey, you may stumble upon a house, walking, hopping, twirling or spinning on chicken legs. The door is made of human bones, the bolts of human fingers; the lock is a mouth of grinning death. Around the perimeter is a picket fence with a skull on each stake. One stake stands empty, to receive your head, should you fail to meet the test. This sight alone is enough to shock the seeker out of ordinary perception. This is not a place of rational logic.

The proprietor of this remarkable house is an ancient hag, the Baba Yaga, who may swoop down on you in her mortar and pestle as you ride. A broom trails behind her, wiping out any traces of her comings and goings, for she cannot be pinned down.

With cackling laugh and eyes that become like points of fire, she inquires what you seek. You must stand up to her boldly and declare what it is that you want. "The kingdom ten times ten"; "a knightly horse, Grandma, to retrieve my lost bride"; "the well with the waters of Life and Death"; "I have come to ask for fire."

Now these are no ordinary requests. One does not venture deep into the forest without good reason. One has already felt some loss, something missing, in the ordinary routines of life. One has begun to search in the depths of the unconscious for what is essential to growth, to change, to wholeness. In fact, the hag, the sorceress, the wisdom energy of the Goddess, does not appear in dreams until the traveler is strong enough to be vulnerable. The ego has to have surrendered some of its defensive control before it can tolerate confronting such energy. Then she appears, without ceremony, and, after determining whether your search is legitimate or not, she has one more question, "Do you come here of your own free will, or do you come by compulsion?" or "Have you come to do deeds, doughty youth, or to flee from deeds?"

This is the test of how ready you are to proceed in your quest. If you say, "I have come of my own free will," your bones will become part of her adornment. If, on the other hand, you say, "I have come by compulsion," your head will, likewise, go on the post awaiting it. The test is simply this, "Have you become conscious enough to go beyond duality?"

Duality belongs in the ego development stage. It is the tree of the knowledge of good and evil, which symbolizes humanity's fall *up* from an unconscious Eden. While Eden is characterized by *participation mystique*, duality has to do with differentiation of energies—a necessary step in the progression toward higher consciousness. Things are identified by their parts—good or evil, black or white, strong or weak—in an either/or world. The ego world in which we live exercises power *over against*, thus perpetuating the neurotic either/or dichotomy discussed in chapter I.

The Baba Yaga challenges us to go beyond that immature stage of development to a both/and world. Neither the undifferentiated world of early matriarchy, nor the overly differentiated world of patriarchy allows for a conscious world that can contain the opposites. The right answer for the Baba Yaga would go something like this, "I am here seventy-five percent of my own free will, sixty-five percent by compulsion."

This answer implies that we have a humbler, more accurate understanding of our own nature. The truth is most of us are where we are partly through overwhelming circumstances that have landed us here and partly because this is where we want to be. Seventy-five percent one way, sixty-five percent the other. If we see the opposites in ourselves, we are less likely to judge and blame others. If we have identified too closely with the light, have too idealized an image of ourselves, then our shadow will surely come up and hit us on the backside. The same is true if we have identified with our negative side: we could be struck from behind by our goodness. Either position is a denial of our wholeness.

The impulse toward false virtue is well understood in the Buddhist tradition, where the *dakini* energy manifests itself in order to create balance. In her study of the *dakini* (fierce feminine energy), Allione finds that "in almost all the stories of great saints in Tibet, the dakini appears at crucial moments. The encounters often have a quality of sharp, incisive challenge to the fixated conceptions of the practitioner. They may occur through a human dakini, or through a dream or mirage-like appearance which vanishes after the message is communicated. These encounters often have a grounding, practical insightful quality that is sharp and wrathful. This is the primordial raw energy of the dark goddess."[1]

To illustrate this raw energy, Allione tells the story of Abhaya-karagupta, a famous high-caste scholar. "A young maiden approached him in the courtyard of his monastery and shoved a piece of bloody meat at him, saying that it had been slaughtered for him. He was taken aback and replied: 'I am a pure monk. How can I eat meat that has been so blatantly prepared for me?' At once she disappeared.

"Tantric Buddhism urges its adherents to go beyond all restrictions, even those imposed by the Buddha, such as not eating meat that has been killed for oneself. This is because in Tantrism all habitual patterns, even 'golden habits,' must be relinquished so that we may *experience reality without conceptuality* [italics mine]. . . . In any situation we must not be conditioned by concepts of good and bad. . . . By not recognizing this girl who acted as a dakini to test his understanding, he [the monk] cut off his progress in the practice. The next time she appeared to him she was in the form of an old hag. This time, having consulted with his guru in the meantime, he recognized her and confessed his failure to acknowledge her before. This was a turning point in his practice. He went on to become an accomplished yogi rather than a strict monk."[2]

By breaking through the either/or rigidities, the Black Goddess creates the space for spontaneity, for new experience, for new insight. Intellect can give us knowledge, but wisdom is based on experience that, if reflected on deeply enough, leads us to paradox and the recognition of the unity that exists. It is to bring forth wisdom that goes beyond conventional concepts that the dakini works *"directly with the energy of the body, speech and mind."*[3]

A duality in which one valence is valued over the other causes dichotomies within our perception of ourselves and others. We begin to live a one-sided reality, an illusion created by our own mind. Among our most dominant dichotomies are masculine/feminine, mind/body, thinking/feeling, and life/death. Feminine, body, feeling, and death have all been subjugated by their opposite. Distinctions are indispensable, the recognition of differences is necessary. It is only when we identify exclusively with one side of the duality and dissociate or repress the other that we begin to have a false view of reality. Clinging neurotically to our chosen identification, we cannot move to a position of wholeness. In choosing mind over body, we have cut ourselves off from the rootedness of our past body consciousness out of fear of falling into it. A new balance must be found if we are to proceed wholly into our future evolutionary growth.

Being the consciousness in matter, the unifying light in creation, the Goddess symbolizes the energy we need to become whole, to proceed toward consciousness. This is not an easy task for ego consciousness to pursue, because all change, all growth, presupposes the death of the old. It is for this reason that Kali is represented as dancing in the cremation grounds, or the dakini as dancing on a corpse. This is also the reason we fear such images as the Goddess wielding her curved sword.

The essence of the journey and the true nature of the sword of the Goddess have been captured in a poem by David Whyte entitled "No one told me."

No one told me
it would lead to this.
No one said
there would be secrets
I would not want to know.

No one told me about seeing,
seeing brought me
loss and a darkness I could not hold.

No one told me about writing
or speaking.
Speaking and writing poetry
I unsheathed the sharp edge
of experience that led me here.

No one told me
it could not be put away.

I was told once, only,
in a whisper,
"The blade is so sharp—
It cuts things together
—not apart."

This is no comfort.
My future is full of blood
from being blindfold
hands outstretched,
feeling a way along its firm edge.[4]

The feminine leads us to the sharp edge of experience. There we have to feel our feelings in our bodies; there our secrets become visible in the darkened, unvisited corners of our psyches. Claiming the unswept corners of our psyches leads us to compassion for ourselves and for others. Knowing we have done our best and it simply wasn't enough opens our hearts to other human beings whose best has likewise failed. The mind has its logic; the heart alone can know wisdom, bridge chasms, make peace.

Again, this is illustrated in a story, told by Allione, of a famous Indian Buddhist teacher.

Naropa was the greatest scholar at the prestigious Nalanda University. One day as he was reading a book on logic, a shadow fell across the page. When he turned around he saw a hideous old hag. She asked him if he understood the words or the meaning and when he replied that he understood both, she was furious and told him that he only understood the words, not the meaning. She recommended that he find her brother, who understood the meaning and then she disappeared into a rainbow. Because of contact with the dakini he decided he must seek true realization outside the monastic university. The dakini appears as an ugly old hag because she is primordial wisdom, ancient beyond conceptuality. She is ugly because Naropa has been repressing and rejecting this part of himself. This ambassador of primordial wisdom appears in a hideous form because he has been deluding himself, thinking that he really understands when in fact he has been building a deluded castle of intellectuality and prudishness.[5]

Much of what we learn at universities is related to "head knowledge." When we have the words, we think we have the meaning. Words and ideas are necessary containers, but they take on meaning only through reflection on lived experience.

Allione goes on to tell of Naropa's journey and the fact that his habitual thought patterns were slow to change. This is something we can all relate to. We have the desire, the quickening of intuition about what we must do or say, but it dies under the weight of habit. Without the intuitive, symbolic language of the feminine soul, the seamless mirror of the mind is easily shattered by conceptuality and literalness.

"Due to his [Naropa's] lack of relationship to the dakini, who exists beyond duality and speaks in a symbolic language, he acted as if there were a 'self' to act. He saw everything external as being separate from himself, and fell into the trap of dualism, rather than seeing the mind as a mirror with the capacity to reflect without dualistic notions of good and bad."[6]

It is only by recognizing and healing the dualities that exist in ourselves that we can come to a true sense of interdependence with the rest of creation. We are just beginning to have some understanding of the interdependence of nature and all natural systems. If we pollute the earth, we are polluting ourselves; if we destroy the rain forests, the lost of oxygen affects every living thing. Weather patterns change; habitats change. This has always been true: over the millennia, the earth's systems have changed dramatically for one reason or another. What is different now is that we are aware of such systems and are, therefore, compelled to take a conscious position towards them and towards ourselves.

We are, likewise, beginning to recognize the interdependence of economic systems. The realization is dawning that on this planet, seen as a whole for the first time from space, we are all part of an interdependent system. We are inextricably tied to each other. But interdependence, as the necessary state for community, calls for something more than knowledge and logic. We can, and do, conceive of it in conceptual terms, but living within a world community interdependently calls for compassion, for feeling about the particular other, the particular situation. Once we realize that the particular "I" cannot have justice unless the other "I" has justice—that others cannot have clean water to drink unless I respect the earth—we begin looking at things differently, through the eyes of wisdom born of embodied experience. Justice is no longer blind.

THE JUDGMENT OF MAAT

In her book, *The Crone*, Barbara Walker presents some of the laws of Maat, the Egyptian goddess of justice. The list includes such commandments as:

1. No one should cause pain to others.
2. No one should make anyone sorrowful.
3. No one should steal, cheat, bear false witness, stir up strife.
4. No one should harm animals.
5. No one should damage fertile land.
6. No one should befoul waters.[7]

As Walker points out, these laws foreshadowed "by many centuries the 'golden rule' that appeared later in Buddhist, Jewish, and Christian traditions."[8] What is most striking about them is that they encompass all of nature, in recognition of the fact that humans are dependent upon the Earth. The interdependence we talk about so glibly today was recognized intuitively as early as 2000 BCE, based on the understanding of the Goddess (Maat) as the unifying principle in all of creation.

The Judgment of Maat. In the Book of the Dead of Kenna, the heart of the deceased is weighed in the scale against a feather from the headdress of Maat, symbolic of her role as the moral order of the universe.

Maat, the Mother of Truth, held sway during the Middle Kingdom of Egyptian history, when the kings were known as "good shepherd kings." They ruled by the laws of Maat, which were regarded as "the cosmic force of harmony, order, stability, and security, coming down from the first creation as the organizing quality of created phenomena."[9] The forms (order, justice, truth) arise out of the creative matrix. This order that rises out of chaos (as archetypal truths rise out of the unconscious) is attributed to the Goddess; it is not the imposed order of the patriarchal (ego) world.

The judgment of Maat, as depicted in Egyptian papyrus paintings, is an apt representation of the individuation process. Most depictions show a tall central pole with seven nodules on it. Across the top is a horizontal pole with a pan attached at each end to form a scale. At the bottom is a large composite creature with a crocodile's head, its open mouth placed between the third and fourth nodules. At the top of the vertical pole sits a hawk-headed bird. When a person is to be brought before Osiris, the god of death and resurrection, he or she must first pass the judgment of Maat. The person's heart is placed in one pan of the scale; an ostrich feather from the headdress of Maat is placed in the other. The ostrich feather depicts truth and justice, since the feathers on an ostrich are all perfectly equal. Now if the heart is too heavy, too densely packed with matter, it will fall into the jaws of the crocodile. If, on the other hand, it is too light from lack of embodied experience, it will fly into the talons of the hawk-headed solar god. Similarly, in the process of individuation, when we experience the world with a transparent heart, when there is truth in the body as well as in the mind, we are raised to a new level of consciousness.

The struggle between instinct and spirit, body and mind, presents itself today in many dreams. A man dreams of a crocodile swallowing his masculine instinct; a woman dreams of tiny crocodiles coming out of her skin; a dreamer dreams of voiding his bowels, and brown crocodiles come out; eagles circle ominously overhead, or carry off something of value. Frequently, these ancient images appear in the forms of their modern counterparts: submarines and planes. A dreamer is out swimming while planes are nose-diving at him, or, additionally, dropping bombs. Submarines, often with a malevolent captain, menace the dreamer.

This motif of the eagle and the crocodile comes through clearly in the dreams of a gifted five-year-old boy. Children tend to be more open to archetypal dream patterns than adults. The following dreams capture the essence of the human struggle between instinct and spirit. Young Sean had three sets of recurring dreams. Here is the first one:

I am skipping down the sidewalk. My steps get bigger and bigger so that I begin to fly—almost! I am excited about this because it is a sort of secret power I am discovering. But then the time between steps gets too long. I start to get scared that I can't control them. I am too high above the trees. It is dangerous. I might never be able to get down. Until it got scary it was wonderful.

The details of the dream occurred in the same pattern every time Sean had the dream. He would almost fly above everything and then become frightened because he might lose control. Although Sean was only five years old, his dreams were warning him of the danger of identifying too closely with spirit. Spirit yearns for light; it wants to separate out from the maternal womb in order to gain a new perspective and a release from the weight of matter.

This is the story of Icarus. In the story, Icarus and his father Daedalus are attempting to escape from the island of Crete. Daedalus, a brilliant craftsman, makes a pair of wings for himself, and a pair for Icarus. The quill feathers were threaded together, the smaller ones were held in place with wax. Daedalus warned Icarus neither to soar too high, lest the wax melt, nor to sweep too low, lest the feathers become wet. He begged his son to follow him. Icarus, rejoicing in the sweep of his wings, soared toward the sun. His father looked back and saw the broken feathers on the waters below. Young and inexperienced, Icarus could not resist sweeping toward the light, and was destroyed by his arrogance. Old Daedalus understood the necessity of holding the balance.

Falling into the abyss was the second of Sean's recurring dreams. Dreams of falling are not uncommon, especially in childhood, because this is a time when the emerging ego must adjust its feelings of omnipotence to the demands of reality. The ego is often bruised in its daily encounters with the real world. The higher it flies, the deeper it falls. All of us—children and adults—have to face our inflations.

Here is the third in Sean's trilogy of recurring dreams:

I am out on the sidewalk in front of my house. A horrible creature, like an eagle, chases me. I am very frightened and wake up, and cry in the dark.

The child feels endangered by power structures that he feels are assailing him. Already, the eagle has become a part of himself. The eagle represents the spiritual ascendancy of consciousness in its positive aspect; in its negative aspect, that ascendancy overreaches itself and becomes domination over and against that which belongs to the earth.

Many young children are given a dream or an experience, or develop a passion for a particular fairy tale or story that prophesies their task in life. Young Sean had another powerful dream that may hold the secret of his life's journey. In this dream, he is again on the sidewalk outside his house. All his dreams take place there, because it is the limit, the frontier of his experience at this time.

> I am standing on the sidewalk in front of the house holding a little piece of paper in my hand that was a great secret and important for me. A witch (like Witch Hazel in the comics) comes along and snatches the paper out of my hand, and laughs at me and takes it away to the far side of my grandparents' house up the little sidewalk that goes up to the side entrance. Under a little shelter in front of the door, she stands holding the paper up to me as though saying "Oh, you want your paper back? Well, here it is, come and get it." I go up to her and reach out my hand to take it. Just before I get it she snatches it away and pushes it down into a hole in the ground, like a drain. Then she cackles and laughs. I go down the hole after it. I find in a room down there another witch, who has got hold of the paper, and she is standing holding it in the same way! When I reach out to grab it, she snatches it away and stuffs it down another hole and laughs, and I go down this hole and there is another witch, and the same thing happens over and over and over again and I keep going down deeper and deeper, and finally I climb down into the place that is absolutely the bottom. There are no more holes that go any deeper, and when I go to grab the paper from the last witch, she throws it into a pit full of crocodiles. The only way I can get it is by walking out on a little metal rod like the towel rack in our bathroom. All the crocodiles want to eat me and I am very scared, but I start walking out like I'm on a tightrope . . . and then I wake up.

This is certainly the journey of the archetypal hero, down into the matrix of matter, down into the core of the unconscious to the primal material. In both men and women, the task of the masculine is to incarnate. The "great secret" of importance is in the jaws of the crocodile. At five, the young hero has an instinctive flash that may become his life's task, and he wakes up.

The devouring crocodile represents the life-death cycle, the ego's greatest fear, which lurks in the depths of the unconscious. Yet rebirth to a higher level of consciousness is not accomplished by flying through the air. The ascent is balanced by the descent. The treasure is recovered through encountering the chthonic devourer, the dark side of the Great Mother. In Jung's terms, this is working at the deepest level of the somatic unconscious in order to bring to consciousness the subtle body.

In this dream the witch, while seemingly malevolent, directs the young hero through the underworld toward the task he must appropriately fulfill before he can safely know the great secret. The witch here is not a negative figure to be feared, although the process, whether one is young or old, is fearful. She is equally the wise witch, who "tricks" us into doing what needs to be done to stop us from languishing in duality. It is by going to the deepest depths and finding there the treasure, the subtle body, that we realize that the very fear that kept us from going there is the fear that has been hiding the treasure all along.

Nearly all advanced spiritual traditions deal with ways in which the energy, the light, hidden in matter can be transformed before the spirit can be embodied as wisdom. In the Eastern traditions, the seven chakras, or energy centers, have been studied as a way of transforming energy into consciousness. The pole holding Maat's scales of justice with its seven nodules suggests that intuitively, the Egyptians may have had some knowledge of these energy centers. Knowledge of this energy flowered in cultures such as India and China, and is now making its way into the West. Since this book focuses on the transformation of energy into consciousness, a brief outline describing the transformation of the energies of the chakras may be of value.

The lowest, or root chakra, is the *muladhara* situated between the anus and genital region. The second lotus center is the *svadhishthana* in the region of the genitals; the third is the *manipura*, in the region of the naval. The three lower chakras have to do with instinctual urges. This recalls the crocodile beneath Maat's scales of justice, whose jaws yawn between the third and fourth nodules on the vertical pole of the scale.

The fourth chakra, in the region of the heart, is *anahata*. Here the lotus center has twelve red petals and within it a six-pointed star composed of two uniting triangles, one pointing upward, the other

The seven chakras

downward. At the center of the star is a golden lingam-yoni symbol, representing spiritual rapture, or the eternal embrace. The third chakra, below the heart, has a fiery red triangle to symbolize the passion of the instinctual forces, or blood as the power of the feminine. The fifth chakra is the *visuddha,* located above the heart, in the region of the larynx. It consists of a white triangle, which points downward, connoting the spiritual power of the descending masculine energy. It is in the heart that the two are brought together in dynamic interaction, producing the divine marriage of masculine and feminine energies within the individual. *Ajna* is the sixth chakra, located in the forehead, between and above the eyes. "The lotus here is of two petals, white and radiant as the moon, supporting a supreme vision of the Goddess, or of a God-with-Form."[10] The seventh chakra, *sahasrara,* is represented by the Lotus of a Thousand Petals, inverted over the crown of the head. This symbolizes a rapture beyond any form.

The chakras may also be interpreted in developmental terms. The root chakra is the survival chakra, a kind of primal hold on life, desiring food, desiring comfort, desiring love—all the basic needs of the young child. Sexuality, the second chakra, unfolds at adolescence, followed by the achievement of the third chakra, the solar plexus, which propels us into our identity in terms of *doing,* which is the goal of early adulthood. This is the realm of the developed ego consciousness. It is in midlife (the fourth and fifth chakras) that most people are compelled to seek a further identity in terms of *being*. The energy, as it moves upward, ideally resolves into a heart of flesh, a heart full of compassion for self and others, a heart grown wise from having struggled with the energy's inner transformation.

If, however, the ego becomes the basis for a split in the evolution of energy on its rise to consciousness, we are likely to develop a heart of stone rather than a heart of flesh. If the ego consciousness, in its will to power, represses the lower levels of energy, they become distorted. Then, the root chakra, symbolized in kundalini by the coiled serpent, becomes seemingly evil. What is repressed becomes negative when the energy of the root chakra is blocked; the "I desire" withdraws because it knows it will not be fulfilled. Unconsciously, that withdrawal can become a withdrawal from the desire to live consciously. It may appear as a fierce possessiveness—holding on to an idea, a project, a person. But the possessiveness is based on the terror of annihilation. Out of it arises rage, jealousy, greed, clinging codependency, parasitic feeding on others, as an infant is forced to feed.

Beneath these seeming passions lies dread—dread of life, dread of chaos, dread of the fundamental feminine cycle (i.e., dying to be reborn). Beneath that dread is frozen despair, the archetypal darkness that lies at the core of the negative mother complex. That is why Kali, the dakini, the Baba Yaga—even the Black Madonna—are so often perceived as totally negative. It is also the archetypal darkness at the core of much of our daily news, even our daily addictions. As our ideals fly higher in to the sky, our reality is faced with a deeper abyss in the earth.

Having a heart of flesh means being able to feel with, suffer with, the other. The heart that is in balance has to find its source in the root chakra. Its root is love, love of life and trust in life. Psychologically, the enlightenment of the root chakra leads not to possessing the other, but rather to commitment to the wholeness in oneself and, therefore, to the wholeness in the other. This involves standing alone, which requires being grounded in the *muladhara*. From that standpoint, one can desire what is best for the other, even if it means surrendering one's own desires and letting go of the other. Within oneself, it means suffering the death that brings new life.

If the energy of the root chakra is fundamentally afraid of life itself, transforming this energy into the very basis of life and further evolution is a daunting task. If we remain in the ego world, the externalized world of concrete reality, death in any form is unthinkable. In the Old Testament Book of Wisdom, this is set out as the patriarchal reality that exists without Sophia.

> For they said among themselves, thinking not aright: "Brief and troublous is our lifetime, neither is there any remedy for man's dying, nor is anyone known to have come back from the nether world. For haphazard were we born, and hereafter we shall be as though we had not been; because the breath in our nostrils is a smoke and reason is a spark at the beating of our hearts, and when this is quenched, our body will be ashes and our spirit will be poured abroad like unresisting air. . . .
>
> Come, therefore, let us enjoy the good things that are real, and use the freshness of creation avidly. . . . Let us oppress the needy just man; let us neither spare the widow nor revere the old man for his hair grown white with time. But let our strength be our norm of justice; for weakness proves itself worthless.[11]

Ego consciousness has difficulty going beyond this attitude. Religious systems hold out a hope of immortality, but if we are split, we can grasp that hope only with our heads. We have not *experienced* immortality opening up within us. We have not seen death for what it really is—a transformation—and we are, therefore, unable to enter into a process wherein that transformation can be experienced consciously at each level of growth. We may, consequently, be very fearful of our ultimate encounter with the Great Goddess. Without experiencing the light energy within us, either we see death as final and meaningless, or we surround ourselves with rituals, talismans, or plenary indulgences, which assure us a place in heaven through their power, rather than through our own transformation.

In the Book of Wisdom, Solomon the Wise provides the clue to finding the balance of the heart. "Seek Wisdom," is his plea. Wisdom combines experience with knowledge. Experience is lived through the passions of body; knowledge is learned through the discipline of mind. Wisdom connects body and spirit in soul. "Resplendent and unfading is Wisdom, and she is readily perceived by those who love her, and found by those who seek her. She hastens to make herself known in anticipation of men's desires. . . . For the first step toward discipline is a very earnest desire for her; then, care for discipline is love of her; love means the keeping of her laws; to observe her laws is the basis of incorruptibility."[12]

Keeping the laws of Sophia, like keeping the laws of Maat, is different from keeping the laws of the masculine. Wisdom, "the artificer of all," is praised by Solomon as "mobile beyond all motion, and she penetrates and pervades all things by reason of her purity."[13] In approaching the temple in Egypt one must bathe in the waters of Maat and repeat, "I have purified my breast and body with clean water, I have purified my hinder parts with the things that cleanse, and my inward parts have been [dipped] in the Pool of Maati; no one member of mine lacks Maat. I am pure, I am pure, I am pure, I am pure."[14]

Residing in Wisdom or Maat is not a literal undertaking. It means allowing consciousness to move constantly within oneself. "And She, who is one, can do all things, and renews everything while herself perduring."[15] This is the worship of the Great Goddess, who is incarnate, who builds up the body of incorruptibility or what Jung called the subtle body or the somatic unconscious. Only in building up this body of incorruptibility can we come to a point of soul consciousness capable of receiving and experiencing spirit.

Part of the feminine task in its journey toward wholeness is a recognition and reception of masculine spirit. This meeting can occur in some moment of numinous experience—a moment when timelessness intersects time. For many it comes in dreams.

A woman dreams she is looking at the stars, which suddenly form into the shape of a dove that hovers over a church. A young blond man comes to lead her into the church. Another woman is watching an animal in her garden rooting in the mud. As she watches, it transforms into a Christ-like figure. A more frequent kind of dream is that of an egg that gives birth to an eagle, or an egg that cracks in the dreamer's hand and reveals a beautiful young boy. A recognition of spirit takes place before the building up of the "body of incorruptibility" can take place. If it is not there as an experience of spirit, then the person will continue to cling to a concretized perception of life over against death. Body work will not be an embodiment of spirit, or a release of spirit. The root chakra, for certain, will remain closed.

Jungian analyst Nathan Schwartz-Salant points out that in alchemy "the first stage is a consolidation on a spiritual level, the creation of the so-called *unio mentalis.* Only then is there a descent back into matter, whence the body is transformed."[16] The transformation he is talking about is the reality that Jung called the somatic unconscious, or the subtle body. Body work or body exercises, however beneficial, will not bring about this transformation. The body will remain essentially concrete. Without the building up of the somatic unconscious the soul is not liberated and the feminine task has been circumvented. This is such an important undertaking both for understanding the role of feminine energy and for our own evolutionary growth that it will be dealt with more fully in chapter 5.

In a transformation that may take place over a period of years, the sexual chakra becomes an energy center not of rage or lust but of creativity and ravishment. Already rooted in commitment, love can find its expression in a sexual union that is free of possessiveness and jealousy. Here essence meets essence in the intense embrace of the moment. One temporarily moves out of chronos, or chronological time, into kairos, the eternal moment.

This timeless moment is characteristic of all acts of creation, where the tension of opposites is resolved into a new unity, a higher consciousness. The opening of the two lower chakras allows detachment and passion to come together into a harmony capable of transcending time. T. S. Eliot writes of this moment in the *Four Quartets:*

Men's curiosity searches past and future
And clings to that dimension. But to apprehend
The point of intersection of the timeless
With time, is an occupation for the saint—
No occupation either, but something given
And taken, in a lifetime's death in love,
Ardour and selflessness and self-surrender.
For most of us, there is only the unattended
Moment, the moment in and out of time,
The distraction fit, lost in a shaft of sunlight,
The wild thyme unseen, or the winter lightning
Or the waterfall, or music heard so deeply
That it is not heard at all, but you are the music
While the music lasts. These are only hints and guesses,

Hints followed by guesses; and the rest
Is prayer, observance, discipline, thought and action.
The hint half guessed, the gift half understood, is Incarnation.[17]

It is this experience of union in self-surrender that has to be supported by the sexual chakra or love cannot find its flowering in the heart.

The energy of the third chakra transforms control and will-power into intentionality. Rollo May defines intentionality as "the structure which gives meaning to experience."[18] In most people, will power is used to control experience—particularly the experience of the body. Over against perceived loss, it strives to shore up possessions, relationships, whatever is needed to give the ego a sense of security. Undifferentiated power emanating from the third chakra is in the service of the ego, maintaining the split between what Freud called the id (biological drives) and the superego.

We try to control our actions and our thoughts through will-power, or what we sometimes call intention. The word "intention" actually comes from the Latin root *intendere*. *Tendere/tensum* means "to stretch" toward something, not to block it off. In May's experience, "what is most interesting is the times in psychotherapy when strong voluntary intention—correlated with 'will power'—blocks the way to a person's intentionality, and is just what keeps the patient from communicating with the deeper dimensions of his experience. Intentionality . . . goes below levels of immediate awareness, and includes spontaneous, bodily elements and other dimensions which are usually called 'unconscious.' "[19]

May goes on to quote Paul Tillich:

Man's vitality is as great as his intentionality: they are interdependent. This makes man the most vital of all beings. He can transcend any given situation in any direction and this possibility drives him to create beyond himself. Vitality is the power of creating beyond oneself without losing oneself. The more power of creating beyond itself a being has the more vitality it has. . . . Only man has complete vitality because he alone has complete intentionality.[20]

Intentionality in itself does not lead to an enlightened heart. It is better thought of as a way of giving meaning to experience. It is open to both conscious and unconscious information.

Idealization is a projection of childlike energy onto persons or institutions seen as omnipotent or perfect. Often, individuals get caught up in trying to express that state of perfection in their own lives. The perfect body, the perfect wife/husband, the perfect teacher, all become disembodied images of the ideal, in whose light they inevitably fall short. Sons and daughters of patriarchy are very susceptible to this light. Women trapped in anorexia love and dread the light. They are in real danger of being swept off the earth by their perfectionist ideals and demands for perfect order. In dreams, these standards at first appear as a light figure, even a Christ figure. As the anorexic becomes more ill, this figure becomes demonic. Men, too, are vulnerable to being carried out of reality by the light. Their ideals, their hopes and dreams and artistic endeavors, can carry them right out of home, children, wife, and bills to be paid. Fantasy is one of the most dangerous addictions in our society. What is missing is embodiment.

Schwartz-Salant makes this distinction between the energy and the child-like expression of it: "The proper reception of idealization involves knowing instinctively, if not consciously, that the energy belongs to the young child: the object of the idealization is not god-like but the energy is, and that energy belongs to the child's emerging Self structure."[21]

What is necessary and adaptive in the child becomes maladaptive in the adult. The child's energy (capacity) for realizing the Self is projected onto parents, or teachers, or in the case of teenagers onto rock stars, athletes, TV characters. Projection in adults is still essential, otherwise analysis would not work. In recognizing what is being projected, people learn to know what is in their unconscious. Realization, on the other hand, is the internal process of taking off the projections and accepting responsibility for one's own potential.

In analysis, this process toward self-responsibility is the key factor if any growth or transformation is to take place. Until we recognize and accept that change is up to us, we are stuck in infantile judge-and-blame games. "So-and-so should be different, then I would be all right. If the workplace were different, I would be fine. Why don't they change? I try to give them everything and they are indifferent, stubborn." The list can be quite long. Everything would be so simple if the object of our projection would just carry out its proper role and if others would just conform to our projections and needs. Granted, a situation "out there" may be far from perfect from an objective point of view—the hysterical wife, the alcoholic husband—but the fact remains that the only person we can take responsibility for is ourself.

We know we can change ourselves when we realize that we are not dependent on how we feel, nor on how others feel about us, nor on what the situation is around us. The values we hold, the choices we make within ourselves and for ourselves remain our prerogative. In most situations, if we begin to change, to do our own inner work, to accept our own darkness and work toward consciousness, the situation will change. We will begin to emanate a different energy, one that exudes a sense of autonomy and authenticity.

This process of self-realization is the embodying of spirit in the fifth chakra. This is the throat chakra, and has to do with being able to speak one's own truth. Here one's truth becomes the expression of a journey already undertaken, of facing the fear of aloneness, of refusing to listen to the voices of conformity that would smile and suck our lifeblood, and lay us in eiderdown to die.

This is an inward journey that usually begins on a wild, stormy night. It takes great resolve to enter into the darkness of our own chaos, to give up the familiar path and begin to trust our own experience. The recognition and unconditional love of oneself is never a selfish journey. Most people, if challenged to love themselves unconditionally for fifteen minutes, reel in embarrassment. "What is love without judgment? How can I love myself so long as I am this assertive little prick? What does that mean—love unconditionally?" Ultimately, *that* is what the journey is about.

In our yearning to be perfect, we have mistaken perfection for wholeness. We think we cannot love ourselves until we and others meet some external standard. Depression, anxiety—in fact, most neuroses and compulsions—are ultimately a defense against loving ourselves without condition. We are afraid to look at the damp, dark, ugly yet exquisite roots of being that stretch deep into our survival chakra. We are fearful of finding that the spirit is not there, that our Home is empty, even as our outer home is empty. Yet it is in that place of survival, where the dark mother has been abandoned, that spirit longs to be embodied so that the whole body may become light. Ego wants to be the god of our own idealized projection; spirit wants to be incarnated in our humanity where it can grow in wisdom through experience.

The sixth chakra is related to the higher, spiritual, realms of perception, namely, to the form of the Divine that the soul seeks. In patriarchal monotheism, the Divine is widely perceived as Creator, Dispenser of Truth, Law Giver, Ruler of Humanity. He is the "beyond" of ego consciousness, who must be interpreted by the theologians, who claim to know what he wants. In his most benign form, this God is a superego figure that espouses civilization over anarchy, love over hate, peace over war. At his worst, he dictates carnage in order to preserve his "kingdom." Such a God-image may function to keep an individual or culture in check, but it cannot bring about the transformation of consciousness.

The great limitation of ego consciousness is that it tends to concretize reality in order to make itself feel secure about its own place in the scheme of things. Thus, it perceives life in terms of doing, and doing implies being able to control or manipulate. From this perspective, life is safe and secure—and static and dead. If, on the other hand, we can root our identity in being, in trusting the Great Mother, who cherishes all life—our own included—then the door is open for spontaneity, for something new to burst in with the security of those roots. Spirit blows where it wills. It is agile and quick, playing within the spaces of matter, constantly changing color, changing form, changing language, moment by moment open to new beginnings. The third eye, or Ajna center, at the core of the sixth chakra, has been called the perception of the imagination. Imagination is without limits, constantly bringing forth myriads of possibilities. Soul and spirit delight here in the garden of creation.

Laughter, joy, and ecstasy are associated with this chakra—and sorrow as well. These are not the personalized emotions of the ego, with its depression and anxiety, or pleasure and excitement. The emotions of the soul are real—intensely real, but they are not personalized. The soul can weep over injustice or the stupidity and greed of humanity. It can rejoice over the budding of a flower, or a little act of kindness. These are the keenly felt emotions of love devoid of self-interest, love that perceives the possibilities and grieves the inability to respond. When we meet someone who loves in this way we know immediately that we are in the presence of a great soul.

Beyond this chakra is the source of pure light, the God/Goddess without a form. If the chakras are dark, if the energy is not flowing, one cannot image this possibility. Ego consciousness cannot go beyond a God with form. Some mystics in the West, like Meister Eckhart, realized the need to go beyond the form of God, but this concept was quickly repressed.[22] On entering this realm, the vibrations in the soul/body become so intense that the individual becomes one with light itself, light beheld consciously. With the death of the gross material body, according to spiritual accounts, the soul enters this realm of light.

An analysand who was to leave for South America to work there was hesitant to go because his mother was hospitalized and becoming quite frail. One day he visited her, and she told him of a dream she had had the previous night.

> There was a boat and a lot of people jostling on the wharf. It was dark and I went to sleep. When I woke up I was on the boat. There was a bright light shining from somewhere above and a voice said, "Are you there, Margaret?" I thought, "Well, at least they speak English, wherever we are." There were other people lying in the boat head to toe, alternating like sardines, and I saw Marge and said, "Are you here too?" She said, "Yes," and I thought, "It's nice to have company." Then the light shone again, and the voice said, "Margaret R——, are you all right?" Then the boat went on, and I didn't know where it was going or why I was on it.

In her dream, the dreamer falls asleep and awakens in a boat, a mythical vessel for crossing over into another life. She is awakened by a great light and a voice coming out of the light indicating that she is known by name. She recognizes a friend who has recently died. The feeling is not one of fear but of comfort and even a sense of adventure into the unknown. This movement into the light seems to be the way the unconscious prepares the soul for the next step in the journey. In this case, the analysand and his mother were able to talk of her approaching death and take their leave of each other. This being done consciously, both felt free and the son was able to leave, although he knew he would probably never see his mother alive again.

Mystics of many traditions have written of this experience of entering pure light, or of going into the void. Since it is beyond our normal experience, description becomes very difficult. Those mystics who have entered the light while still in the body warn of the dangers: the body can hardly stand the intensity of the energy vibrations. Unless the body has become a "pure" vessel, that is, the energy centers are all open and in balance, the physical body will collapse.

The sixteenth-century Spanish mystic, John of the Cross, expressed it this way: "As, however, this sensual part of the soul is weak and incapable of experiencing the strong things of the spirit, it follows that these proficients, by reason of this spiritual communication which is made to their sensual part, endure therein many frailties and sufferings and weaknesses of the stomach, and in consequence are fatigued in spirit."[23]

In today's language, we would say that the soul, which is embedded in body, needs to be released through an increased suppleness and consciousness in the body, so that spirit may be more and more embodied. When this happens, all external phenomena disappear. This experience of light is also given credence by the experience of those who have been pronounced clinically dead and then been resuscitated. Dr. von Franz in *On Dreams and Death*, tells of Victor Solov, who was "dead" for twenty-three minutes.

> I was moving very quickly toward a bright shining net which vibrated with a remarkable cold energy at the intersecting points of its radiant strands. The net was like a lattice which I did not want to break through. For a brief moment my forward movement seemed to slow down, but then I was *in* the lattice. As I came in touch with it, the light flickering increased to such an intensity that it consumed and, at the same time, transformed me. I felt no pain. The feeling was neither agreeable or disagreeable, but it filled me completely. From then on everything was different—this can be described only very incompletely. *The whole thing was like a transformer, an energy-transformer, which transported me into a formlessness beyond time and space.* I was not in another place—for spatial dimensions had been abolished—but rather in another state of being.[24]

This dream is particularly interesting because it features the net, which "vibrated with a remarkable cold energy," a characteristic of the yin (feminine) force. The dreamer touches an energy field so powerful that he is at once consumed and transformed. From that moment everything is different—another state of being arises. If we compare this transformation to shamanic healing or healing through imagery, we need to take careful note of the words "like a transformer, an energy-transformer." Psychic healings happen when the imagination is so charged that it can heat a metaphor to an intensity powerful enough to change the energy in the body. *Metaphor* means "a crossing over." If we really believe that psyche and soma are one, then we need to ingest our metaphors with as much respect as we ingest food. Both act as transformers.

This changing of energy is the subject of a hypothesis formulated by Jung in a letter to Raymond Smythies.

> It might be that the psyche should be understood as *unextended intensity* and not as a body moving with time. One might assume the psyche gradually rising from minute extensity to infinite intensity, transcending for instance the velocity of light and thus irrealizing the body. . . .
>
> In the light of this view the brain might be a transformer station, in which the relative infinite tension of intensity of the psyche proper is transformed into perceptible frequencies or "extensions." Conversely, the fading of introspective perception of the body explains itself as due to a gradual "psychification," i.e., intensification at the expense of extension. Psyche = highest intensity in the smallest space.[25]

Commenting on the existence of a subtle body, Dr. von Franz writes: "If we take the hypothesis of the existence of a subtle body seriously, then this would suggest that the transformation of the coarse material body (and its energic manifestation) would continue gradually into the psyche. This would mean that what we call physical energy and psychic energy today could, in the last analysis, be two aspects of one and the same energy. . . . We would therefore be dealing here with a form of energy which *gradually* changes, from the physically measurable to the psychically immeasurable."[26]

In another letter, Jung makes clear that space and time have no influence on a certain part of the psyche.

> What is commonly understood by "psyche" is certainly an ephemeral phenomenon if it is taken to mean the ordinary facts of consciousness. But in the deeper layers of the psyche which we call the unconscious there are things that cast doubt on the indispensable categories of our conscious world, namely time and space.[27]

In referring to the irrelevance of time and space to certain parts of the psyche, von Franz writes that "at a certain threshold in the increase of frequency, the psychic functions which produce our perception of time and space seem to cease functioning."[28] The physicist David Bohm postulates a projected model of the collective unconscious based on the suggestion that the "observable material universe is just the unfolded or 'explicate order' of existence as the surface of an underlying enfolded or 'implicate order.' "[29] Dr. von Franz concludes: "This new image of the physical world can very well be associated with Jung's hypothesis of a single energy, which physically appears to be unfolded in space-time but coexists psychically as pure spaceless-timeless (enfolded) intensity."[30]

The wholeness out of which the manifest world unfolds is the perception of the sixth chakra, which leads to the experience of such reality in the seventh chakra. This is the reality that for many people seems to present itself at death. It is also the reality toward which Eastern meditation practices such as kundalini yoga, as well as the process of individuation, are oriented. Both are directed at transformation of energy to higher and higher levels of intensity so that ultimately the material body becomes more and more subtle in its ability to receive spirit or light. This is the process towards which the Goddess, or feminine energy, is directed.

Kundalini power, the symbol of raising the energy coiled at the base of the spine upward through the chakras, is called by Sri Chinmoy "the power of the Supreme Goddess."[31] Repressed or coiled in a circle, she can be poisonous both to the body and the psyche, but once risen and standing upright, she is beneficent. The power of the serpent, rightly understood, is one of the ways the Goddess overcomes duality.

One of the ancient understandings of creation in Chinese philosophy is: "The Tao begot one. One begot two. Two begot three. And three begot the ten thousand things." The dynamic between the two is a pulsating rhythm, a vibration. Bonheim, in an article on kundalini, sees this as the primordial wave, which "developing into consciousness, . . . appears in the form of a snake. For what is a snake other than a single, undulating, pulsating wave motion?"[32]

The inherent rhythm in the body becomes an important step in the journey toward the "ten thousand things" represented by the

crown chakra. It is this snake power that lies deep within the unconscious and deep within the body.

> Where, then, does the snake-wave appear within the human being? It
> dwells, first and foremost, within our very center, the spine, which,
> viewed from the side, looks like a snake, and moves like a snake.
> Further, it presides over the entire underworld of the body, governing
> many of our involuntary movements: the swallowing of food, the
> pulsating flow of blood, the peristaltic movement of the intestines,
> the pulsating rhythm of orgasm, and the tiny undulations that ripple
> through muscle tissue. The snake symbolizes everything within our
> bodies and minds that moves under the surface, hidden from the light
> of consciousness.[33]

As the movement becomes more enfolded at the deeper levels
of the cell and finally at the quantum level, we can, through various
movements, dance, drumming, or meditation, "align our conscious
mind with the unconscious psychic forces."[34] In this way, we are
"utilizing duality as a gateway into the consciousness of at-oneness."

Even among yogins, few achieve the highest form of kundalini,
and those, like Sri Chinmoy, who have achieved this experience of
the void—or acausal light—through kundalini, warn against approaching it without the appropriate sense of spirit awareness. As
Chinmoy states: "Kundalini power can perform all kinds of miracles;
but when it is a matter of elevating someone's consciousness, it won't
be able to elevate the consciousness even one inch. For that we need
spiritual power, the power that comes from the Supreme Goddess at
Her highest level."[35]

If we are trying merely to achieve a spiritual supremacy, a kind
of going for the light as if it bestowed some power or recognition,
we can put ourselves in danger on at least two counts. First, if someone does not have a deep spiritual commitment and the body has
not "surrendered" or unfolded consciously to receive that energy, it
is in danger of collapsing with the influx of such great power. Gopi
Krishna gives an account of unconsciously awakening the kundalini
power and almost going insane, feeling that his body was about to
be destroyed. The great mystic writer, Teresa of Avila, cautioned that
the health of the body is liable to deteriorate with the influx of such
energy. She also warned of the moral danger involved. In describing

the spiritual journey, she talks of the interior crystal castle, with its seven levels, or rooms. She tells us that once the sixth level has been reached, the spiritual awakening is such that there is little danger of falling back or relapsing to an earlier state. However, in the fifth mansion, there is a great temptation to use the knowledge gained thus far, and the ability to express it (this corresponds to the throat chakra), for personal power or aggrandizement. The spiritual sense can be subtly eroded by the ego's demands to gain personal recognition or to exercise power or influence over others.

The spirit has to be embodied, reunited with the soul, in order to move toward the sort of consciousness Sri Chinmoy is talking about. Without this reunion, this embodiment, the consciousness necessary to move forward cannot exercise power within an interdependent framework. This is what love means in its truest sense. The evolution of the soul/body to a state where it can become the chalice, the Holy Grail, that can allow Spirit, the creative masculine, within or without, to give creative expression to the world seems to be one of the particular concerns of the Black Goddess, at this point in our history. Without our recognition of the sweetness and sadness, rage and hope, in our bodies, and our honoring of our limitations as human bodies, we have no way of experiencing our compassion for one another. The wisdom of the Goddess manifests in the love we feel rather than in what we think.

BUILDING THE SUBTLE BODY

Spiraling up and spiraling down, the transformation of masculine and feminine, above and below is a constant theme in analysis. This comes through in the following dream. The dreamer was Anna, a high school teacher in her early thirties.

> I was in a plane, and it took off slowly, circling up around a mountain. The plane was suffocatingly crowded, so I eventually got out and stood on the roof. I felt exhilarated and secure standing there with my arms outstretched. It was as if I could reach out at any time and touch the face of the mountain as we circled upward. Then I was going down deep winding stairs into the earth. I came to a place that was like thick yellow slime. It was awful! It was blocking my way, so

I began to shovel it out. People ran over to me shouting, "Stop! This is God." But I kept shoveling. I circled down the stone stairs further, and came to another obstacle of red, flame-like leaves that were damp and matted together. I began to tear them out, and again people were angry and telling me to stop, that I was tearing out God, but I kept going in spite of their anger. Finally, I came to the bottom, and there were fresh green shoots coming up out of the watery earth—like a rice field. People were trying to tear the shoots out, but I said, "Stop! *This* is God."

The first part of the dream is about getting out of the suffocating security of the collective to discover the freedom of spirit. With her arms outstretched, Anna feels as if she is flying on the back of a great bird, perfectly free and yet perfectly safe.

The second part of the dream relates to the dreamer's own process in a very personal way. When this young woman first entered analysis, she would start to talk and immediately go into spasms of uncontrollable coughing, constantly bringing up thick yellow phlegm. This went on for weeks, until she was able to recount the oral sex-abuse that she had been subjected to as a young child. She had, in effect, been forced to swallow the false, demonic spirit, just as many today are being forced to swallow false masculine power, false spirit, in the home, at school, in the workplace. They, too, are being told, "This is God."

Red flames of rage can emanate from the first and second chakras when victims realize what has been done to them. The release of this rage is necessary, for only then can its repressed power be transformed into creativity. Patriarchy fears this potential for power and tries to suppress it. "Nice people don't get angry!" The second chakra is related to the sixth—or throat—chakra, that is, to creative expression. It is the generative power of embodied spirit.

Anna has been working on her rage. She is now ready for the creation of something new. She comes to the root chakra, where she discovers the new green shoots. This is the new life that is beginning to grow in her, with its need to be nurtured and protected. These are the tender shoots of her own unique truth, the beginning of her soul energy that, with care, will eventually blossom into a consciousness that is capable of standing firm in a love of self and of others. This new life she must protect fiercely against the systems and injunctions that would try to persuade her that her own feelings and perceptions are false.

Without an experience of safety in a loving relationship, Anna could never have reached this position. "To protect the soul, the Self seems to set up a block, so that the unendurable pain is channeled into the body, where nature deals with it as best it can. Because the pain is somatized, its psychological component is not consciously experienced."[36] Often, it takes a long time for the soul to trust, to reveal its new green shoots.

The process of embodying spirit is unique in each person. That it requires sensitive timing and understanding is clear from the experience of Sarah, a woman in her early forties. Sarah had engaged in the discipline of meditation since her late teens. At thirty, she found herself "caught up" in an intense white light every time she sat down to meditate. It was as if the natural energy of her body would fail, and her soul would burn with an intense heat. In such a state, she had no sense of time, but she knew she had to "get back" at some point or she would die. Although such awesome moments were a great consolation to her, she intuited that this experience should be set aside. The only way to do this was to avoid meditation, since she had no control over what happened to her in that state. Then, an eminent Spanish spiritual director happened to visit her town, and she took the opportunity to ask for his advice. Should she set aside such a rare gift? He sat silent for a while and then proceeded to describe for her the images that came to his mind. They were related to the story of the three apostles on the mountain witnessing the transfiguration of Jesus. Awed by such an experience, they wanted to put up tents and remain there forever. However, the time for that had not yet come, and they were instructed to go down from the mountain to live out their incarnate reality. "Yes," he said, "I think you should follow your intuition to forgo such experiences."

A short time later, Sarah was sitting outdoors, overlooking a valley, when she had an intense vision. A figure that she interpreted as Christ, "dressed in his wedding garments of white and gold," approached her. Standing to one side was his mother, and behind him stood a multitude of people rejoicing. He seemed to be making a proposal, which she understood to be an offer of divine marriage. She did not tell anyone of her experience, passing the next forty-eight hours in turmoil and terror. The vision had been, at once, awesome and awful. The ego recognized that in accepting such a proposal she would undergo a profound transformation, one that was tantamount to death—not immediate physical death in a literal sense, but rather, the death of the ego. Some heroic response would be required of her: she would be given some cross to bear, some unimaginable suffering to endure. Sarah had a great love of life and all the pleasures that life was calling her to pursue. To use her own words, she was "a very passionate and sexually oriented young woman." She felt incapable of making the sacrifice that would be required of her. But yet, the allure of the vision was irresistible. Timidly, she uttered the word: "Yes!"

For Sarah, this was the beginning of the embodiment of spirit, of going from the pure radiant light to the "god-with-form." On being "reined in," the intense psychic energy took the form of the Divine Lover, an archetypal masculine figure—the masculine spirit seeking union with the feminine soul. The visitations of the Divine Lover lasted for about three weeks, a time in which Sarah experienced such ecstasy that she hardly knew whether she was in her body or out of it.

For the following six years, Sarah was away, pursuing a professional career that required much discipline and intellectual energy. Meditation and spiritual awareness took a back seat to the more pressing demands of her professional life.

Returning home at the age of thirty-six, Sarah took the summer off before taking up a new position. During this time, she experienced some regret at having neglected her spiritual life, and she resolved to regain her balance through prayer and meditation.

Shortly thereafter, while she was in a gathering of about two hundred people, Christ appeared to her again, this time in the red robes of a martyr. He gently chided her for her infidelity to her inner quest, but then he said, "Do not be afraid, for I have prayed for you." Moving toward her, Christ placed a martyr's crown on her head, not the crown of victimization, but rather, a "knotted crown of fire" that turns suffering into love. This is how Sarah described her response:

> A wave of incredible joy went through me. I realized instantly that this was a promise that in spite of my fiery sexuality, my drivenness, and the many things I had come to regard as selfish, I would love completely—at least before I died!

The more Sarah grew in consciousness, the more she realized that what we so often call love has little to do with the ability to love consciously with our whole being—selfless surrender to a higher purpose, becoming love. She was more aware of her dependence on others, mistaking it for commitment; her fear, which asked for assurances; her indifference to the pain of others, which lurked beneath the surface of her own best efforts.

She was no longer tied to the literalness of the ego's interpretation of what was happening in death. The symbolism pointed more sharply to the ego death that would be necessary if love was to be achieved. This was an intuitive soul response to the symbolism of the gift of Christ. The gift had to do with the heart, and it made Sarah impatient for the transformation that would release her capacity to love. Although not consciously aware that anything had changed during those six years, Sarah now began to realize that she had undergone a transformation, because she had remained open.

Two summers later, Sarah had a very different vision. This one lasted for eight hours and gripped her in a kind of transpersonal fear. Difficult to describe because of its intense feeling of chaos, it was a vision of the world without spirit, without consciousness—a vision of matter without light. Out of this apocalyptic nightmare of boiling oceans and crumbling mountains, the only distinct image that emerged was of someone caught in a whirlpool, completely submerged in the spiraling waters except for a hand reaching up and grasping a large rock. Sarah realized that it was *her* hand. *She* was the person in the whirlpool. In the midst of the chaos that was swirling about her, all she could do was try to hold onto some kind of consciousness, some kind of center.

Morning came, and Sarah went out to the lake. Sitting under an overhanging tree and listening to the birds, she had the profound realization that *everything* is connected in love. The others were in the kitchen, getting breakfast ready. As she walked over to join them, she suddenly experienced her own being at one with love. This deep awareness of Self, this experiencing of her own true identity was to become the bedrock of her experience. In the hurly-burly of daily activities, we are apt to lose sight of our real identity, but an experience or a dream can become a reference point to return to in regaining that lost vision.

Sarah's energy now went into an extension of her core experience, although she did not do this consciously. She spent the next seven years exploring the writings of Thomas Berry, Joseph Campbell, and Carl Jung, whom she called her "three wise men." Thomas Berry, who writes and speaks so compellingly of the spirituality of the universe, brought an evolutionary perspective to her thinking. Joseph Campbell gave her an appreciation of myth and symbol, a way of interpreting that evolutionary experience. Carl Jung brought her to the nature and structure of her own psyche in its heights and depths. She was now in touch with the masculine energy that would take her out into the world.

The influx of masculine energy (spirit) resulted in a flurry of extroverted activity. Enthusiastic to empower others, she got involved in training people to minister to the elderly. For ten years, she gave workshops and served on the boards of directors of several charitable organizations—all in addition to her regular job. Inspired by spirit, she was trying to live out an ideal, and inadvertently flooding her soul with too much light. Then, on three successive nights, she dreamed. The vividness with which she recalled these dreams startled her. Up to this point, she could not remember ever having had a dream. For the first forty-three years of her life she was not "a dreamer."

> Night One: I am deep under the earth, inspecting some kind of missile site. My parents are there, and my sister. Suddenly there is an earthquake, and the earth begins to cave in on us. I grab my sister and we take a high-speed elevator up to the surface.
>
> Night Two: I am with my sister in an airplane that is sitting on the tarmac. It is engulfed in flames. My sister and I manage to get out.
>
> Night Three: I am up on some rugged coast (like northern Scotland) and I notice an enormous (10 feet high) tidal wave bearing down on us. (I am aware of a friend in the background.) I turn my back to it and get down on my knees. I let it wash over me, and when it has passed I look at my hair, which is hanging down with long strands of seaweed. I say, "Oh, this is how seaweed is made."

A few days after having these dreams, Sarah awoke one morning unable to breathe. Her body was finally protesting. She had developed pleurisy and pneumonia. This was not surprising, given her dreams. The earth's caving in was a good indication that Sarah's body was reacting against her drivenness. In the dream series, the dream ego is assailed in turn by earth, fire, and water—all the elements except air. Earth and water are feminine elements; fire is masculine. Too much disembodied masculine "air" (spirit) had taken over her waking life, crowding out the feminine elements and embodied fire. Sarah's dreams and her body were telling her that she was suffocating the other elements with too much concrete activity; her subtle body could hardly breathe, hardly take in pneuma, spirit, and was suffering from pneumonia. Psyche and soma, Maat's scales, were out of balance.

Sarah associated the underground missile site of the first dream with unconscious rage. As the earth quakes in fury, she and her shadow sister are carried by the high-speed elevator to air. The plane on the tarmac in the second dream represents her intuition: it burns (with rage and passion) on the spot, unable to take off into the air. However, she and her sister escape. The tidal wave in the third dream represents the danger of being overwhelmed by her unconscious. She deals with it by kneeling with her back to it and letting it wash over her, choosing to react passively to save herself. As she kneels with her head on the ground, she inadvertently takes on the prayer position, which the goddess so often demands in dreams. In lowering her head to the earth, she allows the water to cover her hair with seaweed. Its long tendrils are the exact gift she needs to ground her headiness. The female figure rising out of the water is like Venus born from the sea, a baptism by water.

The Goddess wakened Sarah from the depths of her unconscious with the following dream:

I am in bed, lying in the dark, when I am awakened by a bright full moon. I am looking at the moon, when a cat leaps up on the bed. It becomes evident that I am to follow it. I start down a dark, steep staircase, and when I come to the second landing I see a young man and woman embracing and gently making love. They are quite primitive looking (dressed in skins) but they have an innocence and gentleness about them. My task is to bring them up into the light of day.

The full moon symbolizes the Goddess in her role as a nurturing mother. She it is who wakens the dreamer from her state of unconsciousness. Once the dream ego is awake, her feminine instinct is aroused (the cat leaps onto her bed), and she, wisely, follows its promptings. She is led deeper into the unconscious until she comes to the second landing (the second chakra). The "primitive" young couple she finds there are gently making love. Sarah was able to see them as a reflection of the divine marriage that she had earlier seen in her vision. As above, so below: what happens in the psychic realm is mirrored in the somatic realm. Instead of being obsessed by lust, she now has an image of love. Sex is innocent and the body is pure in this young couple. This innocence and purity, however, can be distorted by lust, which leads to repression of instincts. The body is then made to appear evil, and the gratification of its needs condemned as sinful. Sarah's task was to differentiate her own driven and repressed sexuality, to recognize it as part of her body's greatest gift. The wounding is ultimately the blessing.

Another dream that was important in presenting the Goddess's role in embodying spirit was as follows:

> I am sitting in the middle of a huge field in the lotus position. A large bright moon makes it seem almost like day. I am holding an enormous white snake upright in front of me. All around, as far as I can see, white snakes are standing upright as if they are coming right up out of the earth.

Again, this dream takes place in moon time, the realm of the Goddess. At that point, Sarah knew little of the meaning of the symbols, particularly of the white serpent. She did not know that the white serpent represents the sacred life force, the power of the Goddess. The snakes in her dream portrayed divine energy in its incarnate form, coming right up out of the earth, as *prima materia*, as virgin mother energy. This was an image of the energy in matter (mater) and of the feminine role in releasing, directly from the root chakra, this energy into the earth and in her own body.

This moon dream seems to bring into balance upper and lower chakra energy. In the first moon dream, the release of moonlight into the young couple mirrors the earlier sunlight of the divine marriage. In this dream, the rising of the white snake from the earth mirrors the inundation of pure light that preceded the image of the divine marriage. The stronger the spiritual energy in the top chamber, the stronger must be the somatic energy in the lower chakra. The light has to be grounded.

Sarah continued with body work, daily meditation, voice workshops. As her body became more conscious, the light from within was released, and the symptoms that had manifested themselves when she first embraced spirit began to disappear. At seventeen, Sarah had developed a chronic bowel problem diagnosed as "spastic colon." She had lived with this for most of her adult life, controlling it, when necessary, with a narcotic-based medication that inhibited the peristaltic activity. As might be expected, this strategy invariably backfired the following day. As the lower chakras began to open, through body work and dreams, Sarah's bowel ailment completely and permanently disappeared. The problem had been so chronic that she continued to carry her medication in her purse for almost a year before she finally flushed it down the toilet—a "ritual" she thought very fitting.

Sarah's dreams illustrate the relationship between the above and the below: the release of energy in the lower chakras provided the grounding necessary for embodying spirit. Before this embodiment could happen, before the primitive young couple on the second landing could be brought into consciousness, the split in both the feminine and masculine energy had to be dealt with. The split feminine surfaced first in a dream in which a wild, dark whore was lying on her back on the sidewalk, offering her services to anyone who came along. The dream ego stood by, looking embarrassed. In a later dream, Sarah encountered the same dark figure outside her analyst's office. The whore asked Sarah how she might get into the office. There followed a heated debate as to the propriety of letting her in. Only reluctantly was she granted admittance. Similarly, Sarah's powerful sexual energy came into consciousness gradually and was transformed into the great white serpent.

The repressed sexual passion symbolized in the whore archetype appears in many contemporary dreams. Sometimes Mary Magdalene or Lilith or even a madonna figure appears. Because she does not belong with the faithful wives of the collective, she often appears sadistically beaten, brutalized. But, as every woman who has realized this energy knows, for better or for worse, it carries huge transformative power.

In her outward life, Sarah had reached the point where she was ready to forsake the patriarchal system and her own addictive drivenness. She resigned from boards, gave up her charitable work, even discontinued religious practices as she had understood them. The end of these practices was depicted in one of her dreams as a group of robed monks sailing into the sunset.

> When the ship leaves with the robed monks on it, I begin to climb a river bank on the other side and come out onto a lush meadow. A small rabbit hops by. Then a fox goes by, and we eye each other warily. After this, I turn around and see an enormous bull charging straight at me. I break off a tree branch, and as the bull charges I run the branch through his left eye and bring him to the ground. Suddenly, a black-caped demon figure springs from his body.

As long as Sarah had sought to please others, her sexual energy had remained buried in her unconscious. In stepping out of her Pollyanna role, she realized that this latent energy had been manipulating her from within and undermining more conscious experience of the divine marriage. Now that this threatening energy of the bull was coming into consciousness, what would she do with it?

The following night, she had a second dream.

> I am walking at the edge of a woods with a male friend. Suddenly a fox goes by. Immediately, I become wary and reach for a shovel that is at hand. Sure enough, an enormous bull comes out of the woods. This time, however, a shaman figure dressed in skins and feathers also comes out of the woods dancing and chanting. I realize that he is here to teach me how to tame the wild bull.

This enormous energy cannot be killed, as Sarah had tried to do in the first dream. In fact, it would be psychically damaging to persist in trying to kill it. In a transformed state, it represents powerful creative masculine energy that needs to be integrated.

Sarah began to connect with the bull when the young Dionysus came on the scene in the following dream. Sarah finds herself in a farmhouse up on a hill with an intellectual male friend, having a boring discussion. She leaves the farmhouse and goes down into the valley, and there she sees another friend (a creative shadow figure) riding bareback on a horse, expressing great glee. Then she looks and thinks she sees an animal, possibly a bull. However, as she approaches she sees a curly-haired young boy of four or five, with a goat at his side.

The solar masculine no longer held any interest for Sarah. She went down into the valley, the deeper regions. Her shadow side was no longer wild whore energy. She was now a creative woman connected to her body (horse) in a playful, creative way. The black bull chthonic energy, the polar opposite of the divine lover, had now been transformed into a third—a new, young masculine, connected to the instinctual realm but not overwhelmed by it. The connection with the goat points to Dionysus, now no longer repressed. When Dionysus is repressed he becomes a raging bull. "The Bull, the underground Dionysian power, has been unleashed."[37] If Dionysus is held in bondage, he destroys us. He turns into addiction and madness. When he is honored, "[w]ine streams forth, vines with swelling grapes appear, ivy grows, honey trickles down, water or milk gushes forth. The mystery which calls forth nourishing or intoxicating streams is the same mystery which splits rocks, bursts chains asunder and causes walls to crumble. Dionysus is the god of ecstasy, dance and song; he is also Lysios, the loosener, the liberator. He brings plasticity and flexibility into what is rigid and hard; he frees us from old bondages; he dissolves old claims; he lifts the age-old barriers that conceal the invisible and the infinite. And the infinite vitality that has been locked away wells up from the depths like the milk, honey, and wine that spurt forth from the earth."[38]

This young masculine points to a new Christ consciousness and seems to be where Sarah's energy wants to go. This is the Christ figure of Sarah's earlier visions, but restored to the vitality of the earth, the ecstasy that causes springs to flow within us, the creative masculine. This is the repressed vitality of the underworld and the light energy of Christ coming into a new third creation within consciousness.

Sarah had experienced great ecstasy following her early vision of Christ. Such an experience can become a cornerstone for one's life, but it does not become a way of life. The experience of the divine lover, once it is embodied, does become a way of life. Rather than singling out an isolated moment, it becomes a flame in every moment of every day.

Sarah had been a nun. She had left the convent not because she had lost her faith in Christ, but because the patriarchy that contained him had become increasingly oppressive. The constraints of the convent had finally become impossible to endure. She could no longer put her energy into the institution. After several months of analysis, the following dream showed Sarah where the energy wanted to go.

> I was with my analyst and we had found a wild horse that had been running in a field. We tamed it and took it up to the door of a convent/monastery. They said it did not belong there. However, they had some dresses that they wanted us to exchange for some other dresses at a neighboring convent. This seemed like an imposition so we went further on down the road. I looked through a large opening in the rocks and there in a deep underground cavern I discovered a large golden cathedral. The walls, everything, were bathed in gold. The priest was dressed in gold robes and had the gold chalice raised in the sacrifice of the Mass. Then I walked on further and I saw an old woman and a female friend up on a roof. The roof was made of a board like bristol board and there was a large green S painted on it. The women had been planting grass, individual blades about 3 inches long into the holes in the board. They were about two-thirds finished.

The instinctual life, the passion of the body, had been tamed and was now available to Sarah to live a more whole life. The convent, however, was not a place that could receive this passion. The nuns were interested in exchanging the outer garments: different works, different structures, a deeper embracing of idealism. The fire of inner transformation was not understood. Sarah's energy had moved away from the nunnery.

In the second part of the dream, Sarah looks through a large opening in the rocks and there, in a deep underground cavern, discovers a large golden cathedral. The walls are bathed in gold. The priest is dressed in gold robes and has a gold chalice raised in the sacrifice of the Mass. Here, the golden cathedral and the gold chalice are not common gold but alchemical gold, or congealed light, the interplay between the masculine and feminine within, transcendence and immanence. It symbolizes the work that goes on in the center, the Self. The feminine chalice in the Mass constantly receives and issues forth the incarnate God of life, death and resurrection. Sarah began to experience the light of her earlier meditations as an energy emanating from within her body, an interiorized spirituality.

The energy of the dream then moves into the realm of the Crone who is supervising the work that lies ahead. The roof, the sheltering feminine principle, on which is emblazoned the identity of the dreamer—a large S—is being covered with grass. The grass roof is reminiscent of the thatched roof in many cultures or the sod roof of Irish cottages, familiar to the Irish friend who is helping in the dream. In Ireland, the grass roof was often thought of as a putting on of the earth, of putting oneself under the protection of the Goddess, as if in a cave.

This putting on of the goddess is still a work in progress for Sarah. The S, her identity, must still become more fully incorporated into her feminine consciousness. The work that began (eighteen months earlier) with the seaweed covering her hair is continuing consciously with the grass on the roof. The value in studying Sarah's dreams is the insight they give us into the Black Madonna, whose love is bound to nature and to the earth. Her love becomes a covenant with psyche. The consequences of this bonding lead to embodiment of light and relationship to reality.

Sarah's dreams show the spiraling up and the spiraling down of the energies within our psyche. Like Jacob's ladder, they reach between heaven and earth. Here the angels are ascending and descending; the divine energies are circulating along the spine and vibrating in the body, conscious energies that can transform dense matter into subtle body and disembodied light into subtle body. Ultimately, their union is the divine marriage.

The twelve-petaled lotus of the heart contains the ascending and descending triangle with the golden lingam-yoni. The integration of masculine and feminine energies within symbolizes the divine embrace, which includes all creation. It is the source of our creative response to life. Here is the heart of love.

Over a space of several years, with total commitment to her process, Sarah transformed her lust into a love that could embody lust, refining the energy that becomes a deep commitment to other people. No longer driven energy, it is now an energy that stands in a little hallway every morning and takes time to surrender the day to Sophia.

The movement toward empowerment through love can be seen in two subsequent images. In one dream, Sarah was seated on a chair, and, as individuals came up to her, she draped each with a silk cloth of an appropriate color. In the second dream, she was on the side of a hill; hands were reaching out, and from a basket of flowers she gave each hand a flower, which turned into a jewel that symbolized exactly what that person needed. This is no longer a desire to love that can be driven by willpower. Rather, it is a love that comes out of the center, a love that can see others clearly and give what is necessary to each.

Anyone who has gone into the flames and been touched by the Goddess knows the many deaths the ego has to undergo in order to experience the uniqueness in oneself and in others. Learning to love is a life-long task. Only in an eternal moment can we experience our true identity. As we begin to understand who we are, we can begin to see the essence of others, an essence that is uniquely lovable.

Sarah's dreams are guiding her toward leaving behind the narrow confines of conventionality and duality. Leaving duality means living in paradox. Paradox is the core of wisdom and the core of the Goddess. Wisdom holds the balance of life/death, mind/body, masculine/feminine. By holding the balance of both, she allows them to transform into something new. *Paradox, presence,* and *process* are words we associate with the Goddess, she who "renews everything while herself perduring."

This is the judgment of Maat. She does not assign any judgment or rewards for keeping rules or practices. She weighs the heart. If the heart is in balance, the process is complete; if it is not in balance, the process will continue. On whichever side of her scale we are trapped, we must start again painfully from there. In the Old Testament, she is Wisdom. She is the supreme treasure.

> I have directed my soul toward her,
>   and in purity have found her;
> Having my heart fixed on her from the outset,
>   I shall never be deserted.[39]

PASSING AN ORCHARD BY TRAIN

Grass high under apple trees,
The bark of the trees rough and sexual,
the grass growing heavy and uneven.

We cannot bear disaster, like
the rocks—
swaying nakedly
in open fields.

One slight bruise and we die!
I know no one on this train.
A man comes walking down the aisle.
I want to tell him
that I forgive him, that I want him
to forgive me.

—ROBERT BLY

MEN HAVE NOT ESCAPED patriarchy's bludgeonings. While women are presently more articulate in expressing their demands for equal rights, increasing numbers of men are becoming conscious of their wounding. They are recognizing how deep is the hole at the center of their psyche because their father was not present to them. He may have died; he may have disappeared; he may have worked hard every night at the office or at his computer at home. Life may have been too much for him and he drowned himself in alcohol. He may have been a tyrannical father, who always knew what was best for his son and, therefore, never saw or heard his child. He may have been the perfectionist, for whom nothing but top grades, top scores, top performance were worth bothering with. Or he may have "opted out" and let "Mother" take over—Mother, who was also shaped by patriarchy; Mother, whose judgment was more severe than Dad's, her eyes soul-blind, her ears soul-deaf; or Mother, who in her essential hatred for men, sucked her son's life out. These are patriarchal parents, who may be doing their very best but who are totally unaware of the unconscious devouring complexes that destroy life around them.

Men are no less at risk than women. They, too, even as tiny children, had to "measure up." As little boys, there is something in them that wants to make Dad proud and Mom happy. As adults, their bodies are often forsaken and their feelings buried. Loving words may be on their lips, but they do not feel. If the floodgates open, their hearts may break. In this chapter, we will look at the dreams of some sons of patriarchy who have done their utmost to understand their wounding.

Daniel was a successful, forty-year-old filmmaker when he first came into analysis. Like many successful men, he was propped up with addictions. All the unresolved issues of his life were begging for attention, and he felt that life was slowly eroding from under him. His unconscious resistance made him late for everything. The spaces that should have been vibrant with creativity were dulled by alternating indulgences of coffee, alcohol, cigarettes, and sexual fantasies. Daniel's preanalysis dream was about the death and resurrection he would go through in order to find his inner feminine.

> I am the captain of a ship—a huge ocean liner, sitting in the harbor of a large city like New York. I have been given an order that the ship is to be sunk because it is contaminated in some way. I am very sorry to have to do this. Then I am a worker on the ship. I am down in one of the deepest cabins—my room I guess, and I have a lot of things to do, but I am late and resisting the inevitable. I become overwhelmed by a wild panic; my mind races in all directions at once trying to figure out what to do. I don't know which way to go or what to do first. Suddenly I am calm as I realize that the ship is going to sink, and there is nothing I can do about it. I resign myself. But when I start to see water seeping in under my door, I get a deep sick feeling in my stomach, and then there is blackness.
>
> Now I am the captain again, on the top of the ship, and it is up out of the water again, all washed and sparkling clean and bright. I am overjoyed because my ship had sunk, but now it is floating and clean. I run from place to place, ecstatic. Then I remember that I had been trapped in a lower cabin as a worker and had drowned, and I start down towards that cabin feeling a horrible dread. I hesitate outside the door, dreading the wreckage and destruction inside. When I open the door and look in, everything is neat and cozy and a young woman is sitting at a desk with a light on, her head lowered on her arms. A voice says: "She's fine. She's just sleeping."

Daniel is the captain of an ocean liner: a large ship often symbolizes a large mother complex. In life, his mother had been absent since his infancy, and therefore, her absence became his dominant fantasy. His ship (the container of his life) is contaminated and must be sunk. Here is the archetypal theme of baptism: a symbolic submersion in water, a death and rebirth from the womb to a new life. In the second phase of the dream, Daniel is a hired hand, running around in confusion, accomplishing nothing. His split masculine in his dreams was putting his life in jeopardy. In his waking life at the time, Daniel was no longer in charge of his life. While this part of the dream images his current condition, the final phase of the dream points to the future, unveiling a rechanneling of energies in a very creative way, with his inner feminine firmly located at his center, though still dormant. When he approaches the lower cabin, he finds, not the wreckage of his inner masculine, but a young woman deep in the hold of the ship with the light on. She is not dead, but sleeping. When she awakens, "the light on" suggests that the process of inner transformation will be further illuminated.

Daniel felt that he was trying to protect the young feminine from the addicted captain with the polluted ship and the ineffectual shiphand. A death and resurrection would be needed before he could safely waken and relate to his own inner feminine, and, indeed, this turned out to be Daniel's process over the coming months. Before the inner feminine can safely emerge within the unconscious, she needs a strong, discerning masculine partner, who can maintain the boundaries, create the sacred space where feelings can emerge and be listened to. The intuitive wisdom that arises from the body, the creative matrix, needs a focused masculine that can release the creativity of the soul. The danger in waking up the sleeping feminine whose lamp is lit is that the masculine as captain will be flooded by her presence so that the ship may sink again. What is constellated in the dream is masculinity standing as captain before a feminine figure who has not yet awakened. Archetypally, the scene constellates the sleeping princess of the fairy tale, about to be awakened by the prince's kiss. Here is the young feminine who needs to be free of the mother complex.

Conscientious as Daniel was about his dream work, the following dream shows how easily the neglected feminine can be abandoned. The dream takes place in a day-care center, where all the adults are either eating or watching television—two common addictions in our culture.

A little girl, sort of gray-looking, wanders over from a large table to where I am doing something. She puts herself head first into a garbage can. Like a suicidal person, she proclaims herself to be garbage and throws herself out. I take hold of her feet and lift her out of the garbage can and carry her upside down to someone else. He takes hold of her hands and lifts them up so I can put her on the ground right side up. I lead her over to her friend, who is in the adult room and is supposed to be looking after her, but is actually watching some show on TV and ignoring her. I tell him that she needs a medical check-up (as though he is a doctor) but he says she's fine. I point out that she's so feverish that there are beads of sweat all over her forehead. He agrees to give her a check-up. He stands up and I lead her over to him and although she is gray and sweating she does a little skip of excitement at the fact that she's going to be looked after. When I see the joy she feels from such a small display of caring, I put my head in my hands and cry.

Sick though she may be, the child brings joy without any demand to Daniel. She proclaims herself to be garbage. For the dreamer, this is a wake-up call to do something about the obsessive drivenness of his life. Coffee, cigarettes, and sex had kept him from feeling anything beyond an artificial high interspersed with bouts of depression. Like so many men and women at midlife, he had run headlong into the aching emptiness he had tried so desperately to avoid. This dream was his soul's plea to be heard and cared for.

In the following dream, the archetypal depth of the split in the masculine energy is evident at an individual and collective level:

> I am making my way down a deep, mazelike cave. It is quite dark and I am very apprehensive. I am urged on, however, by a medieval-like sorceress, who is behind me, pushing me forward. I am drawn toward a light in the distance and find my way down to a large opening in the middle of the maze, where two huge figures are seated at a table. One seems bathed in light; the other was equally dark. I become very frightened that I will be seen. The sorceress turns me into a cat so that I can creep forward to the table at which they are seated without being noticed. I look first at the face of the light figure and then at the face of the dark figure, and realize that they are the same. Then I realize with shock that it is my face. I want to get out of there because I am afraid that I will turn back into my usual form and be caught.

Daniel woke up from this dream with an enormous pain in the area of his heart, the center of the cave in terms of his body. It was in the heart that this stand-off of energies was taking place. He could hardly breathe, and was sure he was having a heart attack.

The dark feminine, whom he didn't know yet, made Daniel face what was for him the core issue: his potentially creative masculine and his repressed dark shadow. The task was to hold the tension between these two enormous energies until a third could emerge. The temporary bridge was in the power of the sorceress to change him into a cat (feminine instinct), which could face both parts of himself and allow his ego to remain invisible and, therefore, safe.

The feminine instinct (in the form of a cat) had often appeared in his dreams. It was a part that he had saved from the devouring mother and patriarchal father that gave him his interest in art and kept him from carrying out the death wish that was very real for him. In his dreams this cat began to take the form of the homosexual shadow that would bridge the gap between the negative parental complexes.

> A young girl and I were prisoners with a group of people. We were waiting in an upper room to be taken somewhere. We were waiting for the guard, a big, fat, slobby, disgusting, animal-like man. When he arrived, he picked a young boy from the group and made him come into the next room to have sex with him. There wasn't really a door on the room, so we all knew what was happening, but nobody did anything. We were all afraid. I was horrified and terrified that he would spot the young girl with me and want her too, so I tried to get her to kneel down next to me so she would look smaller than she was, or not be noticed. When the pig had finished, he and the child came out. I was amazed that the boy appeared to be flirting with him. Then we were given the order to start out. He went first, down the stairs, and we all followed in a line. I spotted a pair of scissors on a table by the stairs, and I was determined to grab them secretly as I passed by, so that if the slob tried to take the young girl, I'd kill him with them. As I passed by the table, I tried to reach for the scissors without looking back, so no one would notice—but I missed them. Then somebody tapped me on the back, and I was terrified that I was going to be told on. I turned around and X (a gay guy who works as a shipper at the studio) handed me the scissors.

This dream is certainly about Daniel's trying to protect his young feminine from the brutish, Nazi-like part of himself. But it is also about the betrayal of his young masculine. The young boy is raped, and in being raped he identifies with the power figure in the dream. Many child psychology studies show that children often identify with the perceived parental power figure in the family whether it is mother or father. Children are essentially helpless, and they naturally compensate for this by identifying with power. This was part of the constellation of Daniel's shadow side that blocked the development of his creative masculine.

The final image is that of the homosexual shadow, who gives Daniel the scissors to protect the young feminine. Scissors may also enable Daniel to cut his way out of the web, the collusion with negative energies. The homosexual shadow often appears in dreams in this bridging role. It seems to carry a natural sympathy toward the feminine, while at the same time, being very effective against the tyrannical male and female figures locked in either matriarchy or patriarchy. The brutish Nazi is the power that constellates fear. Buried deep in the unconscious, it would rape both the little boy and the little girl. This is evil, the shadow side of God that the Crone showed Daniel deep in the core of his unconscious. Why is such demonic energy, masquerading as the "super man," so prevalent in our culture?

While violence against women and children has become symptomatic of the present state of our culture, and has recently received much attention, the real problem often goes unrecognized. At the root of this social malady is a pervasive feeling of male impotence, a psychic impotence that most men are loath to confront, let alone confess. Such feelings of inadequacy or impotence are either buried or acted out as aggression or rage.

In another dream, Daniel is twelve or thirteen years old and has a pet snake with which he plays games. This snake is a secret pet. If anyone approaches, the snake immediately turns itself into a rigid square frame, like a picture frame. One day an old priest knocks on the door and walks into the room. Immediately, the snake assumes the guise of a picture frame, and young Daniel throws a newspaper over it. The priest quite heedlessly knocks the frame (snake) to the floor and steps on it. After he has left, Daniel picks up the snake, which is near death, and takes it to a swamp in Florida in hopes that it can be revived.

At twelve, Daniel was coming into his own phallic power. He did not have a strong enough ego, nor strong enough inner support to transform this emerging power, now relegated to the Florida swamp. He was born into a working-class family of six children. Shortly after his birth, his mother was admitted to a sanitarium and, except for infrequent visits, he did not see her until he was ten. His siblings were older. Daniel was raised by his father, an Irish Catholic, a hard-working man who did the best he could. Daniel's father was unable to recognize his young son's imagination and creativity.

Daniel's snake dream takes him back to puberty. This is a time of burgeoning manhood; it must be nurtured in secret and integrated into the personality gradually. The snake carries the potential for wholeness, but this potential is hidden behind the rigid square frame of tradition. In ancient cultures, puberty was recognized as a transition time, when the men of the tribe introduced the young boys into manhood through initiation rites. In this dream, however, the old priest (symbolic of the old patriarchal system) offers no such recognition of the boy's phallic power, but heedlessly steps on it. The emerging phallic power is crushed—in this case not cruelly or deliberately but unconsciously. There is no masculine consciousness that can initiate the young boy into manhood, nor is there a feminine container within or without that is strong enough to withstand the onslaught of patriarchal power.

In the face of this assault, the only thing Daniel can do is take the injured snake to the swamp. This is an ambivalent image; the swamp suggests a place of stale water, where one could become bogged down, inert, passive—a place of the devouring mother, the crocodile. At the same time, it is a place of chaos, teeming with life. It is a dangerous place. In taking his snake to the Florida swamp to resuscitate it after the priest's near-fatal assault, Daniel is attempting to nurture his young masculine, now entering manhood. At this crucial juncture in his psychic life, he has no masculine guide, no positive father figure to show him the way. He consequently finds himself among the dangers of the swamps, where, as Blake points out in his *Proverbs of Hell,* we should "Expect poison from the standing water."[1]

Temporarily, the phallic energy is driven into the unconscious, where its strength manifests itself negatively as rage. The real source of this rage cannot be acknowledged, because it would open the pubescent male to a further threat of annihilation by, for example, the patriarchal priest of the dream, who would inadvertently kill the snake. Often, this rage is directed at the feminine, which confronts the masculine with its woundedness. In this century, the impotence of patriarchy, disguised as power, expresses itself in genocidal behavior.

The packs of young boys stalking our city streets today display untransformed, raw instinct being acted out (phallic power being relegated to the swamp). They are stuck at an infantile level of raw reactions being projected onto other people and "the system." Had they had fathers to attend them in male situations (as the elders of the ancient cultures had done), they would have heard stories of their own forefathers and realized that their fears and dreams were part of an ongoing heritage; they would have been put through challenges with nature that would have demanded their all for survival; they would have sung and danced until their raw instincts were transformed into music that could contain them. In other words, they would have experienced profound respect for nature and the equally profound process of transforming raw instinct into culture. In our society, the decisive transformation rarely happens and the result is an alarming growth of anarchy in the streets, with no respect for nature, law, or culture.

What is evident archetypally in this brutal, regressive behavior of street gangs (though in a very different way and coming from a very different place), is Antony's descent, in Shakespeare's *Antony and Cleopatra*, into the Alexandrine swamp of Cleopatra, where the mud of the Nile, though potentially fertile, buries Antony. If the man fails in the initiation that would take him out of the incest, he falls into negative aggression toward the Mother. He fails to step into his own manhood. Then it is difficult for him to harness his masculine energy to the energy of the matrix that would move him ahead into new creative energy.

As a young man, Daniel married a very beautiful woman—the idealized feminine that he carried within him. This unconscious liaison soon became a collusion of negative projections that served only to further his own feelings of impotence. He gave up his art career and found himself holding down two jobs in order to supply the material possessions he felt his wife was demanding. She looked for the Dionysian in other men, and left him feeling that she would leave him if he did not meet certain standards. He finally freed himself from her. In subsequent relationships, he felt some degree of potency only when he had sex without any feeling for his partner. While this freed him from his sense of inadequacy, it did not connect him to his own Dionysian side; it drove him further into his addiction to work, cigarettes, and alcohol.

At the same time he began to have homosexual fantasies in which he would attract or dominate other men, or sometimes turn the relationship around and become completely dominated by them. Had Daniel had access to some kind of male initiation, he might have had some way of breaking free of his early emotional bonding to his father and been put on a path toward his own creative masculinity (the powerful positive energy he saw sitting at the table in the dream of the cave).

Daniel's emotional impotence is the subject of a dream in which he was to be married.

> I am to be married. Before the wedding, I am having sex with someone. I am not able to penetrate, and I can't tell why. I notice a sore on someone's penis. The wedding is also a shooting of X [a film that Daniel was working on at the time]. I am to sing a solo part, but there is no time to go over it before the performance. I am extremely nervous about the wedding and the solo. Then everyone arrives. The whole crowd is watching me. I notice a sore on my own penis. I am worried that I won't be able to meet anyone's expectations. I'm afraid I will fail.

Daniel's phallic power was wounded, and his anxiety about his inability to penetrate governed his life at this time, not only in his relationships, but also in his work. The film he was working on, which was the cause of a great deal of his anxiety, was his first attempt at going "solo." He could not get away from the expectations of others because he had no firm grounding in his own reality. He did not have confidence in his own ability to stand alone and direct his own life from within his own center.

In patriarchal culture, men are burdened, perhaps even more so than women, by the expectations placed on them to be active and successful in the outside world. Competition is the operative word from the schoolyard on. A man has to find a channel for his own sense of potency, or mastery. If he is not an athlete or a scholar, and does not have the support to develop his own potential, his woundedness can easily translate into some kind of covert or overt violence, a usurpation of power through manipulation, or at the point of a gun.

A gradual shift in Daniel's energy is seen in a dream he had one year later to the day.

I am some sort of god-king, yet confined within a long narrow pen with rounded ends. (It resembled a large penis.) A youth passes by, and I desire him sexually; but I am disappointed when he finishes his business and returns to where he came from. Later, he returns to pass by the pen again, and this time I command his attention. He is nude, and I secretly blow icy blasts of breath onto his nipples and onto his genitals in order to arouse him. I am able to get him close enough to my pen so that I can kiss him on the mouth, and I began fingering his asshole. I tell him that I want to fuck him. He says, "But I shouldn't go back to my wife with an asshole all red and raw." I reply seductively, "Will she really notice?" Then I stopped kissing him, realizing that there is no passion in it for either of us.

Here we have the identification with the old god-king, the symbol of the whole patriarchal system. This is the distillation of internalized patriarchal energies in Daniel, who wants to have intercourse with the new young masculine energy. Interestingly, the breath that comes from his body is not warm. Its icy blasts do nothing to arouse the youth. For the time being, he is still imprisoned in the patriarchal pen. Patriarchy has tried—and continues to try—to seduce the new masculine, to lure it into a sphere that promises power and all its illusory trappings. But, as the dream suggests, this sphere is really a prison.

This juxtaposition of power and imprisonment can be interpreted on the cultural level as well. The prison is not just a prison—it is a *phallic* prison. The king-god (the Sun God) is a symbol of rationality, logic, reason, by which the world is to be governed. What then is the meaning of the phallic prison?

The answer to this question may lie in a study done by Carol Cohn, a Senior Research Fellow of the Center for Psychological Studies in the Nuclear Age, affiliated with the Harvard Medical School. She studied the language of defense intellectuals, "the creators of strategic doctrine [who] actually refer to members of their community as 'the nuclear priesthood.'"[2] They have, after all, the esoteric knowledge, a grasp on power and reality from an objective, empirically-minded, scientific point of view. This technostrategic language is very compelling in its logic, and Cohn admits to becoming seduced by it. However, even false systems can appear compellingly logical, given their starting point, their underlying premises.

Technostrategic language is based on a logic devoid of values, feelings, and humanity. It makes it possible to think the unthinkable, to speak the unspeakable. The horror of a possible one hundred thousand charred bodies is reduced to sustainable "collateral damage"; the incineration of cities is sanitized to "countervalue attacks." Even something as innocuous as peace does not escape the euphemizing influence of technobabble: peace is now spoken of as "strategic stability."

Whence comes the power of this mighty priesthood? According to Cohn, "[M]uch of their claim to legitimacy . . . is a claim to objectivity born of technical expertise and to the disciplined purging of the emotional valences that might threaten their objectivity. But if the smooth, shiny surface of their discourse—its abstraction and technical jargon—appears at first to support these claims, a look just below the surface does not. There we find the strong currents of homoerotic excitement, heterosexual domination, the drive towards competency and mastery, the pleasure of membership in an elite and privileged group, of the ultimate importance and meaning of membership in the priesthood, and the thrilling power of becoming Death, the shatterer of worlds."[3]

The phallic-shaped missile is, perhaps, the ultimate symbol of patriarchy. Cohn recorded conversations in which the unconscious imagery involved "penetration aids," or "more bang for the buck." In talking about the placement of the new missile, one professor said, "Because they're in the nicest hole—you're not going to take the nicest missile you have and put it in a crummy hole." She attended lectures that "were filled with discussions of vertical erector launchers, thrust-to-weight ratios, soft lay downs, deep penetration, and the comparative advantages of protracted versus spasm attacks—or what one military advisor to the National Security Council has called 're-leasing 70 to 80 percent of our megatonnage in one orgasmic whump.' There was serious concern about the need to harden our missiles, and the need to 'face it, the Russians are a little harder than we are.'"[4] While she sat in disbelief at the transparency of the images, no one else (with the exception of another woman) seemed to notice.

Cohn also noticed among the "priesthood" an obsession with what she calls "patting the missile." Their inordinate delight in this activity was so obvious that she had to ask herself: "What is all this 'patting'? What are men doing when they 'pat' these high-tech phalluses? Think about what else men pat. Patting is an assertion of intimacy, sexual possession, affectionate domination. The thrill and pleasure of 'patting the missile' is the proximity of all that phallic power, the possibility of vicariously appropriating it as one's own."[5]

What Cohn unearthed in her research was the unconscious split in patriarchy between the head and the phallus, in other words, the tension between power and imprisonment. Here, then, is the meaning of the "phallic prison" in Daniel's dream. While the head goes about constructing its stratagems of power, assured of its own logic, the repressed phallus (the missile) carries out its destructive activities, driven by its own instinctual needs, which have nothing to do with logic and objectivity. Neither the head nor the phallus is, of its own accord, able to break out of this disjointed relationship. They are both held, as it were, in a prison.

The concern over phallic power is carried in the unconscious of many men. Recall Daniel's dream of a year earlier. Daniel was extremely nervous about the wedding and the performance (his work). He then noticed a sore on his own penis, and was worried that he wouldn't be able to meet anyone's expectations, that he would fail. There is a homoerotic element associated with this concern about phallic power. Recall Daniel's sexual fantasies of wanting to dominate other males as a way of experiencing his own masculinity, or sometimes of submitting to another "powerful" male, that is, participating in the other's phallic power.

Men today are no less seduced by power or imprisoned by fears of impotence than they were in the witch hunts of the fourteenth century. At that time, many husbands denounced their wives to the Inquisition, accusing them of having secret liaisons with the demon lover, who could satisfy them better than they themselves could. Today, as then, underneath the paranoia and propaganda that drive the patriarchal power system is the fear that someone else will have a bigger, more effective penis than one's own. This is the tyranny to which men have become conditioned: they have to compete with each other in a tournament that has only one measure of success.

Another notion pertinent to this discussion is that of "nuclear virginity." The initiation of a country into the "nuclear club" is looked upon as a deflowering, a loss of virginity. If a country, such as New Zealand, rejects the invitation to initiation, the response (as it was in the case of one Air Force General) is that of "a man whose advances have been spurned. He is contemptuous of the woman's protestations that she wants to remain pure, innocent of nuclear weapons; her moral reluctance is a quaint and ridiculous throwback. But beyond contempt, he also feels outraged—after all, this is a woman we've *paid* for, who *still* won't come across. He suggests that we withdraw our goods and services—and then we'll see just how long she tries to hold onto her virtue."[6]

This is the language of the virgin/whore split that has existed for centuries. To lose one's virginity, as India did in testing a nuclear device, is to be looked upon with scorn and alarm. If, on the other hand, a country chooses to remain a virgin when the "protector" wants to make a whore out of her for his own purposes, her refusal is met with anger.

Defense strategy is not formulated on the basis of objective, logical, rational premises, even though this may appear to be the case. Rather, the language it uses suggests that it is shaped by an unconscious desire for sexual domination—a situation that is even more dangerous, since what is actually going on is unacknowledged. All the technology that we are developing will bring no real change to the human condition so long as we act out of a mind/body split that leaves both attempting to function outside their natural totality.

Discussing the mind/body split at the level of language is not a digression. Language mirrors our metaphors and those metaphors are our spontaneous revelations of ourselves. The dichotomy between mind and body in military strategists is no different from the dichotomy in most contemporary men and women, including the individuals whose dreams are related in this book. Daily exercise may produce excellent bodies, but those bodies may live quite cut off from feeling and thought. Most of us know very little about our vital organs and are quite unable to pick up their important messages. In working with dreams, the body's organs and symptoms are essential to a full understanding.

Daniel discovered that the god-king imprisoned in his penis-shaped pen no longer held any attraction for him. His energy was moving toward his own seeds of creation. Two months after the god-king dream, Daniel had another dream, in which he was in a "wonderful, home place," preparing to frame some Book of Kells pages. In the background was some exquisitely beautiful Irish music played by two instruments, and Daniel was intrigued by the way the two instruments interacted to produce the music. Daniel's male friend T. had brought over a book that revealed the secrets of waxing the pages he wanted to frame. Here, in Daniel's own words, is the end of the dream:

> I am looking through the book, and it has wonderfully beautiful designs with exactly the colors I want to work with—dark turquoise and bright rust, gold ochre and kelly green. As with the music, looking at the book is like looking at my art, which has never gotten done—I am impressed. T. tells me that the first step in the process is to have a tiny piece of skin snipped off each of my balls! I am quite uncertain of this, but he goes ahead and does it. I examine the little pieces of skin, puzzled.

The energy in this dream is moving toward a wonderful home place, home as the symbol of belonging to oneself, the place within us that each of us is journeying to. There is the realization of two energies playing together to make beautiful harmony—a foreshadowing of the integration of masculine and feminine. He wants to restore the Book of Kells, a spiritual document linked to his heritage. He is given the exact colors he needs to work with in order to restore this spiritual heritage. There is also the allusion to his work as an artist, which he gave up in his first marriage. The first step in the restoration process is a symbolic sacrifice of two tiny bits of skin from his scrotum (which contains his testicles). That is, he must contribute his own creative power to the process of spiritual restoration. No one else can do it for him.

Nowhere has the woundedness of the creative masculine been symbolized more powerfully than in the legend of the Holy Grail. The legend tells of a whole land laid desolate because the Fisher-King has been wounded in his generative capacity. One version tells us that he was wounded in the thigh, another that he was wounded by an arrow that pierced both his testicles. The arrow through his testicles is not a phallic wound. Rather, it is a wound that precludes the giving of life-producing seed. The phallus is a means of penetration, a vehicle readily linked with performance. If it is cut off from the feminine within a man, from his feelings and values, the loss is destructive. True potency, however, lies in the testes.

The identification of new life with the sacredness of the testicles goes back at least as far as Abraham, the father of many nations. When men were about to swear an important oath or enter into a covenant, they placed their hands on each other's testicles. Thence came the custom of swearing on the father's testicles. (The words *testicle* and *testament* are derived from the same root.) Not surprisingly, the testicles often feature in the dreams of men who are beginning to reconnect to their potency, to the possibility of being creative, of delivering the seed of life.

Early in his analysis, Daniel's dreams often centered on two themes. The first had to do with the link between his ego and his shadow: in his dream, he was both criminal and detective, both murderer and hero. The second involved the feminine in some precarious position that the dream ego was unable to do anything about.

Following the dream of reconnecting his potency to the creative, spiritual realm, Daniel made changes in his outer life. He quit his job and genuinely began to honor his own creativity. Naturally, his dreams also changed. Instead of passively allowing things to happen to him, he began to shoulder his responsibilities. He became more patient and, with his growing confidence, more assertive. He was able to stand up for himself without hurting anyone else. He began to state both his masculine and feminine needs clearly, without manipulation.

The real healing of the split in Daniel's masculinity came around the time of his father's illness and death. He had gone to be with his father during the time of his illness. One evening, as he was massaging his father's back, he was able to tell him that he thought of him as "a good guy." "Thank you," his father replied. "That's all I have ever tried to be." By now, Daniel had sorted out his personal father from his own interiorized father and the Great Father. He was thus able to see his father for the human being he was, a straightforward man struggling with his own circumstances. That night, following this simple exchange, Daniel had a dream.

> I am sitting on my father's front porch. There are people coming and going in and out of the house. The party seems to spill out into the street. Across from the house, there seems to be a carnival going on, with games, and rides, and booths. The people on the porch with me start out to the carnival, and want me to come too, but I realize that I prefer to sit quietly on the porch.

After they leave, I am sitting, looking at a large picture of myself as a baby. The longer I look at the picture, the more I see what a beautiful baby I was. I seem to fall in love with the baby. Suddenly I become ecstatic as I perceive that this baby is more than beautiful, more than wonderful—this baby is exquisitely perfect! The love I feel is so great that I reach right into the photograph and lift the baby up out of it and hold it to my chest. I feel a beautiful bond of love between us. He lies against me completely contented, and I sit quietly, feeling overjoyed. Eventually, I decide to take him for a walk and look around the carnival.

As we are walking, a man running some kind of thrill ride pressures me to take a ride on his machine. He is quite negative, and reminds me of my uncle, with whom I had a fair amount of tension and conflict when I spent my summers working on the family farm. I maintain a careful calm so as not to disturb the baby resting peacefully on my chest. I avoid confrontation with the man, and get on the ride, even though I don't particularly want to. When he gets it going, he seems to make it go faster than it is supposed to. I think he is deliberately trying to make me lose my balance; nevertheless, I maintain it perfectly. When the ride is finished, I simply get off and walk away, still feeling calm and happy with my baby. I decide the carnival isn't very interesting and start to walk back to the house.

In this dream, Daniel is no longer in his father's house. His presence on the front porch suggests some separation from the old bonding. Other people (the less differentiated energies in Daniel's psyche) are going in and out, and finally decide to go to the carnival—a place of play, but also of shadows and distractions. In saying "no" to the distracting energy, he is able to contemplate his own newly-born masculine, reconnecting not only with his past innocence but also with the new possibilities in his future. His early innocence and potential had been frozen in time, as symbolized by the photograph. The beauty that was once his—and every child's—had been lost, obscured, besmirched by life's experience. Now, this innocence is reclaimed—not by a regression into the past, but rather, by a movement forward into the world, the carnival.

The ride keeper is Daniel's patriarchal shadow, associated to an uncle from his childhood. In contrast to the stormy relationship with the uncle, this time Daniel does not lose his balance. His responsibility to his own innocence and potential is strengthened by his genuine love of self.

To become innocent is not to be naive. The child holds a naive innocence, which is lost through family relationships, through the school system, through the competitiveness of work, through any of our experiences that demand conformity at the expense of the soul. From within, our own fears of failure, rejection, or loneliness cause us to give away so much of our self that we eventually can no longer recognize our own uniqueness, our own beauty. As we gradually re-claim the "I am,," we begin to move toward a conscious innocence. Our opaqueness dissolves into a transparency that allows us to com-municate honestly and directly with others. We recover the spontane-ity of the child. We have burned our way through the debris of life to simplicity.

Twenty-three days later, Daniel had a dream in which he was wandering through hallways in a maze-like structure with a homosex-ual friend. The friend says he is leaving for good. Daniel is shocked, but realizes there is nothing more to say. He goes on by himself. Then the dream changes.

I am a religious novice in some kind of "celestial" novitiate, with a group of novices, being put through vigorous gymnastic exercises on free-floating scaffolding way up in the sky. We are quite giddy from the height. Our teacher is an extremely stern and sober master, who gravely stresses the precise importance of every exercise we go through. At that height, his instructions are literally a matter of life and death. We pause briefly, and I am not paying very close attention. Suddenly the Master heaves the swinging ladder at me and shouts, "NOW!" I freeze, terrified, as I watch the ladder swing toward me, because I've never done this exercise by myself and I am not prepared for it. However, I leap into the air at exactly the right moment, grab the correct rung in exactly the right way, and swing through the entire maneuver perfectly, flipping over and landing beside the Master. Since I pass the "test," the practice concludes for the day and we all go inside.

Then I am in a living room, and a group of people is buzzing with excitement at some news. "Have you heard?" they ask me, "The Master is leaving!" I am stunned. I walk away by myself, full of grief. "How could he do this to me?" I think. "How could he decide to leave, and not even tell me?" I go outside his office and sit down, waiting to talk to him. Many people come and go, all settling their affairs with him, and getting instructions. Because I am a novice, I have to wait until they are all done before I can see him. At last he comes to the door and looks out and sees me. He says, "Oh, yes, I suppose I should talk to you before I go." I go into his office, very sad and hurt. He knows I am upset. In the privacy of his office, he turns into my father, but he looks quite different. He is calm and wise, and has a certain radiance and power. He tells me his decision to leave is not due to a loss of faith. It is not a bad thing, but a good thing—a decision he had made with God. He tells me that now it is up to me to carry on without him, on my own.

This dream is primarily about assuming responsibility for oneself. In the first part of the dream, the homosexual shadow leaves, and Daniel journeys on alone. The second part of the dream is about saying good-bye to the father. The evening Daniel had this dream, his father died. What is extraordinary about the dream is that the unconscious put forth the positive things that Daniel had learned from the "stern master." He had been taught to grab hold and to let his spirit soar high above the Earth. He had learned self-discipline and industriousness. Daniel had yet to accept that there are no perfect parents and no perfect children. He still had pain to acknowledge and pain to let go before he could completely forgive his father and fully integrate the message of the dream.

In this dream, there is no judgment or praise on the part of the master. He allows his student to trust his own insights and intuitions without being dependent on others for validation. The transformed father, who has made his own decision to die, leaves Daniel to carry on without him. The son must become his own man, the father of his own inner child. Understandably, this dream was a very special gift for Daniel on the morning of his father's death.

In sorting out his life within and without, Daniel might have thought that he could breathe a little more easily. With the unconscious, however, the more we move toward the light, the more the darkness attempts to constellate against us. It is as if the negative energy is saying, "No, no! Not that easy!" One day, Daniel arrived for his session with a nightmare. In this terrifying dream, he is in the living room, when he feels a cold, icy blast blow through the house. Everything becomes menacing, and a horrific figure appears, dressed in black. The figure comes after him, and Daniel tries to shake him off. Finally, in the hallway, the figure pins Daniel to the wall, choking him. In the end, Daniel is able to muster the spiritual strength necessary to defeat this demonic figure, who then loosens his grip on Daniel's throat and flees.

In the dream, a death wish is constellated. The demon personifies highly charged energy emitted, as it were, from the clash between the tyrannical father and the helpless anarchist son—a negative trinity. The demon is a negative spirit that must be confronted if the killer energy is to be transformed into something more creative.

We can never bring the unconscious shadow energy into full consciousness. Rather, in holding the tension between the positive and negative energies, we make room for a new, "third" entity to arise. Early in his analysis, in what he called "the crone dream" (p. 91), Daniel saw the two huge figures at the table—Christ and Satan—and recognized his face in both.

An apparent resolution of these opposing energies took place in Daniel in a dream he had close to the end of his analysis.

> I am in a medieval-looking town with old cobblestone streets that lead to a large public well in the middle of the main square. There are people down the well, and I am lowering a rope and pulling them up one by one. Finally, at the very bottom of the well, there is only one person left. I pull and pull on the rope, and finally he comes bursting out with great energy, shouting, "I want a good fuck!" I am appalled. He goes right over to a young woman and begins dancing with her. I tell him to stop, but neither of them pays any attention to me. They just keep dancing with abandon all around the square, laughing. N. (his new wife) is there, and I say I don't trust this man, but she thinks he is wonderful. I want to get on my bicycle and ride off.

At the very bottom of the well, in the unconscious depths, underlying the other archetypal energies that Daniel had to pull up, is the "Lord of the Dance," often referred to as the Horned God. Daniel had difficulty accepting him in his dream. He wanted to put distance between himself and this dancing, singing, ecstatic image of unself-conscious sexuality.

This is Cernunnos, Lord of the Animals. It is Shiva, or Dionysus—archetypal energies long repressed by Christianity. Repression turned the Horned God into the Horned Devil, the root of all evil.

For Daniel, however, this dream signified transformation in the split-off part of himself and the possibility of unity within.

The Horned Devil is energy so repressed and cut off from the earth that it is best symbolized by Mephistopheles, that light and airy creature that floats above the earth. The Horned Devil is the disembodied spirit that manipulates, usurping situations for the gratification of its instinctual desires for domination—sexual or otherwise. The Horned God, as Gary Lingen points out ". . . is a positive model for male power—free from the patriarchy and all other authoritative

The Devil. The horned god was associated with nature and the feminine. Since being banished to the unconscious, he has become the disembodied horned devil.

models—as he grows and passes through his changes during the wheel of the year, he remains in relationship to and not separate from the prime life and nurturing force—the Goddess."[7]

The Horned God, moreover, is an archetypal figure quite unlike most masculine images as they appear in our culture. He is difficult to understand because he does not fit into any of the expected stereotypes, neither those of the "macho" male nor the reverse-images of those who deliberately seek effeminacy. He is gentle, tender and comforting, but he is also the Hunter. He is the Dying God—but his death is always in the service of the life force. He is untamed sexuality—but sexuality as a deep, holy,

Cernunos, Lord of the Animals

connecting power. He is the power of feeling, and the image of what men could be if they were liberated from the constraints of patriarchal culture.[8]

The Horned God, the wild man, symbolizes everything that the patriarchal persona disdains, because he plunges people into change, uncertainty, freedom from conformity. He is spontaneous, not rational and controlled; he is honest and straightforward, not devious and manipulative; he is in service to life, not in domination over it. He is confident of his own potency and does not need to compensate with phallic missiles. He is creative, not destructive of the earth or of relationships. Whereas Apollo, the Sun God, turned women into trees, or stones, or made them lose their voice, Dionysus, the god of ecstasy and dance, was, perhaps, the only god on Olympus that remained faithful to one woman, Ariadne.

The real reason Dionysus has been banished from our culture is that he is the God of death and resurrection. Patriarchy, with its unrealistic faith in the goals of this life, is built upon the denial of transformation and death. It cannot tolerate a god who dies—an Osiris, a Dionysus, or a Christ. For men and women, allowing the Horned God to live within us means accepting death as transformation. It means living an incarnated life—a life in which spontaneous spirit is allowed to transform matter. It means allowing spontaneity to burst through outworn patterns of thought and behavior, recognizing that these patterns are dead, and allowing them to die to make room for the new. Daniel was appalled by this energy in his dream, although the women were not. In reality, however, his whole journey deep into the realms of the unconscious demanded many deaths.

Stark honesty, however painful, is needed on this journey toward the Self; the unconscious will not tolerate anything less. One must be willing to face many cruel truths, those we keep hidden from the light of day, and those we keep hidden from ourselves. Not only do we have to die to a false image of ourselves, but we have to change our outer life accordingly. Change *means* change. We may have all the insights, but if we do not incarnate them, they are all in vain. We may have to die to our job, to a particular relationship, to our faith. Death is agonizing, lonely, risky. We have to be willing to suffer the loss of those things that stand in our way to freedom. It is the Horned Devil who says, "No, there is an easier way, a pain-free way. Come fly with me." For the pain of an actual transformation, the Horned Devil would substitute the delusion of an addiction. Instead of flying, one has first to crawl.

Once Daniel began to integrate this energy into his own experience of self, his own sense of potency, he could turn his energy to embrace the feminine both within and without. During, and after this time, he made many changes. Through swimming and body work, he could feel the energy rising from his root chakra. He began to walk differently. Outwardly, he established a new career, and though he was not driven to win awards, his creativity was honored by those around him. He married and eventually had a son. One day he was holding his infant son in his arms, when suddenly he remembered the dream he had of lifting his own infant child out of the photograph. Tears of joy fell down his cheeks at the thought that now he would be given a chance to more consciously father the young masculine. This experience gave new meaning to the phrase "a dream come true."

The Horned God can come back into the culture only in relationship to the Goddess. He is the embodied, incarnate masculine, the rightful consort of the Goddess who is also incarnate, the Divine Immanence. Shiva was the consort of Shakti, as Osiris was the consort of Isis. Christ gave voice to Sophia's wisdom. Incarnate life is the coming together of masculine and feminine in both men and women. A man who is not in relationship to the Goddess has no choice but to project his soul needs onto a woman. No woman can carry this projection, but if she seems to reject the man, or fails to comply with his wishes, fails to be the womb or the nurturing breast that he is projecting, then he feels a loss of potency. Violence against women springs from the deepest insecurities in the male, because, in the absence of the Goddess, the woman carries for the man his soul projection. His experience of the woman, because she is not the Goddess, is a betrayal of his soul needs. To lose her is to lose his soul. If, on the other hand, he wins the woman by pleasing her, his rage is equally great, even if it is repressed rather than acted out.

Daniel's mother was absent; he was raised by a strict father. James's mother, on the other hand, was a devouring mother and his father a passive agent in his upbringing. Although their backgrounds were so antithetical, both experienced the healing power of the Horned God.

James was in his early forties when he came into analysis. He could be very charming, sensitive, and gentle—qualities that attracted many women. On closer examination, however, his relationship with them turned out to follow a predictable pattern: sexual conquest followed by repressed rage and disappearance. He was married and, although he was estranged from his wife, he used his marriage as an excuse not to make a commitment to anyone else. Always, wife (mother) was in the background. As he entered midlife, the unsatisfactory nature of these swiftly abating relationships became increasingly apparent to him. They were, he realized, driven by a compulsion he did not understand, except as a repressed rage, the real source of which was unknown to him.

Upon entering analysis, he had the following dream:

> A tenant farmer has killed someone and has returned to me with a rifle. He was driving along the beach and now comes up a path towards me with the gun. I take it from him and he talks. I am an editor of a newspaper and often publish his comments. He shaves a large broken thumbnail with a chisel. Then he turns from me and starts down the path towards the shore/beach again. Something warns me not to get too close to him—for my life.

The tenant farmer, the shadow figure, does the dirty work. He tells James about it, but James doesn't want to get too close to him or acknowledge him in public. In talking about the dream later, James said that he felt that the farmer had buried his victims on the beach. The buried corpses represented the relationships that James was involved in. Every time a relationship was aborted, it was buried so that he could go on with his socially respectable life. Psychologically, we unconsciously project onto others what is in our own unconscious. We may fall in love with the person who carries the projection, in which case we are bound to our own projected image. We may equally hate or fear another person, in which case we are also bound to our projection. As we become conscious, we recognize and take responsibility for the aspects of ourselves that the other person has carried.

What is missing in the dream is a feminine figure—someone who will carry a soul connection. Until a man has drawn back and integrated his projection, he cannot recognize or embrace his own inner feminine; he constantly looks for it outside himself. Because his own feminine is so undifferentiated, he will unconsciously seek out "mother" on whom to project his soul. Men tend to remain content within this mother-bound projection so long as they are emotionally "little boys" consistently seeking to climb back into the womb. This son-mother bonding will continue so long as mother/ wife is equally unconscious, making no demands that son grow up. Her own inner masculine is still a little boy over whom she has power. In their unconscious collusion, both partners are denying themselves and each other their own truth.

When a man enters emotionally into early adolescence at the age of forty, he may rebel against "mother" and turn his sexual fantasies onto "mistress," as was the case with James. Throughout his life, James had been unconsciously bonded to his mother. While his father was physically present, he was psychologically absent and failed to ground his son in his own manhood. James could not leave mother, nor could he copulate with her any more, since his own manhood was beginning to assert itself. A split occurred in his own feminine; therefore, while in the external world he remained essentially mother-bound in his social roles as husband, father, churchgoer, within himself he rebelled against his bondage to the mother in a series of affairs that affirmed his own late-burgeoning manhood but at the same time threatened his social position.

Only after many years of this split existence (which was a failed attempt to assert a manhood independent of the mother) did James realize he was stuck in a cycle that was hurtful to everyone else and totally unsatisfactory to him. He was stuck in a role in which his acting out in the series of affairs became a burial of the very energies he sought, in the name of his manhood, to release. He did not recognize in the release of these energies the operations of the anima (his inner feminine) in its struggle to break out of the mother. His anima remained mother-bound. For this reason, in the dream version of his affairs, he encounters not a woman, but a man with a gun, who hands him the gun as if to kill the feminine—the mother—in himself. The apparent absence of the feminine and the attendant repressed rage of burying corpses in the sand provides the unconscious representation of his situation.

Given the overwhelming attention he received from his mother, James had to recognize the negative side of his positive mothering. One of his early dreams was of a little boy climbing a hill (Figure I). He came to a great boulder blocking his way. This boulder took

Fig. I

on the personality of a domineering presence commanding and directing his life. It was like an oracle, with the voice coming out of the stone and a finger pointing at him. Then a figure began to emerge from the stone, almost witch-like, with dark circles around the eyes and gaunt cheeks. All the figure consisted of, it seemed, was an enormous head and a menacing vagina. The little boy knew the only way to save his life was to avoid any confrontation.

Fig. 2

James developed the habit of recording the messages from his unconscious through nondominant hand drawings when he awoke, rather than writing them down. Drawing, like writing, with the nondominant hand tends to release the untrained, primal energy of the child, allowing the unconscious to move directly onto the paper without judgment from the ego. The drawing James did of this figure emerging from the boulder is presented in Figure 2. Whatever we fear we tend to concretize, only to find that what has been written in stone continues to oppress us. This figure is, in its fierceness, not unlike the images of Kali, the dakini, or the Baba Yaga. This is the fierce Great Mother that most of us must face on life's journey. To those who see her from a transcendent consciousness, she is fierce because she demands truth, sacrifice, and transformation. For the young boy (the unconscious masculine), she symbolizes death and prohibition. Her energy can guide the masculine to wholeness, if he perseveres. But, like the Medusa, she cannot be faced directly. The masculine must be conscious enough to approach this repressed energy with caution; otherwise, it will devour him.

During the first half of his life, James avoided the confrontation with the devouring mother. He learned how to be charming, how to please women, seeing himself somewhat as a knight in shining armor, ready to rescue the fair damsel in distress. This persona was carried out, however, with a good deal of patriarchal condescension. Outwardly, things were going along the conventionally accepted path—he had a professional career, a wife, and a family; he was an upstanding church member. Then James hit forty. On his forty-first birthday he wrote in his journal:

> I can date the beginning of my mid-life crisis precisely. The moment I pulled open the door and first stood on the threshold occurred on a Sunday morning in June, 1970. As I knelt on the chancel steps in my church and the minister placed his hand on my head, saying the words ordaining me as a deacon, I could feel something like fire coming down from his hand going through my head and throughout my body. At the same time, I could hear myself making a personal vow to follow my emotions and not let these vows constrain my exploration of my emotions and my self. For many years I have felt very guilty about this vow, which I took to be rather Faustian in nature. Today I am less certain that I made a pact with the devil; I did, in fact, make a commitment to finding my inner self. However, shortly after this event [his becoming a deacon], I deliberately let myself get emotionally involved with someone, and [thus] began my first [extramarital] affair.

James's experience of becoming a deacon constellated a classic confrontation between the anointing spirit and the split-off instincts. The spirit could not really be received because there was no conscious feminine container to receive it. His body was not ready, nor was his psyche. What was constellated, then, was the rebel masculine as imaged in the horned devil. Had he made a Faustian vow or a commitment to finding his inner life? In the long term, it was both. He was no longer prepared to please at the cost of repressing his instincts. For many years, and through many affairs, James had little consciousness, if any, that the horned devil was operating in secret while his patriarchal persona was holding onto the old respectable way of life.

Often we learn wisdom by way of disillusionment—with ourselves as well as with others. It was disillusionment that brought James into analysis. Sex had become an addiction. Caught in a repetitive pattern, he could not move forward. Finally, his soul screamed out for some kind of resolution.

In his many affairs, James was acting out the virgin/whore split in his psyche. He needed the comfort and security of his wife/mother, and was anxious that she might reject him. At the same time, he was unable to express his lust to his wife/mother (virgin). In taking up a mistress (whore), he was providing himself with a stand-in as well as a stand-by: he now had someone to project his lust onto, and should wife/mother leave him, mistress would provide him with the comfort and security he needed. For James, as for most men, this split was rooted in the mother complex. This highly charged complex carries with it the need for acceptance, comfort, security, and nurturance, and, at the same time, the fear of rejection, denial, destruction, and death. It sets a man upon the knife edge between womb and tomb. Dependence and fear create a psychic impotence that generates deep unconscious rage. This rage is at the crux of the patriarchal position.

Many of James's early dreams revolved around his ambivalence towards the feminine. Here is one of them:

> I am trying to design a building and am being thwarted, or having permission denied, by a planning officer—a woman—who doesn't like it, or doesn't like the shadows it casts. I talk to a friend, who encourages me and then takes me up onto a bridge, or roof, and shows me over the town to the mountain in the background. The planner is there on the roof, with a jeep with a canvas roof. She is checking the shadows, especially their angle. My friend talks to her and notes the roll of maps she is consulting. "You need the ordinance survey maps to do anything here—they are essential," he says. I look at the sun's shadows on the roof of the jeep and think about getting the map numbers from the roll for future reference, but I don't do it. We look across the rooftop/bridge to land farther on and contemplate moving, but we don't.

In this dream, James is trying to build a new self but feels thwarted because he needs the guidance of the feminine, who has the maps. There is a part of James (the friend) who can talk to her, who is not paralyzed by her. The woman's concern is the angle of the shadows created by the sun (the solar consciousness). Every building (self) has shadows; it's where they fall—their angle—that is at issue. The dream ego is rebellious and looks upon the woman as a barrier, because she denies permission. The friend presents a broader perspective, a new horizon, but, being neither willing nor able to approach the woman, James's masculine ego goes nowhere. It is paralyzed.

A dream two weeks later shows how the ambivalence toward the feminine is acted out in a regression into the negative mother.

> I am in a house (not mine) sitting in a living room chair. A young man is entertaining his girlfriend at dinner with several other friends. Another girlfriend comes and joins them at the table. Then a third girlfriend arrives and is sent to the dining room. I sink deeper and deeper into my chair and laugh, thinking, "This is your life—all your girlfriends together." Then, I am upstairs, talking to a much older woman, who is in bed with the covers up to her chin. We talk and talk, and then she twists and turns and exposes some of her stomach and chest, keeping her arms across her breasts. I notice her white skin. I continue talking and find that I am crossing and criss-crossing my legs to hide a developing erection. She says, "For heaven's sake, stop fighting it and come to bed with me." I rush off into the bathroom, wanting to pee, and turn between tub, shower, basin and toilet. I come back to strip down the bed and lie on it, while she stands at the side, ready to join me.

The first part of this dream has a party atmosphere, with the young man entertaining the feminine. There is nourishment here, around the dining table. The ego, however, sinks deeper into the chair, thinking of his own girlfriends. He goes upstairs (another level of consciousness), where there is an older woman in bed with the covers up to her chin. She tempts him to come into bed with her. The unconscious mother seduces toward inertia or paralysis. He goes into the bathroom and is indecisive about tub, shower, basin, toilet. All four are places where we cleanse ourselves or work creatively with our shadow side. Unable or unprepared to allow the bathroom in the dream to function in this symbolic way, he succumbs to joining the woman in the bed.

Some time later, the mother complex was dealt with more directly. After attending a lecture by a male Jungian analyst, James had the following dream.

> I am in the office of a male analyst. We are standing on either side of a coffee table in front of a fire. Above the fireplace is a large picture of the Great Mother. (She looks like a rather cross representation of Queen Victoria.) The analyst invites me to take the picture down and place it face down on the coffee table. "See what is behind it," he says. I begin to pry the first layer off the back of the picture. It is a young girl looking very dismayed because she has gotten only 49/50 on her spelling test. Father, or teacher, is standing there sternly, holding a ruler. I take off the second layer: it is a dark, seductive woman, looking like Spiderwoman. The third layer is a society type woman, somewhat vacuous, but richly dressed in white with a pastel shawl (or cape) and wearing a red rose. The fourth is a naked, helpless-looking woman trying to cross a field of barbed wire with bullets strafing her path. The fifth is a woman with a large head and small arms but no torso. Her head is fragile and shaped like a tea cup, full of writhing snakes.

In the presence of a strong, masculine figure—a father figure who can accept him—James is able to look at the full dimension of his mother complex. The picture of the Great Mother hangs above the central blaze in the office. When the analyst invites him to look at what is behind the cross queen, he looks at layers of feminine victims and seductresses. The most deeply repressed image seems to sum up all the other images: as fragile as a tea cup, yet as fierce as Medusa (her hair full of writhing snakes), whose ugliness can turn men into stone. In these images, James began to see the projections that he directed toward the women with whom he was having affairs. Some of them called forth the rescuer in him: attracted by dependence and vulnerability, he would gladly rush in to help. While outwardly he played the role of hero, sexual conquest was his hidden agenda. Spiderwoman and Ice Queen called for a psychically aggressive approach. Leaving them could always be justified, since they might either devour him or turn him to stone.

These images are James's projections onto the real women in his life, whom he pursued with much fascination and anguish. Wanting to possess, yet fearing rejection, James put more and more energy into his obsessions and fantasies. Once the conquest was accomplished, the energy level would drop, but sooner or later the pattern would be acted out with someone else.

After three months of obsessive activity, James had a dream (illustrated in figures 3 and 4) in which he confronted his "Horned Devil" shadow.

> I am walking in the forest on some kind of journey, when suddenly, out from behind a tree, a black-caped figure appears wearing a huge, devilish-looking mask. He blocks my path, and at first I am frightened, but then I become angry. When I try to confront him, he seems to merge into the tree. It is as if a huge, pointed mask, with thick eyebrows that seem to become horns, is there among the branches. I try to lunge at him, but then the mask changes into the angry-looking face of a woman with huge breasts sitting in the tree. I back away and sit on the ground.

This dream shows very clearly the collusion between the demon, and the devouring mother. At a collective level, this collusion sums up unconscious patriarchy. The disembodied masculine, which sees its freedom as control over the cycles of nature, matter, mother, puts its energy into dominating her. What our energy flows into, we are captivated by. If love is behind that energy, it can lead to an intoxication with life—the Horned God and the Great Mother. However, if fear is behind the energy, drivenness can lead to captivation by destructive forces—the Horned Devil and the Devouring Mother.

Fig. 3

The underlying fear is what is revealed to James in this dream. The black-caped mask figure operates only so long as the Great Mother is not transformed into a conscious inner feminine energy. Until James confronts the fear rooted in the mother complex, his masculinity as well as his projection onto the feminine will remain split. These energies move in a repetitive cycle, an addictive cycle that stalls any real evolution of consciousness.

Fig. 4

In James, this destructive collusion of energies blocked—as in trauma—his perception of what was going on in his soul. He had, that is, no experience of the inner feminine. She was trapped somewhere, in a cycle of despair, while his suspended masculine, ungrounded and un-contained, repeatedly tried to ground itself by projecting his soul onto an outside woman. At his core was an enormous rage against the mother.

Not until James was strong enough to allow the Goddess/ Crone energy into consciousness was he able to confront this un-derlying archetypal rage. This confrontation took place in the following dream:

> I am at a building site. Suddenly, I notice an old oak door on the far side of the site. I approach the door and go through it. I enter a place that is quite primitive. I see an opening, like the entrance to a cave, with a wooden beam across the top, with "White Bison Woman" carved on it. I am met by a tall old woman, who makes me lay aside the mask I am wearing and enter the cave. When I put the mask on the ground, I notice that it is the same mask that was on the demon shadow figure [in the earlier dream]. We go down a long winding shaft until we come to the center. There, she shows me a large mirror. In the mirror I see myself kicking my mother in the cunt. I am horrified.

Here is the core truth, at the center of things, stripped bare by the Goddess/Crone, who can also appear as an Oriental or Native American woman. It was a horrifying experience for James, but one that he could no longer turn away from. The mask of charmer, of hero-rescuer, the illusory perceptions of self he had used to justify his previous behavior, all had to be left outside the cave. The rage he had never expressed against the huge energy that was taking away his manhood is finally released in the presence of the Crone. It is imperative to note that while this mother in the depths of the cave appears as his personal mother, the energy she presents is archetypal, the magnet that would keep him inert in the mud. This dream has to be seen at the archetypal level.

Fig. 5

The energies that were pulling James into the primal mud had destroyed his capacity to live his own life according to his own values. He was so identified with Mother Church, Mother Corporation, Mother Wife that he could not know who he was. The metaphor in the dream had the power to liberate him into his own manhood.

Later that night, James had another dream, in which he was still in the cave. He felt naked and helpless, lying on his back, almost in crucifixion form, while enormous naked female energies swarmed all around him. Then he was driven out into the wilderness.

The wilderness is a place of reckoning. It conjures up images of danger, isolation, and aloneness. Physically, it is the place where we meet ourselves, undistracted by people or events. We are alone. All our fears rise up to meet us. We are tested to the utmost. If we can endure the terror, the wilderness also becomes a place where we can begin to experience our own strength, our own resources, our own truth. The gospels record that following his baptism, Christ, too, was drawn into the wilderness, where he confronted the temptations of his shadow demon and overcame them.

We can all recognize in our own lives the place of the wilderness: a severe illness, the death of a loved one, the breakdown of a marriage, the loss of a job, the shaking of our faith, the shock of realizing our own limitations. These places are a wilderness because they isolate us so that we cannot be reached by the outside world. These experiences we ultimately have to go through alone. Others may be present on the periphery, but it is as if a veil descends between us and them, leaving us alone, to struggle by and with ourselves.

For James, the wilderness was a long, painful period during which he attempted to withdraw projections and the accompanying obsession with sex. It involved separating, finally, from the wife/mother, whom he had used as a shield against being alone, and, at the same time, hated, because of the emotional dependency this use had engendered. It meant breaking the addictive cycle of possession and fear of loss. Withdrawing of such projections is easy to talk about, but very difficult and painful to accomplish. For many months, James's progress was two steps forward and one back. In the end, James came to realize that he would have to abstain from sex if he was to come out of the wilderness alive.

If we can consciously hold the tension between the opposites, the thwarted desire of the body and the injunctions of the mind, eventually something new will emerge. The emergence of the new implies the death of the old. However, the old cannot die until we

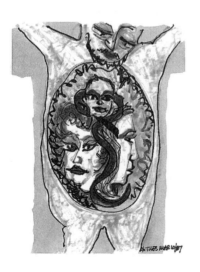

Fig. 6

recognize what it is we have to die to. This was brought home to James on Easter Sunday, in a dream in which he approached the crucified figure of Christ (figure 6). He was standing at the foot of the Cross, contemplating this figure, when suddenly he realized that it was he who was on the cross. As he looked down from the cross, he saw, within his body, the faces of two women facing away from each other, while a large black snake rose up and encircled the head of his own young masculine, as if to strangle him. Then, a knife-like object appeared. He was not sure whether the knife was poised to cut his throat or kill the snake.

This Easter Sunday presented James with an immense challenge. So long as he merely approaches "the crucified figure of Christ," he can stand at the foot of the cross. As his contemplation deepens, he is suddenly aware that *he* is on the cross, his archetypal Self is being crucified. Within his body, the faces of two women look in opposite directions. James saw these faces as two sides of his mother complex—mother and seductress—the energies that kept him on the cross. Then he recognizes the phallic power rising up to encircle his own young masculine. The final image is ambivalent. Is the snake there to protect the child or to strangle it? Is the knife there to cut his throat or to kill the snake? Or—and this is the possibility James does not consider—is this Kali's knife, the sword of discretion that could release him from the cross?

At this point in the process, James still sees the phallus and the knife as dangerous. Yet these are the very energies he needs to release his body and his psyche from the conflict between the two women. His drawing emphasizes the energy of the phallus—the creative strength he needs for his own masculine child. So long as he continues to focus his life energy on one woman or the other, imagining that his problem is his inability to choose the right one, he is avoiding his real issue—his own masculine creativity.

For James, this was a crucial point in his analysis. Two days later, he had a dream in which the new masculine appeared (figure 7). Again, he was on the cross, but this time the feminine faces were facing each other and had receded to the periphery. The black snake was not killed; it had receded to the coiled position at James's feet. The young masculine stood in the center, with an air of inner freedom and a new standpoint from which to approach life.

Fig. 7

This dream seems to be giving James a clear picture of where his energy wants to go. He is still looking down at his body on the cross, but now the feminine faces are no longer in opposition and they have receded to the periphery. The total focus is on the masculine child, who stands with the coiled snake between his legs. James's potential is in the child and the snake.

Following this dream, James began to draw a penis on the figure of himself, something he had not done previously in his drawings. This was not a conscious decision, and it said a great deal about his feelings toward himself. When the power comes from within us and we can claim it as our own, then we no longer have to affirm ourselves by dominating others. The irony is that we are actually afraid of our own power. For James, as for many contemporary men and women, the lost masculine has to do with the Dionysian power, which has been repressed as energy that could go out of control and is, therefore, unacceptable to patriarchy. Repressed, it becomes like a raging bull upon the land, operating outside the realm of rationality, while the disconnected intellect constructs the illusion of a world based on reason.

The recovery and transformation of that energy is essential for men and women. As we saw earlier in Daniel's dream, life was renewed in the recovery of the "wild man" from the well. In James's process, a similar figure appeared (figure 8). In a dream, a horned man came over the brow of a hill and embraced both James and his feminine companion in their old conventional personas: rescuer and seductive damsel in distress. Then, the Dionysian figure laughs at such illusory personas and invites them both to take off these false masks and get down to the truth. Both James and the woman take off their old "skins" and hang

Fig. 8

them on the wall (figure 9). Then they sit down facing each other and begin to talk.

In recognizing the healing powers of the "wild man," we are not overlooking the significance of the Crone in the dreams of both Daniel and James (pp. 91 and 118). When they are strong enough to look at their own psychic truth, both men are guided by the Crone to their place of deepest wounding in the archetypal depths (the cave). There she puts her finger exactly on the wound that has to be healed if they are to be whole. In Daniel, she points out the profound split

Fig. 9

in his masculinity. In James, she forces him to take off his devilish charmer's mask and look at his rage against the Devouring Feminine. Both men are confronted with the truth that can set them free.

Only the man who is truly in possession of his inner power can afford to be "vulnerable," to lay aside his mask and his projections and meet the feminine face to face. This is an encounter with his own soul, she who animates the whole world, inner and outer.

An experience recounted by an analysand illustrates what might be called the "new ground" of relationship. Ian had been married to the same woman for thirty years. They were extremely comfortable together. Indeed, he compared his relationship to her to his relationship to his worn wool sweater that, so long as it held together, he would never consider throwing out for a new one. One day he went into a shopping mall to pick up a pen that he had left at a repair shop some weeks earlier. It was during the lunch hour, and, passing a restaurant in the mall, he decided to go in. To his great surprise, upon entering the restaurant he saw his wife at the back of the dining area sitting alone, reading and eating her lunch. His immediate reaction was to walk up to her table and surprise her, just as she had inadvertently surprised him. It would be fun to have lunch together in this thoroughly unplanned way. Then he suddenly realized that he could not do this. Totally unprepared for this second surprise, he felt completely disoriented. Looking at her sitting alone, Ian knew that he would be intruding upon her privacy. The more he thought about it, the more he realized that the woman sitting alone reading a book and having her lunch was a complete stranger. It seemed as if he had never seen her before. Shyness amounting to embarrassment, embarrassment amounting to shame, overcame him. Though he knew nothing about her circumstances, what she was doing there, where she had come from, what she was reading, he felt such a powerful surge of love that he began to shake. Reeling, he turned and walked out. The surge of love lay solely in this: his wife of thirty years had suddenly been unveiled to him as a complete stranger.

When I asked Ian to explain what he meant by "embarrassment amounting to shame" he hesitated. Slowly he put together his feelings and replied:

> Shame is the recognition of what the old ground was, playing the old roles—persona and tyrant. Ashamed of my whole life. Recognition that the relationship had been in projection and when the projection fell away, the person was a stranger. Feeling the falling away of the mask and realizing the contamination in the projection.
>
> In the radiant otherness is the realization that the reality of the universe is love.
>
> I'd played all the rituals of society, played out the conventional wisdom of the world. Suddenly, that was all gone and I saw that God is love and these roles had kept me from seeing that.

If we, as a collective, continue to be driven by projections and splits between disembodied spirit and unconscious matter, we can never be present to each other beyond the demands of an ego that is trapped in a one-sided need for order and control. When conscious matter becomes a vessel that can receive spirit, this joining together can bring us to a new level of consciousness. The ego can stand in a creative relationship to the Self. To stand in relationship to the Self is to be totally present to oneself. When we are present to ourselves, we are present to others in a totally new way. In the world of the Self, we meet all those of whom we are a part, whose hearts we have touched; here there is no aloneness, only presence. There is no egoism involved here, no need to win or lose, no need to control. The projections have been withdrawn and reclaimed as parts of ourselves. Only when this happens is genuine relationship possible.

The same stream of life that runs through my veins night
and day runs through the world and dances in
rhythmic measures.
It is the same life that shoots in joy through the dust of the
earth in numberless blades of grass and breaks into
tumultuous waves of leaves and flowers.
It is the same life that is rocked in the ocean-cradle of birth
and death, in ebb and in flow.
I feel my limbs are made glorious by the touch of this world
of life.
And my pride is from the life-throb of ages dancing in my
blood this moment.

—Rabindrath Tagore

. . . she is Sophia, which is to say divine wisdom and power,
embracing all the universes. That is . . . why her eternal
person, which is the secret of the world of the soul, is also
its manifestation without which the creative principle of the
world would remain unknown and unknowable, forever
hidden.

—Mazdean Sufi

READING ANCIENT MYTHS and fairy tales can be very helpful because these stories came spontaneously from people who had not studied psychology. The stories came straight out of their unconscious and, therefore, show us how the unconscious works unimpeded by conscious intervention. The images are clear and stark. For those of us who are interested in why we do what we do when we want to do the opposite, the stories are gold mines of information.

If we accept, as Jung believed, that there are what he called "archetypes" in our unconscious, then we can read myths and fairy tales with an open mind. If we do not accept the existence of archetypes, then we have no way of explaining the superhuman surges of energy that magnetize us toward someone or something—or repel us. The word does not matter. What matters is our recognition of the power of these energy fields in our unconscious; they can dictate our destruction (if our ego is weak) or they can be our greatest gift in life. If we cannot tell the difference between human and superhuman (or subhuman) energy, we identify with gods and goddesses, devils and enchantresses, and eventually walk into self-destruction.

We project images onto these energy fields. The god for one generation is Elvis, for another, Michael Jackson. The goddess may be the Virgin Mary, eclipsed by Lilith, eclipsed by Julia Roberts. The task of the media promoters is to find the right image for whatever energy field is floating up from the unconscious mass at that moment. Stars pass by like meteors and are gone.

Some planets, however, we have always with us: mother, father, child. The god and goddess energy that the parents carry for the child is inherent in the infant/parent relationship. "Mother" may be slender, pert, and pretty for one person; she may be big-bosomed, old, and funny for another. Yet, for both, "Mother" carries energy that will influence their lives forever, for better or for worse. In trying

to understand god and goddess energy in ourselves we have to consider our relationship to our parents, since the god is at the core of
the father complex and the goddess is at the core of the mother
complex. In reading the ancient tales, we can recognize the magnetic
interplay of overwhelming energies within ourselves.

In her book *The Golden Ass of Apuleius,* Marie Louise von Franz
shows how the ancient tale outlines the role of the feminine guide in
the development of a man's psyche. The story also has much to say
about the process of individuation in a woman. Lucius, the hero of
the tale, sets out on a white horse, the prototype of the knight in
shining armor. He imagines he can approach his journey rationally,
without any real commitment to feeling.

In the first house in which he takes up lodgings, Lucius loses
his head completely when he sees the servant girl Photis. He regards
her as the prize to be won, and together they are overtaken by lust.
She tells him tales of her mistress, Pamphile, a powerful enchantress.
Believing he will be turned into a bird, he goes with Photis to Pamphile. Instead, he is turned into an ass. He falls into his shadow side.

Lucius is forced to continue his journey as an ass in the company of criminals, usurers, sodomites, and sadists—all the underground characters of his own psyche. As von Franz points out, "It is
an underworld that also opens up today in the psyche of every man
who identifies with only the intellect and its false ideals and who
represses his development of feeling."[1]

In the midst of his confrontation with his own darkest shadow,
he meets Charite, a young girl who has been overpowered by robbers.
Lucius' own wretched condition gives him great sympathy for her.
Through her, Lucius experiences his own compassion. She is a symbol of the woman, usually the wife, who connects a man to his feelings. Often, this woman carries the soul projections of the man, the
values that he does not consciously recognize as his own. Until this
aspect of the feminine is integrated into a man, she may be one-half
of the equation in the virgin/whore split in his psyche—the nurturing, protective wife, who carries his feeling values. The other half
may be a mistress, who carries his lust.

Lucius's next important encounter is in the story of Psyche
and Eros, an encounter Apuleius recounts halfway through his novel.
Lucius hears about Psyche, but in his "ass" state, he does not really
understand her. Still, he is fascinated by the tale of love between

Psyche and Eros. Having been connected to genuine feeling through Charite, Lucius is now able to sense the possibility of love. Psyche is not an ordinary woman. Rather, "[s]he is represented as a girl with butterfly wings, that is, as a spiritual being or as a being not of concrete reality but real enough psychologically. . . . She represents an archetypal aspect of the feminine in Apuleius, that is remote from consciousness."[2] Here the projection is beginning to be withdrawn from the "outside" woman, and Lucius begins to get in touch with his own inner feminine nature. When a man begins to sense the feminine within himself, he begins to experience the possibility of his own wholeness.

Whereas Psyche is one incarnation of the Goddess, she is not the transcendent Goddess. ". . . Isis, who appears at the end of the novel in all her cosmic majesty, personifies the archetypal collective aspect of the anima. There is no longer anything of Apuleius' personal wishes nor of his desire for her. She is the remote, lofty revelation of his deepest, transpersonal fate."[3] Lucius becomes the devoted follower of Isis and serves in her temple. As a man moves deeper into experiencing his inner feminine, he becomes connected to the Self. His feminine is the bridge that allows him to experience his own godliness—his own creative powers in whatever dimension he wishes to create. His projection onto a woman may begin that process, but ultimately, the fire must come from within himself. Paradoxically, his love for the transcendent feminine releases the love that inspires his creativity—painting, sculpture, music, life. Transcendence and immanence are two sides of one deity.

Encountering the Goddess within is not a task for the fainthearted. Only a hero can take the journey to find her. To reach her, he must pass through his own wasteland, give up his false sense of power, and discover what is of real value to him. Only then can he give full expression to his own creative power.

Patriarchy, and the sons and daughters of patriarchy, do know the Goddess. Locked in fear of her judgments, they see her as a negative mother who could destroy them; therefore, they want either to dominate her or please her. In her positive form, the Goddess is the cup, the vessel, the womb in which they need to be protected if they are ever to know the parts of themselves that are not recognized by the collective.

The goddess Aphrodite, in the story of Psyche and Eros, is an excellent example of what many would consider an archetype of the negative mother. The archetype is the white hot or smouldering core at the center of the experience of the personal mother. It may be a voice that ceaselessly judges, ceaselessly sets impossible tasks, ceaselessly sets up death marriages. She leaves her child failed, guilty, and full of shame. Hers is not a friendly womb.

In this story within the story of Apuleius, Aphrodite is jealous because her followers are neglecting her altars and worshiping the exquisite human being, Psyche. She calls upon her son, Eros, to use his wiles to make Psyche fall in love with some odious creature. Apollo, meanwhile, tells Psyche's father that she must clothe herself in mourning dress and set herself upon a rock from which she will be carried away by a fierce serpent. At the appointed time she is left to die, and that night she is carried off by the wind to the castle of her "serpent" husband. He comes to her by night and tells her she must never set eyes upon him. Together, they delight in the ecstasy of love. It all happens in the dark. As in most relationships, the bliss of conjugal embrace, heightened by incestuous attraction, happens in total unconsciousness.

Then Psyche's shadow sisters, jealous of her good fortune, tell her she is sleeping with a monster, perhaps a serpent that does not want his secret discovered. With that seed of doubt planted in her mind, she eventually lights her lamp while her husband is asleep, goes up to him and sees the divine Eros. In her rapture at beholding her husband, she allows a drop of burning oil from the lamp to fall on his shoulder. Instantly, he wakes and flees, and with him, the castle disappears.[4]

Eros returns to his mother's castle. Psyche is left to wander alone and weep. In an attempt to find her husband again—that is, to experience that divine relationship in consciousness—Psyche goes to her mother-in-law. Aphrodite is furious that her son Eros has taken Psyche as his wife. She is angry on two counts: first, she had hoped that he would rid her of her rival; second, she is afraid that he might have learned something of love from Psyche. Despite his failure, she lets him remain in her castle. Meanwhile, she chides Psyche for her faithlessness and rebukes her with the words "So you finally remembered you have a goddess!"

As punishment, Aphrodite sets Psyche three tasks—all seemingly impossible and each carrying a death sentence. If Psyche fails to accomplish them, she dies either physically or psychically. Aphrodite's severe and unfeeling demeanor may seem cruel, but in fact she, as dark goddess, is the catalyst that brings out all the strength and defiance and individuality that sleeping Psyche never had.

The first task is to sort out bushels of different kinds of seeds. Consciously, the task is impossible. But the ants, those helpful, well-organized, tiny energies of the instincts, live in their natural state and are able to spontaneously discriminate. Discrimination—the ability to separate one's own values from those of other people, or true ones from false ones—is essential to Psyche's survival. It was lack of discrimination—that is, failure to separate her own values from those of the shadow voices inside (her sisters)—that brought about her terrible loss. Mother Aphrodite gives her a lesson in surrender to her own deepest instincts, so that she may experience the self-discipline necessary to find her own Virgin within.

The second task is to gather wool from the great sheep, shining like gold. Psyche knows the animals are too wild for her to pick the wool. Totally discouraged, she goes to the river to drown herself. A reed by the riverside tells her to wait until the sheep are resting in the evening; then she can pick the wool off the briars and take it to Aphrodite. This Psyche succeeds in doing. What has Aphrodite taught Psyche here? To listen to the voice of instinct; to cultivate patience, which can prevent her from acting too quickly, thereby bringing about her own destruction. Psyche learns courage, assertiveness, a certain wiliness—all attributes the Virgin needs, even in relationship to the Mother.

Psyche's third task is to take a crystal bottle to the top of a nearby mountain to bring back some of the black water that courses in a river down its slope. As she proceeds up the mountain, she is surrounded by dragons and cliffs, and again contemplates suicide. This time, an eagle, a sun bird, comes to her aid. He tells her that it is impossible for her to go past the dragons. She must recognize her own limitations. He offers to take the crystal bottle and fill it for her. In this way, she completes her third task, and learns, at the same time, the valuable lesson of allowing spirit to take her where instinct cannot. As in the Christian myth, the Virgin surrenders her chalice to spirit and learns her individual strength in relation to the divine.

Having accomplished all three tasks successfully, Psyche returns to Aphrodite. Again, the Mother is furious. Not one to be deterred so easily, Aphrodite presents Psyche with the ultimate task: to go down to Hades and bring back from the goddess Persephone a drop of her beauty ointment. From her adventures in Hades, Psyche learns that she dare not separate her body from her spirit, that she must appease the guard dog at the gates of the underworld, that she does not have enough energy to help everyone she meets, and that she does need specific energy for specific tasks. Above all, she learns that she cannot rescue other people from their destiny and that trying to do so can undermine their strength.

In all of these tasks, Psyche is building her own creative masculine energy as she strengthens her inner virgin. (The two go together). As she nears home, she asks herself, "If this beauty ointment is so precious to Aphrodite, why can't I use it myself?" She opens the jar that contains the drop. Immediately, a vapor rises from the container, causing Psyche to fall into a deathlike sleep. Disobedience toward the mother is often essential to full virginity. This may or may not be the personal mother. It can also be the collective mother—the corporation, the alma mater, Mother Church.

The appropriation of beauty, the "putting on" of the Goddess, is quite deliberate. Up to this point in the story, Psyche had held her beauty unconsciously; she had unconsciously challenged Aphrodite by not acknowledging her gift or what it really meant. Now, she has acknowledged the Goddess, she has suffered through her tutelage. Now, she dares to become like her, not only in her beauty but also in her divine wholeness. For the final integration of the masculine to take place, one has to go into the "land of the dead" (Psyche's fourth task). For a time, one becomes detached from outer reality and surrenders to the inner workings of the soul. This process is echoed in the New Testament's exhortations to put on the "mantle of Christ"—an image of death to the old self. Psyche's deathlike sleep is precisely this experience. Many conscious women who have come far in their journey suddenly fall gravely ill for no apparent reason. This near-death experience is a final surrender, a final initiation into a new level of consciousness, a consciousness that must be "stolen" from the Goddess herself.

Greek author Arianna Stassinopoulos tells us that Psyche's marriage to Eros, the divine son of the Goddess, is the only wedding to take place in the presence of all the gods and goddesses on Olympus. This union brings together all aspects of the divine energy. This is the sacred union of soul with love. Zeus held a great feast to celebrate this union and we are told that Aphrodite danced.[5]

Although Aphrodite may seem stern and demanding, her real purpose throughout the story has been to bring Psyche to the place where she can blossom forth in her full womanhood. Through the tasks the mother assigns, she releases the attributes in the young feminine that are necessary to the maturing. Psyche gives birth to a daughter, whom she calls Pleasure, or Joy. Pleasure is the child of the divine marriage on Mount Olympus. The feminine as Beauty and Love can be the revelation of the Goddess in every human being. This is not the beauty found in cosmetic jars, or facelifts, or beauty parlors. It is a beauty that shines forth when the soul is no longer in exile, but radiates in every living cell. The exiled Russian writer Alexander Solzhenitsyn paid tribute to this beauty in his acceptance speech on winning the Nobel Prize.

> If the all too obvious and the overly straight sprouts of Truth and Goodness have been crushed, cut down, or not permitted to grow, then perhaps the whimsical, unpredictable and ever-surprising shoots of Beauty will force their way through and soar up to that very spot, thereby fulfilling the task of all three.[6]

This is the beauty that radiates from the soul whenever it expresses itself, whether in art, or music, or in the eyes of an old crone. Her eyes may be fierce, or gentle, full of laughter, or full of tears. They always instruct us, guide us, and become a mirror in which we can see ourselves, if we dare to look closely.

So repressed has the Goddess been in our culture that it is very difficult to find a story that illustrates her in her loving transcendent power. Yet she is present—so present that we take her for granted. We do not see her.

Many poets know her. Milton, for example, knew his Urania, his muse, who dictated *Paradise Lost* to him night after night throughout twelve books. Shelley, likewise, communed with his muse and, at her dictation, his winged pen created some of the finest lyrics in our language. The intimacy with an inner Beloved creates the fire that kindles great art. The unconscious is released, the human being is aflame with transcendent energy. The love that is enkindled manifests in the creation.

For most of us, the fire of her love manifests most delicately and most fiercely in springtime. Out of the icy clutches of winter, buds begin to become plump. Each day they are plumper and more colorful. We notice green sprouts, perhaps a snowdrop or a bluebell. Gradually, the whole world begins to vibrate in shades of green, and our own heart swells with the mystery of creation. The Goddess manifests in countless births from her womb. A crocus—purple in white snow—speaks louder than any sermon about the sacredness of birth.

Or perhaps we have been present at the birth of a child. For nine months we have watched the belly become plump, and plumper. And then, we have heard the anguished cries of labor. We have watched the head beginning to crown, beginning to push its way into this world. Finally, the last shriek of the mother, somewhere between death and life. Then a new life with ten fingers, ten toes, nose and ears, moves in, as life has moved in for millennia. Yet every life comes from a silence so profound, we stand in awe, wondering.

As we stand wondering in the presence of death. The life that one day moved through a birth canal with one tiny hand appearing and then another, and two tiny feet, a body that blossomed through all its potential, now withers, breath ceases, and all is silence. The soul shimmers for an instant. Again, we stand before the mystery.

We stand in the presence of the Goddess—God unveiled on Earth. The timeless intersecting time. The Goddess of birth, transformation, and death. Within the container of her power, life happens. She is Immanent within the bud, within the baby, within the soul that moves through yet another birth canal into its next abode. She, likewise fierce and full of love, brings us face to face with the transcendent that speaks to us of mysteries we cannot fathom.

For most people, it takes a lifetime for the psyche to find its relationship to the Goddess. She appears in the psyche in her three-fold nature, sometimes Virgin, sometimes Mother, sometimes Crone. However, it is the Crone that our culture has so brutally repressed. The wise woman, the healer, the transformer has been one of the greatest threats to the patriarchal world. Ironically, with the founding of universities (centers of *oneness*) in the eleventh century, women's natural talents for counseling, healing, and being a source of wisdom were curtailed; women were barred from attending. Public services could be rendered only by someone with the proper credentials and, since women were not allowed to acquire these credentials, they were effectively removed from the intellectual life of the community. Many who were burned as witches were among the most gifted women of the time.

> Our culture's official rejection of the Crone figure was related to rejection of women, particularly elder women. The gray-haired high priestesses, once respected tribal matriarchs of pre-Christian Europe, were transformed by the newly dominant patriarchy into minions of the devil. Through the Middle Ages this trend gathered momentum, finally developing a frenzy that legally murdered millions of elder women from the twelfth to the nineteenth centuries.[7]

As Barbara Walker observes, "Until the Crone figure was suppressed, patriarchal religions could not achieve full control of men's minds. Such religions tended not only to ascetic rejection of the physical experiences of life, but also to fearful rejection of the Divine Old Woman, and by extension of old women generally."[8]

As a symbol, the Crone had to be suppressed by patriarchal religions because her power "overruled the will even of Heavenly Father Zeus."[9] She controlled the cycles of life and death. She was the Mother of God, the Nurturer of God, and, as Crone, the Slayer of God. While Christianity retained the feminine as Virgin and Mother, it eliminated her role as Crone. It is interesting, however, that in this century, her presence at Fatima and at Medjugorje in Bosnia-Herzegovina (where she might well have been heeded) has cast her very much in the role of the Doomsday Crone of old. Her message, that the hand of wrath will fall if human behavior doesn't change, has crystallized her voice in the face of the brutality of the twentieth century.

Since she has not been present in the culture, she has not been readily accessible to the conscious awareness of modern women. Without her, even the dynamic symbols of Virgin and Mother are distorted. The Crone in a woman is that part of her psyche that is not identified with any relationship nor confined by any bond. She infuses an intrinsic sense of self-worth, of autonomy, into the role of virgin and mother, and gives the woman strength to stand to her own creative experience.

In the mythological tale of Hera, the divine consort of Zeus, we can see the transformation from unconscious wife to conscious virgin, she who is who she is because that is who she is. Hera's life was totally bound up with what her husband did or did not do. When Zeus was faithful and attentive, she was the bountiful goddess; when Zeus was promiscuous, as he frequently was, she was a raging shrew, taking out her wrath on the "other woman." Hera's jealousy consumed her life. Today we would say that her marriage to Zeus was one of quintessential codependency. "As long as Hera projects on her husband all her own unlived creativity, so long as she expects to find fulfillment exclusively in her role as Mrs. Zeus, she creates her own betrayal and a marriage that is in a permanent state of war with brief interludes of peace in bed."[10]

It was not until Hera finally decided that she had had enough of Zeus's promiscuity that things began to change. She left Zeus and returned to her birthplace in Euboea. In aloneness she came to terms with her own essential oneness. She had engaged her Crone state. Women are, by nature, disposed to relationship and connectedness; yet true relationship cannot be embraced until a woman has a deep sense of her at-one-ment. Without this essential independence from all roles and bonds, she is a potential victim for servitude.

Once Hera had let this Crone energy in, had accepted that part of herself that is bound by no relationship, she "bathed in the spring flowing through the foothills and emerged with her virginity renewed—One-in-Herself, the Celestial Virgin."[11] With her own creative virgin restored, she could become Hera Teleia (fully grown, complete). She returns to Zeus. "[F]illed with a secret, smiling wisdom that leaves no room for raging jealousy, she is reconciled to him, now ready for the deep marriage for which she has always longed."[12] From now on, this would not be a marriage based on need—something that Zeus undoubtedly understood and responded to. Hera demanded and got her wish fully met, matched, and mated.

In the story of Demeter and Persephone, Mother Demeter is in anguish for nine days and nine nights after the disappearance of her daughter, Persephone, in the arms of Hades, the Lord of the Underworld. In her grief, she allows the countryside to become barren. On the tenth day Hecate, the Crone, appears and assists Demeter in getting reunited with her lost daughter. Hecate has the wisdom that allows Persephone to be daughter to her mother and, at the same time, wife to her husband. The countryside blooms again.

The restoration of the cycle appears in dreams today. One woman dreamed that she was in her Crone state, diving deep and surfacing as she played in the ocean waves (the depths of the unconscious).

> I am swimming carefree in the ocean when I notice a big ship. As I look, I realize it is headed straight toward me and intends to run me over. I dive beneath the surface and elude it. I have no fear. I even seem to be amused. I swim toward the shore, but a huge whale-like creature surfaces and tries to swallow me. I take large chunks of green and gold sod from the ocean and throw them into the creature's mouth. As I approach the shore, I see mothers with their young daughters, playing in the surf; but as I get closer, they are concrete statues. I come up out of the ocean and move among the statues, and as I do they become real flesh and blood and begin playing and laughing. I walk on into a little building, like an office. Three or four men are in there, sitting around. I tell them about the ship coming into the harbor, and urge them to do something about it quickly. They get up and point to a chart on the wall and explain that by their calculations what I told them is impossible. They won't even look out the window. I get disgusted and walk out, realizing I will have to take care of it myself.

A woman in her crone state can easily, and almost playfully, elude two powerful complexes in the unconscious. As she approaches the shoreline, the boundary between consciousness and the unconscious, she sees that the Mother/Virgin energies have been turned into stone. This is the concretization that cements the feminine into stereotypes. The dream ego's appearance as crone revitalizes this energy, restores it to its rightful potential.

In the last section of the dream, the masculine energy is locked in its own patriarchal logic, not willing to open to the spontaneity of the moment. Here is reason that is unreasonable because it refuses to confront reality. The dream ego will have to call in her crone energy in order to deal with the huge complex that is coming in and with the blind stubbornness of her own masculinity.

For many women, the task of confronting patriarchal logic is daunting. In offices and boardrooms, they routinely encounter plans and organizational strategies that they instantly recognize as having no connection to the lived reality. Being more in touch with frontline

reality, women are in a better position to sense what will work and
what will not. Often, there is a tacit understanding among them:
"Well, let them talk. We will have to do what needs to be done to
make it work." Confrontation, however quiet but firm, is always difficult, because the adversary is not just faulty logic, but a power
system. When a woman's crone is strong enough to confront the
Chairman of the Board, and he loses face, she has also to contend
with the sinking feeling inside, "There goes my job!" And even
though she may not lose her job, she still has to deal with the inner
feeling—and with the prospect of earning a reputation as a "bitch."
A man in her position would more likely be praised for his assertiveness. While attitudes are changing, it still takes a strong woman, with
a well-defined sense of her own boundaries, to stand up to patriarchy
and come through unscathed.

We hear a great deal these days about women stepping into
their own shoes, or finding their own voice. In other words, they are
trying to live their own feminine potential and speak with their own
feminine voice. If their voice is coming from their own musculature
and not from a complex, it is a real voice ringing with feminine truth.
Many men, too, are trying to hold onto their jobs and, at the same
time, live from their own inner values. Many of the largest corporations are attempting to recognize the voice of soul within the everyday business world. Psychologically speaking, they are differentiating
the Virgin from the Mother, Psyche from Aphrodite. The young
uninitiated feminine, who is just beginning to know that she exists in
many men and women, inevitably faces the judgment of the Mother.
Mother may be personal mother, the boss at work, the corporation
that refuses to recognize the existence of the emerging feminine.
Often, in a crisis, lip service is paid to the feminine, but, when the
crisis passes, retribution takes over, even revenge. It takes a very
strong Psyche to stand up to the discipline the Mother sometimes
enforces. As the old saying goes, "If it doesn't kill you, you'll be
stronger." The Mother's severity sometimes feels like abuse—and
sometimes it actually is. It is part of the differentiating process to
recognize which of the two it is and to act from that recognition.

For people who live in daily dialogue with the unconscious, the
Goddess herself may make quite clear how she hopes the evolving
feminine will respond in a given situation. And if Virgin replies, "I'm
not strong enough to do that," she cuts in, "I'll help you. Do it.

There's no time for farting around." In the absence of role models for the new feminine in our culture, the Goddess speaks through dreams and creative imagination, giving guidance to those who choose to listen. Her sense of humor always softens the sharpness of her approach. Her compassion for the human being in the human situation establishes a strong, loving container so long as communication is kept open.

Her advice often proves to be a turning point in a person's psychological growth. For example, women who tend to mother their man even after years of analysis may be told that the mothering has to stop when he begins to work with his rejected body. Mothering at this stage can leave a man stuck in a mother complex for the rest of his life, because he is afraid to drop into the deeper primitive areas of his own musculature. The man *may* become angry and accuse the woman of not being sympathetic. She may be irritated or cool and distant. Both have to realize that in times of confrontation, personal response very quickly flies into archetypal response. Anger shifts into rage. When the archetype is constellated, the individuals cease to be present and raw body response is acted out.

Our streets are dangerous because culture is giving way to anarchy. Psychologically speaking, archetypal acting out of raw instinctual energy threatens the place of archetypal containment within art forms disciplined enough to hold the conflicts. Audiences still participate in the grief and terror that is contained within the magnificent poetry and music that is being embodied in the theater. Outside the theaters, churches, concert halls, museums, and art galleries, the container is barely strong enough to hold itself together against the onslaught of archetypal acting out, much art now becoming nothing more than undisciplined acting out. In that situation, the Death Goddess is quickly constellated.

In contemporary relationships, Psyche and Aphrodite are often confused. Women who are genuinely attempting to differentiate their Virgin out from their Mother try to speak their own truth. If their partner is still stuck in Mother, still thinking that femininity is only mothering (mother providing a safe, cherishing container in which life grows), he experiences her truth as a judgment. Or the interchange can happen with the man having a more finely honed feminine voice than his wife, in which case she may experience *his* truth as judgment passed on *her*. As the Virgin and Mother mature into

Crone, and the Crone speaks with the sharp truth that shocks and alarms others, again the woman may be looked upon as a negative Mother voice. As soon as that old pattern surfaces, the infantile judge-and-blame games are resumed. If we can remember that once the old archetypal patterns start to resonate, the individual is no longer present, it may make getting out for a walk an easy journey to the door.

One of the darkest corners from which the negative Mother can arise is angry women in women's groups. After years of closely relating to each other in the loving container of the protective Mother that they have created for themselves and each other, suddenly things may start to turn sour. Everyone is sad and embarrassed. The fact is that everyone has a headache or vomits before the meeting. No one is excited about coming. What is going on? There will be many different dynamics, but one is worth examining here in terms of the Mother. In a group of women, as each begins to feel her own individual empowerment, she begins to move into a position of leadership. Another without any desire to be at the top or in competition also finds herself with leadership ideas. For some in the group, this feels like the return of patriarchy. The ones who are taking the initiative may be honored by the group but required to stay in line. As a result, the best energies that are being born within the best containers are stultified. Initiative and leadership become questionable throwbacks. As the energies of the whole group build, too much may be repressed. Then the group becomes the negative Mother, who will not allow each child to be who she is. Most women are fearful of the judging Mother. They don't need that from this beloved group. So the group dissolves just at the point where each member has the most to give, the most with which to experiment in a group that loves her. Those dynamics need a clear eye and a loving voice to discipline them before they go too far to recover.

The Crone has been missing from our culture for so long that many women, particularly young girls, know nothing of her tutelage. Young girls in our society are not initiated by older women into womanhood with its accompanying dignity and power. Instead, for their models, they look to fashion magazines, where they see the kinds of bodies and faces that they themselves can never have. Paradoxically, these are the ideals that are held up for them if they want to be successful, particularly with men. A recent national survey of teenage girls in North America showed that "while 13-year-old girls are nearly as confident as 13-year old boys, by age 16 the females' sense of self worth has plummeted."[13]

With no inner Wisdom figure to guide them, and no outward model to help them set boundaries and be their own person, young women often fall victim to false and superficial ideals, such as pleasing others. Ironically, they achieve their greatest success at the cost of their own emerging sense of self.

Many women are locked into relationships that leave no room for their own creative expression. In fact, they are not even aware of their own creativity. Without the Crone, that part of us that can stand alone, many relationships stagnate in codependence, in which both partners act out carefully defined roles that block growth. If both partners are not changing and growing, there is no excitement, no challenge left in the marriage. Boredom sets in. A typical complaint from women is, "All he ever does is work and watch sports on TV. There's nothing to talk about any more. Our breakfast conversation yesterday consisted of him reading the nutrient label on the cereal box." Equally typical is this complaint from one man, "Trying to come to a meaningful decision about something is like trying to pin Jello onto the wall." Many couples put up with these stagnant relationships because change might mean aloneness. Without the Crone, the task of belonging to oneself, of being a whole person, is virtually impossible.

When a woman stands her own ground, exercises discipline, or lays down her terms and conditions with "straight talk," she speaks with the voice of the Crone. "Straight talk" is not language that is writhing in a complex. Too often, complexed women unconsciously overprotect, or try to placate, or manipulate others into doing something or into behaving in a certain way—usually with disastrous results, because they do not know their own voice. If a woman becomes identified with any one role—wife, mother, teacher—she has no mirror in which to see the situation objectively. She is hiding behind the role without exploring her own reality. Crone energy is energy that has been distilled through years of attempting to speak straight from our own reality. One day we are surprised by the sound of our own voice coming straight from its ground in our own body.

Take, for example, a professional woman in her early thirties who came into analysis to "talk over" her failure to hold a particular relationship. She had been involved with a married man at her church for about six months when she became pregnant. She decided to have an abortion, and he acted the perfect gentleman by driving her to and from the hospital. Then, he promptly ended the relationship and moved on to another woman. She felt she should react in a "civilized" manner and be understanding of his motives. However, she had a dream shortly thereafter, in which a rabbit is popping in and out of holes in the ground. An old woman comes along and hands her a high-powered rifle. The dream ego looks through the sights of the rifle and sees there the face of the man who had "dumped" her. She pulls the trigger and blows out his brains.

This woman recognized her rage and realized that she had better deal with it. Using her journal as a safe container, she poured out her rage uncensored. It turned out that her rage was directed at all men, particularly her father, and much of it was justified. She persevered in this cathartic writing activity until she came to a "clearing," where she could begin to recognize her own reality and what she needed to do to empower herself. This was the turning point.

It became clear to her that the affairs she had been having were a desperate attempt to have the relationship with her father that had been missing in her life. Unconsciously trying to establish a parental relationship that is missing or distorted, we inevitably choose a person who is like the parent whose love we never had. Not surprisingly, the same distorted pattern of interaction is acted out. This woman began to see how she had reacted to the "betrayals" in her life and how she continued to betray herself because her own motives were not clear. Her attempts at self-assertion, of speaking in her own voice, would often elicit displeasure on the part of the men she had to deal with, whether socially or professionally. She would back off at their displeasure, feeling misunderstood or unappreciated. This betrayal of her own integrity eventually coalesced into an inner cesspool of rage. The only way out of the cesspool was for her to disengage from the old patterns of self-doubt by speaking in her own voice and repeatedly forgiving herself for her own self-betrayals.

Reflecting further, she discovered that her own inner masculine was as fickle and uncommitted as she had perceived the outer masculine to be. When she was working on a project, for example, she would start off with great enthusiasm, but then lose interest and be easily side-tracked. If doubts or questions were raised about her work, she would lose heart rather than take up the challenge. If she encountered difficulties, she would give up rather than try to sort things out. "I have such difficulty penetrating to the heart of the matter," she once said. In saying that, she realized that she was talking about her own uncommitted masculine.

The way unconscious dynamics operate and how they affect our conscious life is clearly illustrated in the experience of Anne, a thirty-eight-year-old teacher. Her work over a period of eleven months shows how a woman who was locked in her head and alienated from her feelings was released into her body by the Goddess archetype manifesting in her dreams. At the time Anne came into analysis, she had just returned to university to complete her doctorate in English literature. Her friends had urged her to seek help for what they thought was her inability to perceive situations correctly. She had acquiesced, more to prove to herself and to her friends that everything was all right than to find out what was wrong. The structured tests she was given showed nothing unusual, but the Rorschach (which delves into unconscious dynamics) indicated that she was using her intellect as a major defense. Everything in her life was rationalized: there was no place in her awareness for feelings, needs, affect. In addition, her profile showed loneliness, rage, and feelings of incompetence. These, it seemed, were on the verge of breaking through into consciousness, and to prevent them from doing so, she was overincorporating her perceptions of what was going on around her and intellectualizing them. So obsessive did her attempts at control become that she would often misperceive the situation and thereby miss the point. Her friends were right—but she was not ready to admit it.

Two months after her initial assessment, Anne had a brief dream, which spoke to her in a way she could not ignore.

I am looking at these strange, inanimate animals shaped this way:

I feel them and inquire what they are called. I don't get an answer, but I'm attracted to them and keep touching them. Their color is an off-white. In the next scene I have a large container, which I set down and begin emptying. It contains clothes, and a separator or divider between the top and the bottom of the container (like a cooler). When I look down into it [the container], the strange animals that I saw earlier are alive and, of course, I'm excited. I take them into my hand and cuddle them. These shapes, in the bottom of the container, are breathing.

When asked what the shapes looked like, Anne said, "Teardrops," and her tears began to flow. Her feelings were alive, but they were buried and barely breathing under the weight of the personas (clothes) she had been carrying around for such a long time. These tears, these feelings, were "strange" to her, but there was great relief, even joy, in acknowledging them. Often, when we get to the point where we can no longer bear the constraints of a persona to which we are enslaved, we are forced to surrender. The unconscious can then begin to reveal to us what is missing, because we are ready to look for it.

About a month later, Anne had another dream, which directed her further in her longing to integrate her feelings into her life.

I'm standing more or less wrapped around a small black-haired, dark-eyed female. Suddenly, she turns on me fiercely, extricates herself, and orders me to move back and give her space. Her eyes are riveted on me and her hands are strong as they push me back. I keep staring at her as I step back. Then I turn around and see a crowd of people standing on the stairs behind me. "I can't move back or all these people will fall backwards," I tell her. I stay put, and suddenly the dark lady starts talking. She says she felt the other parts of my body—they were solid—but she didn't feel my breasts. She begins chatting in an animated but now friendly manner.

Having become aware of her undifferentiated feelings, the sadness of all her repressed tears, Anne is now confronted with her shadow self—a shadow that becomes separated out and therefore recognizable. Having been repressed for so long, her shadow is fierce and demanding, wanting to be recognized by Anne and given some space. This fierce energy constellates and confronts the dreamer as she is being pushed up the stairs by the crowd. All the undifferentiated energy is pushing Anne up into the head. This is the old pattern of trying to keep on top of things by solving them logically.

Anne's parents had come over from Eastern Europe. Her mother had played the traditional role of taking care of everyone's needs while denying her own. She was the silent and compliant partner to Anne's father, a hard-working tradesman with a great deal of ambition to get ahead materially. While Anne had adopted her father's attitude of "getting ahead" and achieving, she had also inherited from her mother the need to please others and be self-effacing. Her religious beliefs, which were influenced by her mother, reinforced her need to serve others at the expense of her own happiness. When we are locked into an ideal, it is difficult to give the shadow side any room, not only because we do not want to acknowledge this part of ourselves, but also because we fear letting other people down by revealing to them our imperfections.

Anne was very energetic in her pursuits, both academic and social. Her energy, however, was a drivenness in pursuit of an unconscious ideal inherited from her parents. The dark woman tells her she felt her body but not her breasts. The breast, the nurturing symbol, is close to the heart chakra. The heart symbolizes the integration of mind and body, of spirit and instinct, represented by the three chakras below and the three chakras above. When energy is flowing freely between the chakras, the heart chakra symbolizes the movement of love. When we love, it is no longer necessary to operate out of will power, nor is it necessary to be driven by the need to be responsible for others, or the need to achieve. What we do out of will power, however noble, falls back into anger and loneliness, if our own legitimate needs are not being met. The body becomes solid, rigid, concretized in its efforts to serve the injunctions of the mind.

The body learns patterns of responding that become locked into the musculature and become a concretized configuration of the repressed or negative emotions. It was at this point that Anne agreed it would probably be good for her to do some work with her body. "[A]lthough a person may have conscious insight into the way a complex cripples his or her action, if the body does not let go of the conflict created through years of habitual tension, half the problem is not solved and the former distorted pattern is quick to re-establish itself."[14]

Anne began to work, on a weekly basis, with a Toronto therapist, Beverly Stokes, who attempts to reeducate the body through the developmental processes and with experiential anatomy. Within a month of starting to work with Beverly, Anne had a short dream that showed that the energy was beginning to flow within her body.

> My attention is drawn to an outdoor stage (like a pavilion). We are celebrating. On the right is a solo performer, gracefully undulating her body, and I'm really intrigued by her movements and want to reach out to her. At the left of the stage are Chinese folk dancers with silk banners and firecrackers. They are very colorful and loud, and somewhat scary. Suddenly, the solo dancer comes closer and becomes a waving, undulating, sky-blue silk banner, moving in and out. I can see the thinness of the banner as it sways like waves moving toward me.

Anne's work in repatterning her body stirred up different energies in both sides of her body. The right side is a dancer with undulating wavelike motion who becomes a blue banner moving toward the dream ego. The left side is also stirred up, but it is represented by sharp, decisive movements punctuated with firecrackers. This kind of energy is foreign to the dreamer, and is, therefore, a little frightening. The two energies are reminiscent of the fundamental wave/particle basis of reality as described in quantum physics. Both have "silk banners," but each has its own special tempo and rhythm. At this time it is the feminine (sky-blue) banner that attracts Anne, as it reaches out like a wave, in a pattern of relationship. Subsequent dreams showed that the release of the feminine was to be the route by which Anne would eventually come to embrace the positive masculine.

Two weeks later Anne came in very excited by two dreams she had had on two consecutive nights. In the first dream, she met the Black Goddess and experienced a release of energy in her unconscious that was to be a turning point in her journey.

> I am on a large blue-black-purple moor walking and stalking, a little frightened, yet curious about my strange environment. Coming toward me from a distance is a huge black figure, and as it gets closer I see it is a woman with black flowing hair, black eyes, and long, flowing black clothes. I stop and turn around to retreat and run as fast as I can. However, when I turn I'm back facing her again. This

happens at least twice (I felt like a swivel neck) and I'm facing her again. This time I hear her say, "Come," and she takes me by the hand. We start walking, and suddenly I feel right in step with her, as if we are gliding smoothly and very quickly. In front of us there suddenly appears a beautiful, round, sparkling (jeweled?) house set amid evergreen trees. We go up the stone pathway. The door opens and I find myself in a magnificent, high-ceilinged room with a mandala on the floor and intricate but delicate markings on the walls (Japanese, Chinese artwork?). I focus on the huge mandala—a very intricate mosaic of figures and designs in vivid tangerine, gold, and azure blue. I think it is the most beautiful thing I have ever seen. As I am staring at it, from its center a black ebony carving shoots up at least 7 feet tall, continually changing its shape. I get closer to the carving, mesmerized and wondering what it is, when suddenly an arm extends from it to embrace me. Just as we are making a hand clasp, it changes into flowing gossamer-like material, with vivid brilliant colors, gyrating in spiral form. Then I hear some music, soft with exotic tones, which seems to keep the sculpture in motion. I sense the sinuous rhythm and feel stirred inside. Spontaneously, I move in slow motion (belly dancing?) toward it. Suddenly, I'm naked and free. It has become water and I'm feeling cleansed and refreshed from head to toe. Then I am wafted up and down and around, dancing in the water flow. I start to laugh with glee, like a little child. It is so exhilarating! Then I wake up.

At the beginning of the dream, Anne is wandering on a moor, a desolate and frightening place. The desert, the moor, is a place of aloneness, a place where the old, familiar patterns give way to the unknown. This is the place of numinous experience; it is here that the Black Goddess approaches the dreamer. This larger-than-life energy is frightening, and the dream ego wants to run from it. She is afraid she will be overwhelmed by it. She turns in every direction, but is always left facing the Goddess, who encompasses all points on the circumference.

Finally, the dreamer follows the Goddess and is led by the hand to the center, the heart of the feminine mysteries. The round, sparkling house represents the enclosure of sacred space within each individual. The great Spanish mystic, Teresa of Avila, had a similar vision of the interior castle as a round crystal structure within us containing all the levels of consciousness. The house is surrounded by evergreen trees, the regenerating principle of nature. On entering this magnificent structure (a symbol of the Self), Anne sees that the floor is a brilliant, intricate mandala. The mandala, or circle, is a dominant symbol in almost every culture and appears as a healing or unifying symbol of the Self arising spontaneously from the depths of the collective unconscious. It serves further as a container of the life energy. From the center of the mandala, this life energy rises in the shape of a black ebony carving that keeps changing shape.

This can be seen as the *prima materia*, the dark center of the unconscious that rises up in the double container of the jeweled house and the mandala. It is seven feet tall. Seven is the number of the Great Mother. It suggests, as well, the kundalini energy rising up the spinal column through the seven chakras.

Moving into the center, experiencing the outpouring of unconscious energy requires a strong container, a safe place, a mandala. This energy reaches out to the dreamer, who has temporarily become mesmerized by it. Suddenly, the ebony transforms into a flow of brilliantly colored gossamer-like material, kept in shape by music. Allowing one's energy to flow from the depths of the unconscious opens the body to new vibrational possibilities, safe within the resonating womb.

Finally, the column turns into a fountain of water. The dreamer finds herself naked, totally herself, and dancing in its clear, refreshing spray. She is vulnerable, but unencumbered. This is a kind of baptism, a restoring of the original wholeness. She goes around and up and down, the motion resembling the quaternity within the circle. The glee of this experience is that of the reborn child, the spontaneous new life within her.

Her initiation by the Goddess into the feminine mystery leads Anne to the navel of existence. The dark wood becomes the crystal fountain. The energy rising from the roots of existence is transformed from the dark matter of the Great Mother to the translucent matter of the Goddess. "Water is the source of all potentialities in existence . . . associated with birth, the feminine principle . . . Water is the liquid counterpart of light."[15] As such it is connected with the transformation of matter. At a more archetypal level this dream points to the Fountain of Life that rises from the root of the Tree of Life in the center of Paradise. To be open to this inner fountain is to be transformed by its life-giving water.

This dream heralds the death of the old life and a rebirth to new possibilities. The Black Goddess leads the dreamer into a safe container, to the place of wholeness within herself. Mandalas, as Jung saw them, are birth places, and in this dream, the transformation of the energy erupting from the center, within herself, led Anne to a place of freedom and spontaneity.

The theme of this dream was counterpointed by a very short dream Anne had the following night.

I am swimming/floundering in water with strange, ugly animals (crocodiles) surrounding me. Whichever way I try to get out or hide under the water they are there just waiting. Suddenly I start screaming, "Eat me, just *eat* me! I don't care! Come on, *eat* me!" Then the crocodiles change into neon-tetra tiny tropical fish (rainbow colored) and swim in and around me and I start to catch them. There are thousands of them all around. The sun is reflecting off them with brilliant, dazzling color! I am hugging them, trying to catch an armful as I come up out of the water.

This dream clarifies what happens in the unconscious when blocks are removed from energy channels in the body. It is an example of what Jung calls *enantiodromia*, the reversal of a psychic situation. If we think of a pendulum swinging naturally back and forth between the poles, action and reaction, we can see it suddenly overstimulated and going instantly over the top from one energy into the other. Such a rapid shift is common in children or in adults when they are drunk or overtired. It also happens when new energy fields are opened: as the energy climbs to new heights of joy on one side, it suddenly flips into new depths of terror on the other.

In this dream, the crocodiles of the chthonic mother are not about to let the dream ego escape. They have been concretized in her body for a long time. No matter how she twists and turns, there is no way out. Then—and here her ego strength is crucial—she confronts them, "Come on, *eat* me!" This encounter provides an interesting contrast to the earlier dream, in which she tried to elude the great dark figure. That struggle ended with a very different "come." In both impasses, the dream ego is strong enough to surrender. Far from a passive giving up, this is an active choice involving huge courage in the face of a supernatural challenge. It goes beyond fear to "Thy will

be done." Here is where transformation happens in the unconscious.
The menacing energy that pulls toward death is suddenly turned into
energy vibrant with light. The Death Goddess shifts into Life Goddess. The body is no longer concretized in fear. Transformation happens at the cellular level, as if the very cells of the body are loosened
from the grip of fear and explode into vibrant multi-colored carriers
of life.

A few nights later Anne had a short, humorous dream that
points to the release of the kundalini energy into the same rainbow
color of the fish.

> I'm standing in line with a large empty bag, waiting for a loaf of
> bread to be put in. I'm in the middle of the line (about 20th). Finally,
> when it is my turn, a man says, "Close your eyes and don't open them
> until you are out of the building." When I finally look into the bag,
> I discover a large snake (3 feet long) coiled at the bottom and start
> to scream. As I do, I see the snake looking at me benevolently. I pick
> it up and begin to pull the skin off from the rear, as one would a
> stocking. Underneath its skin are rainbow colors (like those of the
> neon-tetra tropical fish). Suddenly, the snake winks its left eye and
> says, "Thank you, thank you!"

Anne was expecting an everyday loaf of bread; she received a
gift she could not have chosen, nor asked for. This one can change
her life. The Goddess Isis is sometimes depicted as a coiled snake in
the bottom of a basket. The snake shedding its skin is a universal
symbol of rebirth and regeneration. The coiled snake the dreamer
finds is her own repressed sexual/spiritual energy. On seeing it, she
panics, but then realizes it is benevolent and wants to be released.
The similarity in the color of the snake and the tropical fish points
again to the rainbow connection between heaven and earth. The
image makes a further connection between the transformation at a
cellular level within the body and the transformation of the core of
that energy in the serpent/spinal cord of the dreamer.

In *Antony and Cleopatra*, the same image, a snake coiled in the
bottom of a basket, appears as the Goddess Isis, Death Goddess of
Rebirth. Rising like Isis herself to her full archetypal stature, Cleopa-
tra is determined to die in order to be united eternally with Antony.
As the serpent bites her breast, it confers its sting of immortality.
"Husband, I come!" she cries,

Now to that name my courage prove my title!
I am fire and air; my other elements
I give to baser life.[16]

Free at last of the chthonic crocodile that sleeps in the ooze of the Nile, Cleopatra awakens in death to her full Isis stature.

Anne's release from entrapment in the chthonic Mother is further elucidated by a series of dreams she had in a single night about three weeks later.

I am rushing down the stairs of a cathedral (dark wood paneling). I am searching for someone. Suddenly, I see my mother sitting with a babushka tied around her head. She looks at me; I look at her surprised. We do not communicate because I'm still searching.

I am outside in a large field. I am conscious of the brightness and the blue sky. I am thinking of flying kites when almost in the same moment the sky seems filled with question marks—large red question marks.

The question marks begin gliding down toward me. The first one, as it comes to me, becomes my mother, holding a brightly colored umbrella. She is suspended a little off the ground and beckons me to her. She hands me a small transparent box, in which I can see butterflies. I open the box, and at least six or seven butterflies fly out and circle me. I keep turning north and south. Just as quickly, another question mark comes down. It becomes a circus (midway) with a *large* Ferris wheel. I am a bit apprehensive to get on it because I sense it is almost toy-like—very plasticky and fragile. However, I am somehow transported to it; I find myself sitting in it. It seems comfortable and secure. It starts moving. At different moments I feel the movement up and then down—my feet even touching the ground, and then going up again. It is a very unusual sensation. I feel my whole body one with the Ferris wheel. The dream seems to go on all night, with the question marks continually coming to me. Later, I am in a tall, transparent building with a huge skylight. Still later, I am very small, looking upward at a very bright blue sky and trying to get out of a deep, stark space with steps and steps, climbing endlessly upwards. There is no light. I am counting the steps. Another question mark comes toward me. It is a woman. She seems to be ten feet tall with a flowing purple gown and a big smile on her face. I begin to shout;

"I'm not you, I'm ME—ME! Do you understand? I'm strong too!"
Suddenly, she embraces me. I wake up and start to cry.

These dreams express the downward and upward movement between the opposites of the unconscious and consciousness that are brought into what Jung called the *circumambulatio*, the circular motion that connects all things to the center. Moving down into the old cathedral, Anne encounters her mother wearing a babushka, for her an image of the repressed feminine. This, however, is not what the dreamer is looking for. Consciously, she has rejected this role and sought for her answers in the intellect, in the sky. She is thinking about flying a kite—in this instance, a kind of undisciplined reasoning, a going with the wind. In real life, this is what Anne was getting into and what brought her into analysis. The answers she had previously sought become question marks, burning red questions that now approach her.

The first question is around the mother—her own personal mother, but also the mother complex. As the question mark comes down out of the sky toward her, she recognizes it is her mother, who now offers her a transparent box containing butterflies. Anne takes the box and releases the butterflies. The butterfly symbolizes the soul in its release from unconscious matter. This dream is similar to that of another woman, whose mother was actually dying. The dream ego holds her mother in her arms and does not want to let her go. The old mother (the forces of inertia in the dreamer's body) wants to die. Letting go of those old patterns, however, would mean the dreamer would have to make changes in her conscious life. The mother gives her a gold butterfly, with the words, "Butterflies are free." Then the old mother dies. Subjectively, this dream, like Anne's, speaks of matter (mother) wanting to become conscious. Objectively, both dreams suggest release from matter.

The second question mark becomes a large Ferris wheel. With some trepidation, the dreamer is transported into the round of life, the *circumambulatio*. Jung saw this circular movement as the marking off of the sacred precinct, as fixation and concentration. "Action is reversed into non-action; everything peripheral is subordinated to the command of the centre. . . . Psychologically, this circulation would be the 'movement in a circle around oneself' so that all sides of the personality become involved."[17] All the light and dark forces, the

opposites, in the personality are brought into play within the wholeness of the circle.

The later segments of the dream return once again to the up-
ward/downward task of reconciliation of the opposites. The
dreamer is in a tall transparent building, but this is balanced by her
painstaking climb upward from the depths of the dark unconscious,
step by step.

The last burning question that comes to the dreamer concerns
the Goddess herself. This is the energy that appears larger than life,
and she is clothed in the spiritual color, purple. Faced with this
enormous energy, the dreamer asserts her own individuality. On the
Ferris wheel, all the opposites of Anne's personality were gathered
together and finally in this dream she is able to assert her own wholeness, her own integrity. I am ME! I belong to myself and that is more
important than anything else. It is crucial to reach this stage from an
ego standpoint, because until we belong to ourselves we cannot enter
into a meaningful relationship with the archetypal energy. When
Anne can claim her own uniqueness, then the Goddess rejoices and
embraces her. It is important to remember that dreams give us images
that point in the direction of wholeness. The unconscious moves
ahead of consciousness. In these dreams, for example, Anne is being
given guidance toward her own totality. Conscious action may come
somewhat later.

Two weeks later, Anne encountered the Black Goddess again.

I meet a very tall, graceful, black lady with a black dog under her
arm. She takes me by the hand and we glide to a small stand by the
side of the road. On a table, there are many pairs of hands—long
fingered, short and stubby, tanned, short-nailed, manicured—every
possible kind is there. I am mesmerized for a few moments. Suddenly,
a pair of big, warm hands reaches out and takes hold of my hands—at
first gently, then firmly—and begins to massage them very slowly and
carefully. I feel some pain and cry out—also an energy going through
me. I start laughing and begin to reciprocate and massage the other
hands. Then I realize that all these hands are mine.

This dream recalls the fairy tale *The Handless Maiden*. Through a
tragic relationship with her father, the maiden has lost her hands, her
capacity to take hold of reality. That story is about the feminine

refinding her connection to life through her hands.[18] Anne does have hands in the dream, but they need to be massaged. Her ability to receive life, to create, to give, lacks real energy, lacks connection to the instinctual depths. All the possibilities, represented by the other hands, are cut off when a person is out of touch with the source of energy. Slowly and carefully, the energy must be massaged back into the hands in order for us to take hold of life. Physically and psychologically, this is a painful process. As Clarissa Pinkola-Estés puts it, "As we practice the deep, instinctive knowing about all manner of things we are learning over a lifetime, our own hands return to us, the hands of our womanhood."[19] We are able to grasp life with all its polarities and possibilities, to give as well as receive. This gathering together of all the possibilities lies at the core of Goddess energy.

In the weeks that followed, through analysis and body work Anne "massaged" the energy back into her hands, her body, her psyche. She began to feel the energy in her body, to sense what increased her energy and what drained it. As this energy became more differentiated, she learned what fed her soul and what caused it to shrink into a protective cover. A dream she had about eight weeks later makes this "body learning" conscious.

> I am scuba diving in the Mediterranean (wearing all the gear—wet suit, snorkel, flippers, and tank). Suddenly, I am stripped of all my gear and left naked without breathing support. I panic. Then I take a deep breath and it seems all right. I am swimming *naturally* as if at the water's surface. Yet, I'm under the sea observing coral and again the neon-tetra fish are teeming around me. I find myself floating and frolicking, laughing and carefree. Some dolphins come along and one comes under me. I ride on its back through the water. I feel free and unencumbered, and breathe normally.

In this dream, all the "gear," all the defenses are stripped away. Suddenly feeling vulnerable, without all the patterns of defense, is cause for panic. Walls not only keep others out, but keep us in. Yet, we can afford to tear down those walls only if we are willing to surrender to a sense of connectedness deep within ourselves. There is a way in which we create our own reality. Our own inner dynamics are played out in the people and situations that constellate around us. When we come to a place of openness and connectedness within ourselves, our reality without becomes more open and connected. Trust begins to emerge—trust in ourselves and trust in the universe. This is not naiveté, but an undefensive posture toward life. It is surrendering to the journey that is uniquely ours.

In the dream, Anne begins to breathe deeply, to receive spirit (the breath of life), to let it move within her. She can swim naturally now, not afraid of the unconscious. She merely observes its contents. Instead of whales or devouring crocodiles waiting to consume her, the neon-tetra fish, the tiny vibrant cells, of her earlier dream surround her. Dolphins, these extraordinarily sensitive denizens of the deep, symbolize the psychopomps, or guides in the unconscious. She is buoyed up and rides through the waves, guided now by the natural forces of her unconscious.

It was now nine months since Anne had come to see me and I gave her the Rorschach test once more—something I usually do not do. However, I was so struck by the force of her dreams in releasing emotional content and her openness to the process that I was curious to see what the results might be. The results showed a significant drop in the intellectualization score. This score represents a major way in which the individual organizes his or her perceptions of the world. Intellectualization is quite resistant to change, no matter what the intervention. For Anne, intellectualization had been part of a defensive posture. In letting go of her need to control through rational means, her emotions began to surface. Rage and loneliness became much more evident. With the surfacing of these emotions, her psychic discomfort began to rise. Also, Anne's perception had now moved from external scanning to internal scanning. Here too, she had had a defensive posture toward the world, being overly alert to what was happening "out there." Now she was able to look more for the answers, the cues, within herself. She was now ready to begin working gradually toward achieving an external/internal balance.

I did not share with Anne at the time the "objective" affirmation that she was perceiving and experiencing the world in a different way. I did not want to influence the process. The need to release the emotional content within her body, to focus this energy and give it an outward, creative expression still remained.

Over the next few months, Anne continued to integrate the polarities between her instinct and her intellect, between body and mind. This integration of spirit and instinct was manifested in a dream she had shortly after the Rorschach testing.

> I'm in a large assembly room participating with others in a worship service. A woman dressed in yellow/green plaid, with hair of the same colors (yellow and green), walks up the stairs to a stage to sing a solo. I'm very much taken with this golden/green hair and how it is part of her patterned dress. She is very graceful. She turns toward the audience at the left and front and sings in a most liquid, yet strong and clear voice. I'm really struck that she can sing so well. Suddenly, I hear an authoritative voice (perhaps that of a bishop) telling us to remove the pornographic posters from the walls, because they are offensive and scandalous to the students. I happen to see one of the posters at the back—a beautiful form of a human body. I respond, "This is not pornographic. This is a beautiful human body!"

The green and gold plaid hair and dress symbolize the integration of the natural with the spiritual. With this integration, the feminine finds her voice, a voice that allows her to speak out against the patriarchal restrictions that have become part of her psyche. Having moved away from a position that valued achievement and the superiority of the mind above all else, Anne was now able to celebrate her body in its own natural beauty.

Anne's integration of body and mind continued through a series of dreams in which she was mountain climbing in the Alps in the company of three other women. The climb, with its difficulty, its exhilaration, its drudgery, and its demands for conscious awareness at each step, was to become a metaphor for her life. Sometimes, she would wonder, "What am I doing here? Why am I climbing?" At the same time, she knew she could never go back to living unconsciously. In one dream she had the experience of thinking to herself, "This moment is very special. I feel and *know* I'm in communion with myself, with nature, and with the Divine."

When the Virgin energy begins to mature, new masculine energies begin to appear in the dreams. The old demanding, authoritative, judgmental father may be hovering somewhere in the background, but the presence of the totally new masculine figures attests to different energies. In a later dream, Anne encounters a man in a lab coat, who wants her to really hear her own voice. She described the encounter thus:

He picks up a small round box with VOICE written on it. He presses it gently, and I begin to hear my voice. Qualities that I recognize give way to a deep, very fluid resonance, a timber that I have heard in an opera singer—very different. I am struck by it and begin to question how and where he got my sound. He counters, "Do you want to go on hearing this inside of you?" "Of course!" I exclaim, and then quip, "How are you going to do it? Are you going to stick it [the box] in my throat?" "No," he says quietly, "I want you to drink this slowly." He hands me a glass of clear liquid (water). "And it's yours." I take the glass and begin drinking. At first it is like drinking fire. It sears my throat and gullet, and I feel it going down quite deep, but I don't—can't—stop until the glass is empty. Then, I put my arms out in a questioning gesture, "So?" I begin to feel a change. I try to speak naturally and my voice sounds the same, but I can hear the other voice, the deep fluidity *inside* of me. "Do I have to pay you, or what? Who are you?" I ask. He just smiles with his eyes and shakes his head—no—and continues looking at me. I wake up.

Anne, like many of us, had shut down her creative expression. Her feelings were repressed in her belly, and her mind was working overtime to keep the world in order. Between the two lay—quite literally—a stone in her throat. One reason she was late starting her analysis was that she was diagnosed with a tumor in her throat. Although it was biopsied and found to be benign, it was beginning to interfere with her breathing. Since she did not want to interrupt her sabbatical year, the operation was postponed until May, when classes were over. By that strange law of "coincidence," Anne had this dream in April. When the doctors were preparing to operate the following month, the tumor was no longer there. If, as Pythagoras once said, "a stone is frozen music," then Anne had finally learned how to sing.

What it means to hear one's true voice is poignantly conveyed in a poem by David Whyte entitled *The Fire in the Song.*

> The mouth opens
> and fills the air
> with its vibrant shape
>
> until the air
> and the mouth
> become one shape.

And the first word,
> your own word,
>   spoken from that fire

surprises, burns,
> grieves you now
>   because

you made that pact
> with a dark presence
>   in your life.

He said, "If you only
> stop singing
>   I'll make you safe."

And he repeated the line,
> knowing you would hear
>   "I'll make you safe"

as the comforting
> sound of a door
>   closed on the fear at last,

but his darkness crept
> under your tongue
>   and became the dim

cave where
> you sheltered
>   and you grew

in that small place
> too frightened to remember
>   the songs of the world,

its impossible notes,
> and the sweet joy
>   that flew out the door

of your wild mouth
> as you spoke.[20]

The mystery of our voice lies in the unique vibrational patterns each of us has. The universe itself is ultimately a pattern of vibration.

According to science, "the music of the spheres" can be taken literally. This music can resonate through us, but too often we are blocked. The spirit cannot move within us or express itself through us. In this dream, the masculine spirit appears in modern guise—a man in a lab coat—but his gift, the treasure in the box, is priceless—her own voice, "the deep fluidity *inside* of me."

Two nights later, the same masculine energy reappeared, this time with a different gift.

> I'm back at the lab and the same man [the one in the lab coat] asks me if I would like a "new skin." "Sure!" I reply. "I'll paint your body from head to toe with this purple maximized concentrate," he informs me. Before I know it I am standing naked with a purple body. At first I laugh, but then I get frightened about what is happening to me. As in the other dream, he responds with "smiling eyes" that keep watching me. I look again at my body. My skin is clear and soft, like a baby's. I put my hands over my eyes and dance around. I cannot believe this is happening to me.

Symbolically, to receive a new skin is to be reborn. Here, the dreamer is painted in purple, the color of sovereignty, of the mantle of divinity. The result is a new spiritual body. New wine poured into an old wine skin will cause it to burst. The inner work Anne had been doing in releasing the light in matter required a new container. The light within, the growing consciousness, required a new body, a subtle body, to contain the energy.

The concept of the subtle body draws on an ancient tradition. "The subtle body denies neither psyche nor soma, but brings them together in a *tertium non datur,* a third which holds the physical and psychic tensions and acts as a catalyst releasing energy to both sides."[21]

If we think of the masculine/feminine trinities within, or of the judgment of Maat with the balance between the lower and upper chakras, or of the spiraling up and down in Anna's mandala dream, or of Sarah's journey, we get a sense of what it means to bring the psychic and physical bodies into balance. This can happen only in a body that has a greatly enhanced awareness and sensitivity. The body now speaks, as it were, and we are well advised to listen to its voice. "Once the subtle body begins to become conscious, it cannot be treated as if it did not exist; severe physical and/or psychic symptoms will erupt if it is disregarded. The laws governing the subtle body have to be recognized, usually requiring radical changes in unconscious eating and drinking habits, breathing, sexuality, etc."[22] If a person goes back to the enslavement of patriarchal thinking, the new body will not be able to endure.

In a later dream, Anne's own creative masculinity has found the strength to separate itself from the tyranny of reason and, at the same time, remain connected with the head (intellect, spirit) in a happy, healthy relationship. The setting suggests that joy in the body has contributed to this healing.

> I'm at an assembly and sitting behind a man I think I know. I lean close to his ear and whisper, "Hello." When he turns around, however, and looks straight into my eyes, I realize he is a total stranger. I look on either side to the folks there, but I'm drawn back to the gaze of this man ahead of me. Later, I am with this man in an exercise room, ready for some body movement. He takes his head off and puts it on the floor, and begins dancing and leaping like Zorba the Greek! The head on the floor is laughing at him. I'm pulled into the dance of life.

The stranger is a new masculine energy—one that Anne has never encountered before, but now meets face to face. This is an energy that can consciously lay aside the purely rational and enter into life, body and soul. It can laugh at itself. It is a kind of wild-man energy that many women find irresistible.[23]

Separation from a part of the body with all that the part symbolizes is an old theme in mythology. In chapter I, we encountered Black Kali with the severed head in her hand. To cut off the head of patriarchy within us is to cut off the power drives—the injunctions, the rules, false reasonings, false values that separate us from our reality and take our voice away.

This dream ends with Anne being pulled into the dance of life. Here the opposites are no longer in opposition. Mind and body have a joyful appreciation of each other. Together, masculine and feminine are delighting in the intensity of the flames. Together they are creating subtle body.

As the end of July drew near and Anne's sabbatical was coming to a close, I began to wonder how her unconscious would handle this event and what her last dream would tell us. The night before her final session, Anne had two short dreams.

> I'm just walking naked and carefree along the beach aware of the water and the land.

> I'm playing chess with "the devil." We are locked in an intense "showdown." Suddenly, a cat jumps up on the table and guides my hand to the right move. I sit back and say, "Checkmate."

To walk naked along the seashore, aware of both the water and the land, is to live without defenses, trusting in the inner rhythm of life, balanced between the conscious and the unconscious energies. Anne is aware of both the unconscious aspects of her life (the water) and the conscious aspects (the land). Living in the awareness of both realities bestows a great freedom—freedom from the fear of being caught off-guard by the conscious world and of being overwhelmed by the unconscious.

Fear is the realm of the devil. In the second half of the dream, all the negative forces of the unconscious become locked in a deadly showdown with the dreamer. Such a showdown often occurs in the process, particularly when great progress has been made in dealing with the shadow. The deepest point of regression, in this dream "the devil," gathers all its force for one final attempt to take the dream ego out of consciousness. Fear constellates in the unconscious, with all its seductive moves, whisperings, and mocking laughter.

In the game of chess, a player can call "checkmate" when the opponent's king is in check, unable to release himself. The king's defeat brings the game to an end. Patriarchal values are overcome. Only a Crone would dare to play such a game with "the devil," and only a Crone would so easily trust her feminine instinct (cat) in such a "showdown." Together, cat and Crone defeat the dark side of the Father in the royal game of life.

Anne's analysis had lasted only eleven months—a relatively short time. There was still much to do, much to be incarnated into her lived reality. The dreams told us where the energy wanted to go. They gave us an affirmation of a greater, more meaningful reality—one that Anne had already begun to experience *in her own subtle body.*

She had become open and attentive to the process she was in. The time she had for this stage of her journey was, however, limited by her outward reality—something her unconscious was aware of. This awareness on the part of the unconscious is often evident in working with people who have a terminal illness. The individuation process is speeded up, as it were. Time becomes concentrated.

Although Anne's analysis was short, she left with a genuine sense of her own womanhood. Through her dreams, she had found her own Virgin strength. In spite of fear and anger, she had separated herself out from the archaic Mother and patriarchal Father. She had found a new mother in the Goddess figure who came to guide her and teach her how to cherish herself. Her new masculine energies were released to lead her into areas of herself she knew nothing of. Her Crone strength allowed her to relate to the archetype without identifying with it. Her "I'm me!" was free and spontaneous. Anne learned to dance in the flames and to hear the sweet joy of her wild mouth as she spoke.

Anne continued her journey in an unexpected way. She received a request to teach and work among the native Mayan population in the mountains of a Central American country. Anne's eyes would shine and dance thinking about it. Her doctoral thesis was not finished, but it could wait. She was going to a people who lived in harmony with nature, whose culture was rich in color and symbolism. "Maybe," said Anne, "they will help me to understand more deeply what it means to live from the heart."

Some day, after mastering the winds, the waves, the tides,
and gravity, we will harness for God the energies of love.
And then, for the second time in the history of the world,
humankind will have discovered fire.

—PIERRE TEILHARD DE CHARDIN

The Shalom of the Holy; the disclosure of the gracious
Shekinah; Divine Wisdom; the empowering Matrix; She, in
whom we live and move and have our being—She comes;
She is here!

—ROSEMARY RADFORD RUETHER

She's the joy of the earth,
She's the warmth of the sun,
Dark of the night and the depths of the sea.
She's the brilliance of thought,
She's the sweetness of breath,
She's the love that's forever—Amen.

You'd better believe she's alive
She's alive, she's alive, she's alive
And she lives in my heart
Hallelujah she lives in my heart.

—"Song of Sophia"
CATHY LEE FARLEY

> And all shall be well and
> All manner of things shall be well
> When the tongues of flame are in-folded
> Into the crowned knot of fire
> And the fire and the rose are one.

This is the final image in T. S. Eliot's *Four Quartets*. Throughout the poem, as in musical quartets, various themes have been introduced, developed with many variations in major and minor keys, woven and interwoven to reveal each nuance of tone. The rose and the fire and the dance are three of the major themes that weave the *Four Quartets* together. The "lotus rose," as Eliot first refers to it, suggests the soul flower of India, its roots firmly established in the mud, its stem reaching through the water to support the exquisite blossom opening to the sun—creation opening herself to consciousness.

For us in the Western world, the rose dances with a similar soul value. Delicate, sensitive, vulnerable, the rose with its thorns carries images of intense passion, passion that throws us into the fires of life that "[b]reak, blow, burn, and make [us] new."[1] While it burns in the fires of life, it is not consumed. Throughout the poem, fire has danced its presence as a purifier, destroyer, creator. Having moved through the paradoxes of descent and ascent, movement and stillness, death and rebirth, agony and triumph, flesh and spirit, in the final magnificent chord of the poem, Eliot recognizes that nature and spirit, flame and flower, are one.

The rose in the fire symbolizes the daily round of human passion intersected by the divine, so that what could be meaningless suffering is transformed into soulmaking. Those of us who are conscious at all have experienced moments when the personal has been intersected by the archetypal, time intersected by the timeless: one note in an aria from *Norma*, one triumphant cry from a newborn baby, one flash of ecstasy in lovemaking, one final breath in one we love. Those moments are moments of NOW. They are not moments bound to the past, moments in which we experience ourselves as passive victims of our own fate. Nor are they moments bound to a future that will never come. They are moments in which the soul IS, present tense, NOW, dancing in the flames.

In such moments, matter is seen not merely with the natural eye, but is perceived with the inner eye. Perception requires imagination and creativity and reflection. When matter is *perceived*, the soul has created an image. The moment of perceiving concrete reality as an inner reality, as a soul-image, is a timeless moment, when the mundane meets the divine. This is the process of soulmaking. For example, an older woman is saying a last good-bye to her young lover. Her hand drops almost imperceptibly. An observer may scarcely be aware of the hand dropping, but if one perceives with soul, that simple gesture may provide an image of the story of her life. And the soul will hear her soul. "I have not been killed," it silently shouts. "I won't be killed. Here I am. I have a song to sing, a life to live. Hear me, see me, love me."

What has this to do with the Goddess? What has she to do with transforming meaningless suffering into soul-making? Traditionally, the individual soul has been thought of as feminine in men and women. Matter, too, is thought of as feminine. Spiritual disciplines were meant to guide the soul on its path through creation to consciousness, creation as the ground for consciousness, earth opening herself to sun.

On the journey, individuals recognize their animal passion and, like children, tend to live it out. However, raw instinct tends to become more raw. Society would be anarchy without personal discipline. Feminine consciousness is the transformative energy that can contain the energies of matter and, through the fire of love, connect them to the energies of soul.

To enter the NOW of the soul is to perceive an image. To see, hear, smell, feel NOW. To enter that image is to stop dwelling in the past or the future and to enter the world of metaphor, the creative moment. "One who cannot leave himself behind on the threshold of the moment and forget the past, who cannot stand on a single point, like a goddess of victory, without fear or giddiness, does not know what happiness is, and, worse still, will never know what happiness is," writes Nietzsche in "The Use and Abuse of History."[2]

Jung talks about that single point in his essay "On the Nature of the Psyche":

> Since psyche and matter are contained in one and the same world, and moreover are in continuous contact with one another and ultimately rest on irrepresentable, transcendental factors, it is not only possible, but fairly probable even, that psyche and matter are two different aspects of one and the same thing. . . . Our present knowledge does not allow us to do much more than compare the relation of the psychic to the material world with two cones, whose apices, meeting in a point without extension—a real zero-point—touch and do not touch.[3]

This essay was published in 1947 and further revised in 1954. Much has happened in the world of science in the past thirty-five years, much that is validating Jung's concepts, much that is making the connection between the instinctual images and the dynamism of the instincts more available as empirical data. One analysand, for example, drew a picture of a ferocious black bird nesting on the top of a stunted tree. "It's my mother," she said, "sitting on my sexuality." A few months later, she painted the same Y-shaped tree with an ugly red and purple hand at the junction of the Y. Both of us had ominous feelings about that foreign hand, so she went to a gynecologist, who at first told her there was no problem. However, when he did an ultrasound examination, he was astonished that she had suspected cancer at such an early stage. If we can perceive the inner image of the physical illness, the soul will exercise its own dynamism in the illness. The images it paints are often validated by the finely tuned machines now available to modern medicine.

Another woman, suffering from chronic fatigue, depression, fitful sleep, and breathlessness, drew a picture of her body as she experienced it, after a dream about a black spider. Systematically, the spider moved up, down, around, and through her body, making a solid mass of threads; this was not a healthy web, but the thready mass of a thoroughly psychotic spider. Her lungs, kidneys, bowels, were enmeshed. When the results of her tests returned, she discovered she had a candida infection, a yeast overgrowth sometimes associated with a breakdown of the immune system. Her image had

revealed the dis-ease in her own matter. The Goddess is that energy
in us that transforms matter into consciousness.

Another example of technology revealing the dynamism of instinct is the record which the computerized blood pressure machine
gives of the rate and blood pressure of a breaking heart. James Lynch,
in his book *The Language of the Heart,* gives convincing data concerning
the factors implicated in the development of hypertension, migraine
headaches, and heart failure. Patients with these disorders typically
show virtually no emotion while telling their sad stories; fundamentally they are deaf to the language their bodies speak.

One such patient, a psychiatrist, Henry, suffered from hypertension and took large doses of an antihypertensive medication. In a
controlled monotone, he told about his mother's death when he was
twelve. "Funny, I don't even remember crying at that time," he said.
During the telling of his story, his blood pressure had risen from an
almost normal 155/90 to 225/130. In order to lower his blood
pressure, Lynch asked him to breathe deeply, and shifted the conversation to Henry's wife, who had been listening. She agreed to have
her cardiovascular reactions monitored. She and her physician-hus-
band were shocked to find that her heart rate was around 120 beats
per minute and her blood pressure was elevated to 165/100. Later
in the day, she dropped her calm persona and began to sob: "I don't
want him to die. I don't want him to die." Her heartbeat pounded
at 165 beats per minute. Her blood pressure rose to hypertensive
ranges. Lynch concludes, "Each . . . saw the links between his or her
blood pressure and the painful memories of love lost in childhood.
But, most of all, each began to look beyond the surface calm of the
other's body, and to pay attention to the meaning of its pained and
caring internal dialogue. Henry and Louise's bodies had revolted because neither was listening to or understanding the other's hidden
communications, in part because neither could tolerate the other's
suffering."[4]

One might wonder why all analysts do not have one of these
computerized machines in their offices. Surely it could give analysands and analysts an instant view into the psyche, when someone
quietly says, "Because I expect nothing, I am never disappointed," or
"How often can your heart break?" or "Life is for other people. I am
fat." Behind the controlling mask, the soul yearns to speak its agony

even through a computer. However, there is an inner computer far more sensitive than any machine. The soul knows how to compute its own destiny and, if it is given a chance, how to achieve it.

A few of the conclusions reached by the medical research team as described in Lynch's book are worth careful consideration. These conclusions have to do with psychosomatic disorders, not illness caused by other factors. They are factually correct, but they do not take into consideration the soul of the individual. For those of us who believe that many illnesses are a manifestation of soul suffering, these conclusions are alarming, because they leave no room for dream imagery, not only as the healing power between conscious and unconscious, but as a guide to renewed creativity and new life.

- Psychosomatic disorders frequently are associated with unresolved emotional conflicts outside the patient's awareness.
- Supportive therapy that involves a great deal of reassurance can bring blood pressure down from dangerously high levels but cannot eliminate hypertension.
- In virtually every study, the current interpersonal conflicts could be traced back to emotional conflicts in childhood.
- Psychosomatic patients who have difficulty expressing their feelings are "emotional illiterates." Such patients have so successfully buried their emotional problems in their bodies that they no longer have any capacity for insight.
- Patients [who have no words to describe their feelings] demonstrate a conspicuous absence of fantasy and dreams. Their mental activity is dominated by concrete detail utterly devoid of unconscious fantasies. They do not realize they cannot identify their own feelings. They use words like *love, hate, jealousy*, rationally but have never experienced them. This disconnectedness between language and emotion stems from a lack of some crucial experience pertaining to their birth. These patients are "super adjusted to reality" but beyond their superficial impression of superb functioning, one discovers a sterility of ideas and severe impoverishment of imagination.

These conclusions are based on studies of stress-linked medical disorders.[5] From a psychic point of view, I would understand the "sterility of ideas and severe impoverishment of imagination" rather differently. Stress is a crucial factor in disturbed sleep patterns, patterns that do not allow the person to drop into deep sleep. This lack of deep (REM) sleep may be related to the "conspicuous absence of fantasy and dreams" in patients who have no words to describe their feelings. However, while people often say they cannot remember their dreams because the alarm goes off, instantly plunging them into "superb functioning," I have yet to see an analysand who does not eventually contact a world rich in imagery. The soul may go into hiding, but it does not die.

Moreover, the most stressed adults were once creative children, whose intensity and imagination collided continually with the rational, rigid world of their parents and teachers. Adults who have lost their own creativity and are smoldering with unexpressed emotions are jealous and frightened of the child's creative imagination. They demand that the child "be good," which means, "Swallow your anger, initiative, and creativity and reflect me." Is this a possible root of psychosomatic illness? When the soul decides to live, it releases the creative child, who loves to play, for whom every moment is NOW, the artist whose perception bridges the timeless world and time through imagery.

It is quite true that when most people first begin to relate to their bodies, the flood of lost memories and the accompanying toxins released may be overwhelming and produce severe illness. Soul and body may need time to rest and become acquainted with each other. Surrender to illness may be part of the journey. If body work, or what is better called soulmaking, is being carried out with an accomplished therapist, the dam is gently and patiently removed so the resulting flood does not drown the ego. The body may storm out of control, but it does so in the safe container of someone who loves it and knows how to encourage it to know and discipline itself. The analysand may deteriorate when faced with the buried past, emerging as a terrorized infant, thrashing, spitting, sobbing, but once the ego reconnects with the infant, symbols are immediately present. Far from being "emotional illiterates," these people express their needs and emotions loud and clear. They can one day become highly attuned to their exact physical and spiritual needs. Anne, whose story was told in chapter 4, is a splendid example of a person who came into analysis as an "emotional illiterate" and, guided by images of the Goddess, was reconnected to her soul.

From the soul's point of view, some comment is necessary concerning the "disconnectedness between language and emotion [stemming] from a lack of some crucial experience pertaining to their birth." When a person works through to the deeper levels of pain in the soul (the eternal part of ourselves, which dwells in the body), the anguish surrounding the birth may become manifest. Sometimes the dreams say, "Don't go in there," warning analyst and analysand that the trauma is too intense for the ego to endure. Sometimes the dreams suggest that the mother tried to abort the child, that the child was not wanted, that a child of the opposite sex was desired, or that the father rejected the child. Whatever happened, the child was not welcomed into this world and the bonding between mother and child did not occur. However hard the child tries to be loved, it knows it will always fail, simply by being who it is.

If the mother's emotions are not anchored in her own body, the child has no way of finding that anchoring, no way of relating to the body's loneliness. Nor can the mother mirror the child, since she sees her own guilt and frustration every time she seriously tries to relate. Most children go on living in spite of the grief that may have surrounded their birth, but they do so at a price. Disconnected at their deepest instinctual level, they hang on to life by becoming "superadjusted to reality." They develop a charming persona, perfect their performances, and deny who they really are. They dream of a nonexistent paradise in the past and an equally nonexistent future. Their bodies are so armored against invasion that genuine feelings are not accessible. On the other hand, they may become tyrannical, like a street hoodlum, for example, and brutalize reality. Because they are not wanted, they feel perpetually under siege and force their way in. This kind of behavior is the dark side of their dream paradise. Realizing that paradise does not exist, they become all the more ferocious, because they know they are hanging onto nothing. People who have something to hold onto can relax. People with nothing have to hold on very tight.

The "super adjusted" may one day realize that their perfect performances demand energy they no longer have. They are weary of focusing their whole lives on jobs and relationships that demand everything and return nothing. "If this is life," they say, "I don't want it." What they may not realize is that they have been functioning on willpower all their lives. The rich, deep love of life is not in them because the primal bond is absent. They buried their soul early in life and, with her, they buried their real feelings, their connection to their body, and their imagination—in short, everything that makes life vital and creative. Responsibility, duty, excellence hang heavily about their necks. Glittering at the center of a world that has become ashes in their mouths, their fires are almost out because consciousness and unconsciousness are not in harmony. The metaphors that could bring the two worlds together are blocked.

By definition, *metaphor* means "transformer; a crossing over from one state to another." Just as the body will attempt to heal itself if it is given the chance, so the psyche will attempt to heal itself; often that healing comes about through metaphor—an image that is part matter, part spirit—a physical picture indicating a spiritual condition in the dreamer, like the image of the rose in the fire. Energy manifested on one level may be transported to quite another. Living the metaphors often involves a leap of consciousness, which forces us to recognize not only gifts we buried long ago, but gifts we know not of. The leap involves taking responsibility for our own potential. Metaphor is a gift of the transformative feminine, the energy that connects psyche and soma.

A conflict that is resolved on one level of integration can come up again at another level, particularly when there is a severe split between psyche and soma. People with eating disorders, for example, are quite out of touch with their bodies. Usually, the body has carried the whole brunt of their unconscious conflicts; contrary to their experience, it is the best friend they have, and it attempts to maintain whatever balance it can.

Food addicts—like other addicts—tend to develop a victim complex. Whether the source is a controlling parent or a physical or psychic trauma before, during, or after birth, they tend to experience themselves as born losers. "Life," "the Universe," everything is against them. In their powerlessness, they wonder where the next blow is coming from, or, having given up wondering, they become defiant or resignedly accept whatever comes. They dream of concentration camps, where they are bound and raped by their own ideals (in the form of Nazi officers of the Super Race); of animals being tormented and starved; of their house being devastated by tidal waves, whirlwinds, or nuclear explosions. Their immune system is constantly on the alert, and, after years of stress, the adrenals weaken and the body gradually succumbs to allergies, candida, and other diseases connected with immune dysfunction.

In the course of their analysis, there comes a day when they realize that they are loved. No performance is necessary, no mask. Their soul can be as angry as she is, as spiteful as she is, as infantile as she is, as sweet and coy and playful as she is, and still be assured of the love of another human being. No judgment, no blame. No longer attempting to be anything they are not, they love and are loved.

Sometimes, in this exquisite moment of recognition, I have reached out to touch an analysand. The body has faltered, cowered, and, like a battered dog, withdrawn. Powerless to say why they are so frightened, powerless to feel what is happening in their bodies, they are turned to stone. Consciousness and unconsciousness are locked in civil war. Their darkest night of the soul has begun. The task of releasing a terrorized body is immense and is impossible if not combined with dream work and imagery, because these give meaning and containment to the terror. Body work, like dream work, is soul work; together they illuminate that point where the apexes of the spirit and matter touch and do not touch. The dream that follows a body/soul session usually indicates why the energy was blocked, what complex was involved, and shows where the energy is trying to go. It brings to consciousness what would otherwise be an unconscious, unintegrated process, a picture that will be repeated until consciousness receives the message.

Like a river, the individuation process follows a natural flow, which Jung perceived as a natural gradient toward wholeness.[6] As the process unfolds, it becomes clear that energy blocks, which are personified in dreams, are manifested in the body in encoded patterns, which shape the body, adjust the posture, determine the movement or lack of movement and ultimately produce symptoms in varying degrees of severity. In the fire of analysis, these encoded patterns may be changed, making the repressed energy available to consciousness. The analysand begins to experience his/her own life, begins to feel free to make the choices that are crucial to wholeness. Now the ego is strong enough to face the ultimate question.

At this juncture, the dreams point to a dark pit or a doorway, behind which is an ancient, moss-covered broken staircase, or some-times only an earthen path. Sometimes, the dreamer is told to go into rooms in the basement that are totally unknown. At this point, the body can turn to rock, in a resistance that must be respected. If the ego is strong enough, the Self will guide the dreamer to the loneliest loneliness, there to answer the question: "Do I want to live?" Sometimes, this point is reached through an almost fatal illness. In this encounter, the veils of illusion are ripped off. If there are addic-tions, they are seen for what they are: a suicidal rebellion against life, a running as fast as possible on a tightrope across an abyss, a frenzied drive in a vehicle that crashes into an abutment.

In other words, life has not been lived in the body; the soul has not taken up residence. The body has become a machine, running on willpower, and the soul, the young feminine, has been left to starve in the darkness. At the moment of awakening, the individual has to ask real questions and be prepared to take real action. It doesn't matter any more what mother did to me—or father. Am I going to stay in this job? Am I going to remain in this relationship? Am I going to give my soul time to perceive life? Am *I* going to live? It is common for people who have reached this point to say, "I really want to live but I have no idea what that means."

Here, the dreams reveal the primal loss. For whatever reason, the child did not bond with the mother and therefore cannot bond with life. This is not to put a guilt trip on mothers. We are all the children of a culture that rapes Mother Earth, that rapes the feminine in all of us. However, we do not have to accept blindly that rape. We can choose to rescue the little girl from the manure pile. We can give our soul child time to play; time to imagine, dream, perceive; time to put those images into painting, writing, music, dance. This is the food that will nourish her. In our creating, we are created.

In our dreams, this manure pile may also appear as a black pit. It sometimes contains a fearsome and magnificent image—the great serpent, Kundalini, the life force itself, which rises from the base chakra, the instinctual matrix, situated between the anus and the gen-italia. If we fail to connect with that deepest part of ourselves, we lack grounding in the cherishing Mother. The hips and legs that would connect our body/soul to her are wounded, barely able to stand in a world they cannot stand. However, if only we have the consciousness to perceive it, the hand of the Goddess is in the shit.

Without the soul's perception, the shit is meaningless suffering. The healing power of nature manifests itself in the suffering. At the point of wounding, the Black Madonna may appear in our dreams and take the rejected soul in her arms and rock her with her head against her heart.

So what is the rose in the fire all about? It is about *perceiving* the soul's suffering in the fire of physical pain and passion. It is about the anguish of spirit descending into physical limitations, and opaque matter ascending toward spiritual aspirations; it is about the conflict between these two realms producing consciousness in the soul, which belongs to both time and timelessness. It is about perceiving light in matter. It is about the creation of subtle body.

Most of us try to let our bodies and psyches function instinctively, until we are ravaged by disease or neuroses. Then we realize that the body/psyche cannot function naturally in the concrete, concretized world in which we live. Metaphorically, the body becomes a machine to be driven or a garbage dump to be avoided. At the same time, the magnificent Mother in whose womb we live is mindlessly poisoned and raped. Surely, our insane denial has to be perceived and acted upon. The Great Mother is sending us many messages warning us that her immune system is breaking down. If we are to save her, we must first embrace our own soul in our own flesh.

What we are doing in body/soul work is contacting her light in our own depths, becoming aware of our own subtle body (the body perceived through imagery). Dreams can make quite clear that until the subtle body is connected at the deepest instinctual level (the base chakra) and until it is strong enough to act as a conscious container, the spiritual energy related to the third eye (the spiritual center in the forehead), must remain veiled. Body/soul work is preparation for the divine marriage in which the light of soul opens to the light of spirit.

The rose burns in the fire of love, a love that pierces to the very heart of our own self-destruction and self-creation. There we can weep for what others have done to us and for what we, therefore, have done to ourselves and others. There we meet others in our mutual imperfections and forgive. At the heart of matter we find the mystery—the presence in which we are all one. The meaning of the

rose burning in the fire at the heart of matter is starkly expressed in
the following Zen koan:

> Ride your horse along the edge of the sword,
>> Hide yourself in the middle of the flames,
> Blossoms of the fruit tree will bloom in the fire,
>> The sun rises in the evening.[7]

Let it be Known; today the Eternal Feminine
In an incorruptible body is descending to earth.
In the unfading light of the new goddess,
Heaven has become one with the deeps.

—VLADIMIR SOLOVIEV

The feminine line is not a line but rather a flow in harmony
with the impetus that carries the brush and paint across a
canvas. The impetus comes from within like a fluid flow
through the body, filling my being and flowing out into the
space of the canvas. If a canvas were not present it would
naturally flow into the room and become part of the air and
atmosphere of the room. Such an impetus does not have a
color or perfume to assist in making its presence known but
when working as an artist I can capture its feel and texture
giving it a presence and life on a canvas.

—LINDA BETH

"Dance, then, wherever you may be,
I am the Lord of the dance," said He;
"I'll lead you all wherever you may be—
I will lead you all in the dance," said He.[1]

This chorus is from one of the best-loved hymns in the Christian tradition. Its rhythm and melody dance their way through the pews into the heart. Surely, dance is among the most important metaphors of our end-of-the-millennium culture. Prints of *La Danse* by Matisse are favorites on living-room walls. One of *The New Yorker's* funniest images is of *La Danse* with one change: one dancer has fallen out of the circle. Part of the humor lies in our sudden realization of the power of Matisse's circle. The fall-out of one dancer has sent a new vibration throughout every other dancer as each attempts to hold the momentum of the circle true. The circle creates the sacred space—calm, dependable—within which the dancers dance their own energy, or choose not to dance.

Ballet, jazz, free dance, square dance, rock 'n' roll—all have their place in our memories. And who can doubt that whatever catastrophe is happening in whatever part of the globe, the line dancers in Nashville will be earnestly stepping out their routines on Channel 38?

And metaphorically we dance. In dreams, we dance along a fence, holding our balance between "the opposites." We dance up the stairs, down the stairs, on the sands beside the sea, on dance floors we have known and others we have yearned to know, with bands from our high school formal to ensembles from our fortieth wedding anniversary.

Dance celebrates the body in motion—striding, leaping, curving, soaring, holding. Dance—whether it be religious dance, tribal dance, social dance, one soul dancing alone for the love of the dance—dance is an image of ceaseless energy forever moving toward a threshold that begins in what is ending. And so we dance toward the new millennium.

Science also speaks in images of dance. Astronauts penetrate the immensity of space and the universe becomes a great galactic tarantella danced in slow motion. Biologists describe the dance of the cells. Physicists look into the depths of inner space and see, not inert matter, but a dance of energy.

> The exploration of the subatomic world in the twentieth century has revealed the intrinsically dynamic nature of matter. It has shown that the constituents of atoms, the subatomic particles, are dynamic patterns which do not exist as isolated entities, but as integral parts of an inseparable network of interactions. These interactions involve a ceaseless flow of energy manifesting itself as the exchange of particles; a dynamic interplay in which particles are created and destroyed without end in a continual variation of energy patterns. The particle interactions give rise to the stable structures which build up the material world, which again do not remain static, but oscillate in rhythmic movements. The whole universe is thus engaged in endless motion and activity; in a continual cosmic dance of energy.[2]

Describing the continual creation and destruction of particles in the rhythmic dance is describing the Black Goddess, the Goddess of the Dance. The rhythm of death and life, chaos and creativity, is symbolized in the dance of Kali. "The world is created and destroyed in Kali's wild dancing, and the truth of redemption lies in man's awareness that he is invited to take part in that dance, to yield to the frenzied beat of the Mother's dance of life and death. Redemption lies in the realization that one is in the hands of Kali and that ultimately one is directed by the Mother's will."[3]

To contemplate the Black Goddess as the flux of life, death, rebirth, is to see things as they really are. "[Kali] illustrates strikingly what the world of appearances looks like to the one who has seen beyond. . . . her overall presence, which is frightening, and her dwelling place in the cremation ground clearly mock the ultimate significance of a world grounded in the ego."[4]

To go beyond the ego, we have to turn inward with our own microscopes of introspection; we have to go into our own opaque matter to discover the unpredictability and spontaneity of our true nature. We have to enter chaos, terrifying though it might seem, if we are to find our own creativity. Courage and awareness of the dangers are essential to our entering into the dance of our own dark reality. To let go of the familiar landscape of our own restrictions is to risk madness. "For Kali is said to be mad. . . . With her equally mad and wild lord, Siva, Kali reigns over and impels onward the dizzying creation that is this world."[5]

Change and flux, the decay of the old and the birth of the new is the feminine rhythm. This rhythm manifests in history; it becomes more apparent in periods of transition. Orderly systems, with their manifestos and hierarchies, build and accelerate, then collapse into chaos. Individuals, too, build and accelerate and then collapse. We live in a "high-tech" world; we accelerate our busy schedules; we meet the demands of family, work, and community; our minds outstrip our bodies. Life becomes hectic; we try to exert control; we create secure little pigeonholes; we deceive ourselves into believing we are in control; and all the time we know chaos is leaping at our edges. Feminine rhythms are forgotten. Purses are lost in dreams, and little cats die.

We turn on our television sets; we are stunned by the chaotic images. In the last few years we have witnessed the old order collapsing throughout Eastern Europe. We have seen the Berlin Wall come down. We have seen Poland, the Czech Republic and Slovenia, the former Yugoslavia, Rumania, Georgia, Chechnya, one after another saying "no" to the Great Father. Africa, India, Central America, the United States, Canada—we are all facing our own chaos.

Within and without, chaos reigns. We look on, dismayed, as the natural order buckles under the strain of ecological disruption. We watch helplessly, as the institutions we believe in collapse. We witness the dogmas that gave us faith being challenged. We see the social order totter as crime and violence rock our schools and neighborhoods. We sense our immune systems being assailed, as new and virulent strains of virus emerge. We are overwhelmed by alienation as our relationships fall apart. We feel the Earth move under our feet, and we are terrified at the prospect of an inner earthquake.

In the wake of this social and personal turmoil, many people who are attempting to become conscious are experiencing profound changes in their psyches and bodies. New energies are being released, collectively as well as individually. Countries around the world are attempting to rid themselves politically of the Old Mother and the Old Father, those archaic parental complexes that hinder growth. At the individual level, people are seeking *inner* freedom, psychic freedom. They want to be rid of the old parental complexes—Old Mother Mud, who swaddles us in deadening security, and Old Father Law, who keeps us mired in that mud with traditions and precedents. These two huge complexes, when they are not brought into consciousness, simply say, "No, kid, things are not going to change!" But something is now stirring within individuals as it is among groups. The yearning to be free is, hopefully, a manifestation of a new energy that is driving individuals to take responsibility for their own lives. Unless we can consciously recognize that we have such a responsibility, we are doomed to anarchy.

The freedom we seek does not lie in the patriarchal control we so desperately attempt to maintain. Rather it lies in letting go and descending into the chaos of the maternal matrix where the seeds of new life are waiting to be fertilized. Letting go is embracing the Black Goddess, she who will open our eyes to our illusions, she who will make us see that our treasure lies in the repressed feminine energies that we once labeled weak, irrational, disorganized, supersensitive, and all the other thoughtless labels—naive, stupid, slow, melodramatic. Descending into her territory demands the death of a rigidly controlled life. Dancing with her means finding a new discipline that allows the new life to sprout and grow.

In the following pages, we will discuss some of the ideas and imagery from the earlier part of the book with deeper resonances. If you can imagine a diamond suspended in light so that we can move around it, above and below it, and see the many colors and depths, move and enjoy and accept that we cannot understand Sophia's Wisdom in one gulp, then you'll patiently read and patiently wait for your own unconscious to respond in dreams. Then this will not be an intellectual concept you are trying to understand with your mind; it may come as a "yes" in the cells of your body. Then you will know you are in the creative matrix where the feminine work goes on.

In describing the balances of energy flowing between spirit and instinct in the psyche, Jung used the image of a spectrum. At the infrared end is the dynamism of instinct, in which all the bodily instinctual energies originate. At the ultraviolent end is the dynamism of the archetype, in which originate images, dreams, active imagination, all the activity of the imagination. If we imagine a pendulum swinging from one side to the other in this spectrum, sometimes slowly without much swing, sometimes violently with too much momentum, we get a sense of the energy moving between "the opposites." Jung described the archetype (the magnetic field, as we earlier called it) as psychoid, meaning that its energy can be experienced through both body and psyche. So long as there is a relational balance between soma and psyche, the pendulum swings steadily from side to side—action and reaction.

The Psychoid Archetype

Instincts		*Archetype*
infrared ——————— experience ——————— ultraviolet		
(Physiological: body symptoms, instinctual perceptions, etc.)		(Psychological: ideas, conceptions, dreams, images, fantasies, etc.)

If, however, the balance is disturbed, something quite other starts to happen, and, as with an off-balance pendulum, the whole structure starts to shake. Within the human range of oscillation, the balance can be held. Once the pendulum begins to swing beyond human limits, it pushes toward the poles of instinct and spirit. These hypothetical poles, at the two extremes of the spectrum, are outside the range of human behavior. For example, a bulimic dancer who has been trained to believe that she is a weightless angel, hears the voice inside her head, perhaps outside as well, endlessly shouting, "Not good enough, not high enough, not perfect enough, not light enough." No matter how well she performs, she is never perfect enough. The ante goes up. She as woman, human being, is not seen. The voice does not shut up. It wants light, light, and more light. The pendulum is swinging out of human range. Spirit is becoming demonic, Spirit is controlling ego. Spirit is wiping out ego. Spirit is appearing in dreams as Hitler destroying everything human that is not perfect enough to be part of his Super Race.

Now, action/reaction sets in. Crocodile surfaces when the pendulum, following its compensating balance, swings too far into the dynamics of instinct—the infrared pole outside human boundaries. Desperate for nourishment for her body and her soul, the bulimic wolfs down mother food as fast as she can, chewing none of it. Very little that goes into her stomach has been transformed by the mouth and teeth into energy that can be further transformed, digested, and assimilated in the human stomach and the human intestines. The angel dancer does not want to know they exist. Their shrieks and screams for food, she compulsively obeys as she blindly gulps down her ritual feast. In the orgasm of vomiting that follows, she will release herself from both poles of the insane swings of the pendulum. Then, for a few moments, she will be a human being at peace.

To be trapped in this diabolic rhythm is life in hell. Countless addicts are in it, desperately putting on a pretense of being human for a few hours of the day, waiting to get back to the madness that will take them to their moment of peace. They are swinging between two inhuman poles. The only way they can stop the voices in the chaos on both ends of the swing is to annihilate themselves in the orgasm of their compulsive ritual.

How to find one's own humanity? How to find that still place and live in it? That is the question. Certainly, the violent swing has to be brought under control before anything will change. The Twelve Step program in its many forms is very helpful and in many situations essential. Some additional questions are necessary in order to move the energy out of dead channels into totally new ones—living life from "Yes" instead of "No."

What is the addiction trying to tell me? Why is that wild dog in my dreams desperately biting my hand, almost taking my arm off? How are the symptoms of my illness trying to heal me?

To deal with these questions, let us first look at Jung's statement, ". . . it is not only possible but fairly probable, even, that psyche and matter are two different aspects of one and the same thing. The synchronicity phenomena point, it seems to me, in this direction, for they show that the nonpsychic can behave like the psychic, and vice versa, without there being any causal connection between them. Our present knowledge does not allow us to do much more than compare the relation of the psychic to the material world with two cones, whose apices [apexes], meeting in a point without extension—a real zero-point—touch and do not touch."[6]

If we put that statement in diagram form, it would look something like this.

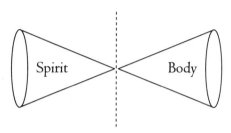

Spirit with its pole as one cone, body with its pole as the other, each reaches out to the other, touching and not touching. Touching and not touching because in 1954 there was very little scientific understanding of how imagery influences the chemistry of the body, or how the chemistry influences the images. Clearly, the apexes *do* touch, because a sick thyroid *does* create depression, and conversely, the loss of a loved one *can* influence the growth of cancer cells.

Fifty years ago, Jung could not see where the psyche-soma connection was biologically, but he knew there was a connector. He understood that the subtle body (the light body, the energy body, the metaphorical body), the home of the soul, was the midground between spirit and body. This midground is the world of the dream. This is the world where we are given a picture of what is going on in our instincts. It is also a picture that gives us a spiritual message. We can see our spiritual condition in the images of our dreams.

In the last fifty years, a great deal of research has been done on the biological connections between psyche and soma. At the Symposium on Consciousness and Survival, sponsored by the Institute of Noetic Sciences, in the early 1980s, Candace Pert, Chief of Brain Biochemistry at the Clinical Neuro-Science Branch of the National Institute of Mental Health in Bethesda, Maryland, presented some truly remarkable findings on the interconnection between the mind and the body. Her research had uncovered the existence in the body of chemical substances known as neuropeptides, as well as receptors for these substances. The interaction of the neuropeptides and their receptors, she believes, is the key to understanding how emotions are manifested throughout the body.[7] Summing up her presentation, she said:

My argument is that there are three classic areas of neuroscience, endocrinology, and immunology, with their various organs—the brain (which is the key organ that the neuroscientists study), the glands, and the immune system (consisting of the spleen, the bone marrow, the lymph nodes, and of course the cells circulating through the body)—that these areas are actually joined to each other in a bidirectional network of communication and that the information "carriers" are the neuropeptides. . . . In thinking about these matters . . . it might make more sense to emphasize the perspective of psychology—rather than that of neuroscience. A mind is composed of information, and it has a physical substrate, which is the body and the brain; and it also has another immaterial substrate that has to do with information moving around.[8]

Subsequent research has gone still further in isolating the chemical intermediaries between body and soul—the neurotransmitters and neuroreceptors. We now know that a highly charged image can create a correlative shift that stimulates changes in the body's chemistry, much as changes in body chemistry can alter moods and stimulate the imagination. As psychoneuroimmunologists and analysts work together to correlate the workings of the body with the imagery of dreams, the gap and nongap that Jung saw between psyche and soma will rapidly narrow and, I believe, eventually close.

In the imagery of the Feminine, this midground between spirit and body, the subtle or metaphorical body, is the place of the Virgin. As an archetype, the Virgin is the transformer. Like the virgin forest that carries all the potential of new life, within her is the seed of the new consciousness that may be quickened by the spirit and brought into life. In Christian mythology, if that seed is nurtured, cherished, reflected upon, allowed to mature into its full beauty, it becomes the masculine energy strong enough to partner the Virgin. It is the Bridegroom in the royal marriage to the Virgin Bride. These are the archetypal images working in the background as we discuss balancing energies.

Let us now look at the Virgin archetype as it manifests in our lives. In doing so, try to let all superimposed images and associations go. Try to imagine the transformative energy that bridges spirit and matter, the energy that holds spirit and matter together, like a rainbow, the energy that lives in the subtle body. If we think of the power in the pendulum violently swinging from matter into spirit without a bridge, and the power of the psychotic corners on either end that may be constellated in the swing, we have some idea of the strength necessary to hold that center point where spirit and body meet and do not meet. The strength lies in the metaphor.

Metaphor is the language of the Virgin. Virgin, as we are using the word, is an image of the soul, the eternal part of us that takes up residence in the body for a few years and connects to the world through the orifices of the body. Soul is from a different reality than body. It is eternal. It hears with eternal ears, sees with eternal eyes, smells with eternal nose—its Presence resonates with that other dimension. It has no language but the language of the transitory body. Therefore, it speaks in imagery, the only way it can communicate eternal truths to beings who are both eternal and temporal. It can, of course, speak through music, paint, clay, marble, arches and domes, arabesques and leaps, and gardens, and other creative forms. Right now we are attempting to understand the power of metaphorical language—a language that our culture dismisses at its peril.

At its peril because our Beingness thrives in the imagination. Children who are given space to imagine dance their days through hours of creative play. Adults who give themselves time to play, time to connect to the energy that they so often repress in their workaday world, go into their chaos and behold, childlike energy is available to them. Their imagination dances with their soul. Without this connection, shorter and fewer workdays, unemployment, and boredom can trap exiled souls in the demonic vision of an archetypal madman or madwoman who promises superhuman light on one side, superhuman sex on the other, with no room for human life in the middle.

More than that, without metaphor, culture is meaningless, dreams are meaningless, symptoms are meaningless (except in terms of curing them), religion is meaningless. Life is two-dimensional, flat, and boring. Drugs, sports, sex may restore metaphor for a few hours before the meaninglessness of life settles in again. Life without metaphor is intolerable.

We have spoken many times in earlier chapters about the importance of embodiment—the release of the repressed goddess in the earth of our own bodies. In relation to metaphor, a released body is capable of resonating. Like a cello, our body is an instrument that vibrates in relation to sound waves. Every cell hears. Let us take, for example, a dream image. An eighty-year-old woman dreams that she returns to her homeland in Europe and stands beside the streetcar stop where she once waited for the streetcar that took her to school. As she waits in the rain of a foggy evening, a child runs up to her, puts her tiny hand in the eighty-year-old hand and says, "I've come to take you home."

Now, dreamers who have forgotten that they have soul ears will respond to such dream with, "Do you think a trip to Europe will help me?" People who are beginning to remember their soul ears will say, "I just don't get it, but I know there's something there." People who hear with their soul ears feel a trembling resonating through every cell in their body and their eyes fill with tears. They recognize the completion of the circle as the soul prepares to go "Home." And Home is Eternity.

Now, if a father says, "My son is coming home. He didn't receive the scholarship this year," the soul immediately senses trouble. How can the son come *home* to his father if his father looks at him and thinks, failure? The father "loves" his son, but he can neither see his soul, nor hear him. The son cannot Be with his father. That sense of alienation may drive him to drink with the boys, and father may wonder what kind of selfish brat he raised. We hear this kind of lost connection everywhere we go, soul genuinely looking for soul and the door slammed in its face. The resonance that would make the feminine connection is not present.

Life is so diminished without metaphor. Imagine going to the film *The Bridges of Madison County* without metaphor. Imagine trying to understand why people are gasping or sobbing in those long, silent scenes. Imagine seeing and not seeing the fingers touching and not touching, the eyes seeing and not daring to see, the body remembering and trying to forget. Imagine sitting at that red light, seeing the left-hand blinker on the truck ahead flashing in the rain, and knowing that all you need to do is push your door handle a quarter of an inch and you'll be Home. Imagine all that with no knowledge of Hecate and crossroads! And no knowledge of Shakespeare!

> And whether we shall meet again I know not.
> Therefore our everlasting farewell take:
> For ever, and for ever, farewell, Cassius!

If we do meet again, why, we shall smile;
If not, why then, this parting was well made.[9]

And no knowledge of Emily Dickinson!

Parting is all we know of Heaven,
And all we need of Hell.[10]

If you haven't seen *The Bridges*, don't worry. I'm only trying to demonstrate the joy of resonances as they vibrate deeper and richer into the body and psyche. They become powerful guides, helping us to recognize the truth or falsehood of people and situations. We all have our own metaphors and our own resonances. The images we choose to ingest determine the daily refinement of the subtle body.

We need now to ask ourselves, "What happens if the metaphor is concretized?" In other words, what happens if the energy comes into the transformer—the Virgin that is strong enough to take the transformation—and instead of transforming and moving into another kind of energy, it is concretized in matter? I can illustrate this with a story from an intensive workshop. Naive or courageous as I was, depending on how you perceive the situation, I announced to the thirty women that we would put our shadow concepts of the last three days into life. We would have a shadow party. We had been doing body work to contact this energy and most of the group were experiencing new ripplings of energy up their spines and throughout other parts of their bodies.

On the night of the party, a splendid turkey had been prepared. Everyone was too excited to eat. Each was putting on feathers or sticks or seaweed or red paint, whatever was necessary to allow the transformation to move into life. Well, it certainly did. The women found themselves with gestures, walks, voices, language that they had never had before. As the party progressed, the energy became hotter and most hot. I was rather glad when it was safely over.

The next morning in session, I discovered that the turkey had been gobbled to its bones at midnight with quantities of wine. Many of the women had severe indigestion and hangovers. Can you imagine releasing all that yearning spirit and feeding it turkey and wine? A body vibrating with new energy is simply unable to digest turkey and wine. This is concretizing the metaphor.

It happens because the body is frightened. With the upsurge of repressed and, therefore, unknown energy pouring in, the body is anxious, perhaps unable to deal with the cascade of rage and grief that surges forth as it begins to experience itself. Chaos breaks out within the body because the energy has not yet found its new channel. If the Virgin container is not strong enough to acknowledge and contain the chaos that is bursting out, then the energy may regress and destroy the new life by concretizing the metaphor—gobbling turkey to quiet the chaos, instead of dancing or playing in some creative way that feeds and releases the soul.

When each woman brought her own psychic conflict to consciousness in the next session, we were able, in most cases, to find the Virgin standpoint that could sustain the new energy without allowing it to run amuck. The value of the experience was in bringing the unconscious conflict to consciousness so that it could be dealt with creatively instead of being allowed to regress into repetitive behavior.

Most addicts cannot hold a Virgin standpoint, especially if their own concretized metaphor is obtainable. To keep their abandonment fears down, they grab for mother (food), spirit (alcohol), divine union (sex), light (drugs). Yet again, they put themselves to sleep and regress to what they hope will be the security of Mother Crocodile. They are terrified to move into her creative side. Instead of holding the still point until the energy has a chance to transform into the ultraviolet side of the archetype, they plunge into the infrared.

The power of metaphor was brought home to me in a situation from my own life. In 1968 I was in a car accident that left one side of my head and face badly damaged. A brilliant plastic surgeon, to whom I am eternally grateful, cut through my scalp and with his delicate instruments went under my skin and pulled my broken bones back into place. Two weeks later, the swelling subsided and I knew I still had an eye. Two years later, I had regained the feeling in my face, but one major symptom remained. Night and day there was a loud ringing in my ear and the sensation of a mosquito continually flying inside—a disorder known as tinnitus. I went to specialists in Canada and England and they all told me they could do nothing. I would have to learn to live with it.

I was in analysis with Dr. Bennet in London at the time. The more intense the analysis became, the louder the bells rang and the faster the mosquito flew, until I thought I was going crazy. I had a dream in which someone and I were working on a machine that transforms one kind of energy into another kind (a metaphor machine). I became confused because I didn't know how to work the very complicated switches. But the other Presence did. Then someone said, "How do you feel on the eve of becoming everything you have fought all your life against?"

The ringing was now so loud that I rushed out of bed and landed on the floor of the kitchen before I knew I was awake. I prayed to God to take away that ringing or let me die. Immediately, a vision of a mock-orange bush in full bloom appeared, with its delicate ivory-colored blossoms that perfume the month of June. I was so enthralled by the beauty of the bush that I was not at first aware of the perfume in my feet. But slowly, slowly the perfume rose in my legs and its sweetness moved into every cell of my body until the perfume and I were one. I became the metaphor. Gradually, unknowingly, I had come to a standing position, with my arms raised. When the vision faded, the ringing in my ear had ceased. It has never returned.

I had gone to the kitchen and was fed: my body was ensouled. This, of course, changed my life. The efficient, clock-and-calendar, always-in-control woman was no more. I realized my empowerment was through concentration on an image, a gift from the unconscious. I realized that the fear and chaos in my rational mind could be stilled by the order in my unconscious. The archetypal image rising out of the depths of my body—the Dark Goddess permeating the orange blossom bush with love—could bring conscious and unconscious into harmony and with each other and with the natural order. Then, I could be whole.

At the time, I did not care much about what had happened psychologically. I only knew that I had been visited by divine light, that I had experienced a love I never knew before, a love within matter that shattered the world as I had known it. Reason was silenced. I could only say, "Yes. Thank you."

Later, when I read Jung, I began to understand what had happened psychologically. Tension, fatigue, pain had taken me into a regression, metaphorically into the dark side of the mother, where death seemed the only way out. The emotion was so intense that the ego had to surrender. At that crossroads where conscious and unconscious meet, the dynamism of the instinct "Let me die" (the infrared end of the spectrum) transcended the conflict, took me right out of the pain. The image, the orange blossom bush (the ultraviolet end), pouring perfume into every cell of my body, brought about a harmony, physically and psychically, that transcended any feeling I had ever experienced. Someone who knew how to work the switches created the metaphor of the blossoming bush and transformed the energy of the distraught consciousness into the harmonic energy embodied in the unconscious. The archetype of the dark mother, Death, was transformed into the archetype of the loving mother, Sophia, she whose light permeates matter.

Knowing that someone is moving you, whether you understand it or not, is an awesome experience. That nonrational knowing, which is *being known*, is what brings the heights and depths together. In that wholeness, healing lies. Every cell remembers its health. Without ego interference, psyche perceives light in matter. That was the dawn of becoming what I had fought against all my life. The sweetness of my body surrendered to her love. In *being known*, I knew myself as part of the one.

Dreams of black snakes carrying light on their heads, golden ants that can eat up or bring life to endangered bones, dreams of transformers that change one energy to another accompanied by shifts in symptoms suggest that the consciousness inherent in organic processes at the biological end of the psychoid archetype are more accessible to consciousness than we once thought. Indeed they are pushing for recognition. Images of animals in the process of transforming into human beings seem to suggest that instinctual matter permeated with light transforms into more subtle matter. To put it another way, the Goddess in matter wants to be made conscious.

Surrendering to the wholeness that comes from harmony with the natural order will make no sense to someone who is wedded to a Newtonian/Cartesian paradigm. Quantum physics, however, presents us with other possibilities. A friend of mine, who is knowledgeable about quantum physics, read the preceding paragraph, and responded with the following statement: "Our very Beingness is the manifestation of energy patterns—a manifestation that is made up of many collapsed wave functions. The energy patterns of 'I' are whole themselves. It is only when the 'I' clings to a part as if it were the whole that the energy patterns become disrupted. This can lead to a breakdown such as illness. Since it is the ego observer who creates a particular reality, to allow the energy patterns to reconfigure, we have to bypass the ordinary ego perceptions. The metaphor machine is one way of doing this, because it acts as a bridge to the non-rational (non-dualistic) reality that we really are."[11]

Metaphor brings healing because it brings wholeness. Take, for example, the word "fire" in David Whyte's poem on pp. 156–157. If we free-associate with it, we come up with words like hot, red, anger, alive, fierce, fire in the belly, fire flaming, exploding through the mouth, loud, untamed, roar, Yessssss. We might experiment with what the poem is describing. If we allow ourselves to breathe into our belly and open our mouth, we might experience our whole voice.

Metaphor captures the passion, the movement, the meaning. In one image, it brings together a total response—emotional, imaginative, intellectual. If we focus the fire of our imagination, our own metaphors begin to heat and transform, opening up new energy channels in our body. In taking the imaginative leap, we embody the metaphor. In becoming the metaphor, we become whole. The wholeness may not last, but that moment rings like a tuning fork that the cells do not forget.

What is the difference between embodying an image and concretizing it? To concretize a metaphor is to literalize and kill it. For example, a woman dreams of making love to her neighbor. If she literalizes the metaphor, she may joyously assume the unconscious wants her to have an affair. She is probably wrong. The dream process is a soul journey, in which all the parts of the dream are a part of the dreamer. The dream is showing the woman a part of her own masculinity with which she needs to unite. If she does have an affair, that masculine energy is still projected, and the fire that should be heating up the imagination in order to transform the energy will be lost in the acting out of the passion. The dreams will probably cease, or the woman will begin to dream of another man. The energy that wants to move toward the inner maturity of masculine and feminine is betrayed. The images become static or cease.

If the image is embodied, on the other hand, it becomes incorporated into the cells of the body, as I described my assimilation of the perfume of the mock-orange blossoms. The image lives. Through relaxation and concentration, the metaphor is taken in so that it opens up areas blocked with fear or anger or guilt. As the new energy opens the darkness of the negative emotions, those areas are purified and transformed. Gradually, the mutilated animals become whole, the darkened house is filled with new light, the devouring mother becomes the Dark Goddess and the tyrannical father a strong and loving guide. If embodied, the metaphor bridges the gap between head and heart. All the cells of the body respond.

This is a lifetime process that requires diligence and hard work and much common sense. Images in the body can dislodge huge complexes and one must be very respectful of resistance against moving into painful areas. Where there is trauma in the body, the company of a friend or professional therapist is essential. The metaphor carries far more energy than anyone who has not experienced it can believe.

Another question. Why do we have to have light in matter? As I understand this process, a body that has never been listened to, never been acknowledged for the courageous pack horse it has been, never been treated as the temple of the Holy Spirit, that body is essentially unconscious. Its messages are not part of the whole person. It carries the unconscious conflicts, because the ego is not strong enough to deal consciously with them. That body is not free enough, or strong enough, to be penetrated by the light of Spirit. Therefore, I think of body work as bringing matter (Mother) to consciousness. What we realize as we work is that we are releasing soul.

If you have any doubt about the power of metaphor, ponder the O. J. Simpson trial as covered on television. Ponder the theme of Shakespeare's *Othello* in relation to the Feminine. Ask yourself why millions became addicted to the trial. The masses are not interested if their own unconscious projections are not being acted out. Did you find your own masculinity guilty? Did you find your femininity colluding? What was your verdict? Could you convict? Reflect on the icons and their effect on our culture.

Another powerful metaphor came to me as I was reworking the meaning of my metaphor machine for this book. A friend of ours, David, arrived at our home on a Sunday morning. He was visibly shaken, as people are when the timeless world crosses their time. He had recently purchased a laptop computer, taken it to the beach with him, and had a profound experience as he wrote the following journal entry.

8:10 PM August 5, 1995

Sitting down on the beach to write my journal with the new Toshiba 400CDT multimedia laptop computer. I want to reflect on the tool itself. I am fascinated by technology and recognize that what is sitting on my lap is a paragon of tools. As my fingers start to hit the keys, it occurs to me that the very mechanism of this machine is based on representation. The machine is literally an embodiment of representation, of metaphor—a metaphor machine.

Take the words I am typing right now. From the keystroke, each letter is translated to a digital machine code comprised of 1's and 0's before it shows up on screen. The inscrutable ROM (Read-Only Memory) does its mysterious work: letters and words appear in train as if impressed directly from the keys themselves, and what was a thought runs a progress from kinetic impulse to binary code to patterns on a screen. I think of the nerve screen in "Prufrock" ["It is impossible to say just what I mean/But as if a magic lantern threw the nerves in patterns on a screen; . . ."[12]]. This marvel of technology can do what it does, thanks to the silicon chip—manufactured from silica, a gritty sand used in ancient Greece to cut the marble temple columns and, in ancient Egypt, the pyramid blocks. Now, in an infinitely more sophisticated form, it embodies the subtle heart of this machine.

Waiting for words, listening to the waves gently washing ashore, I can't help but be filled by their sound and their presence. It's a sound that could have been heard a million years ago, five million, a billion—before there were ears to hear. But here I sit with a laptop computer—a machine built on the ancestor of an old cutting edge—the cutting edge of the contemporary purveyor of the global age. This quintessence of sand, in the form of silicon chips, gives the machine its power to reproduce the world, to organize the flow of electrons through myriad channels so that the world can be rendered back to us. Right now, I can record the sound of these ancient waves or capture video images of them and attach these sensory impressions to this document as objects to preserve the moment. As yet rough cut compared to their "real" counterparts, these images are themselves a virtual reality.

The consciousness that I bring to the workings of the machine before me becomes a mirror of my own consciousness, one that allows me to realize what I am carrying about with me in my laptop satchel. I am carrying the Earth as its silica element emerges in my consciousness of it. My Toshiba multimedia computer mirrors the world I construct, in and as consciousness. Proof rock.[13]

David knows a great deal more about computers than I do. He designs computer programs and teaches programming at a community college. As he read this aloud to us, I thought of Blake seeing "a World in a Grain of Sand."[14] I wondered if Blake's "World in a Grain of Sand" mirrored David's world in the silicon chip.

David sees in the computer a metaphor of the mind in creation. Beyond that, he sees the computer as mirroring the entire creation itself, the world being transformed moment by moment, recreated before our very eyes. The electronic impulses that whizz around a computer's silicon-chip circuitry recall Blake's "Pulsation of the Artery."[15] Every pulsation is the creation (and re-creation) of the world. Something like that is what David experienced on the beach that evening, and something like that is what a woman experiences in her body.[16]

Metaphors act as guides. If you trust in your own dream process, you know the moment when you no longer have a model, no questions, no answers. You have nothing to help you but the images of your dreams. If you want to live your own life, your images and your body are your individual guides. Together, they strengthen your inner core. Think of the images of athletes before they jump, musicians before they play, actors and dancers before they step on the stage. The great ones take the moment to see themselves present in what they are about to do. They concentrate, still at the center. Then, and only then, do they move into the image. The imagination moves ahead of the action.

Releasing matter into light, or releasing matter into energy, is part of living in the atomic age. The c in Einstein's equation $E = mc^2$ is squared, multiplied by itself, and it is a large number on its own. This implies that a lot of E (light energy) goes into making a small amount of m (mass). Sometimes, people are heavy in matter, but because their body is conscious, they fill it and seem to be exactly the right size for what they exude. Think of Pavarotti or Jessye Norman. Others are light in matter, but without light, and they seem to drag an overwhelming burden.

Instead of thinking of matter as dense mass, imagine a picture by Claude Monet. Monet could perceive a water lily. What he saw was different intensities of light on lily, leaf, and water. His orchards in spring, his haystacks at sunset, his pathways—all dance with released light. His world is a garden in which the Goddess delights.

The French Impressionist painters were forerunners of our age, as were the Romantic poets. The Feminine, which was just beginning to push through from the depths of their unconscious, is now fully present and ready to be lived in consciousness in many men and women.

Sometimes she appears in dreams as an old woman sitting on the ground with a cloak thrown over her head, weeping, while armies fight around her. She roars in the symptoms that debilitate us, when the pollution is too much, or we disobey her laws. She also roars when we fail to recognize that our physical attunement must be harmonious with our spiritual insight.

A woman dreams, for example, that she is met by an old woman who firmly offers her a bottle of ointment. She is to apply the unguent to the soles of her feet. As she does so, light begins to move up her legs and into her whole body.

Another dreams of entering a lush green valley. As she stands admiring nature, a large woman dressed in purple chiffon appears on the hill opposite. Immediately, everything in the valley, including the dreamer, is suffused with inner light.

A man dreams he is cutting the grass with a hand mower. As the grass flies off the blades, he sees sparks of light. They become so animated, he stops his mower. He is overwhelmed by a presence. In his own backyard, he experiences the mystery in whose presence we are all one.

In whatever ways the process of bringing the body to consciousness develops, a strong container in which the energies can transform, physically and psychically, is essential.[17] With concentrated work, opaque matter gradually transforms toward more subtle matter. Jung understood the subtle body as the soul body or energy body present in matter, always in a state of flux, moving up or down the spiral.

The effect of subtle body is delicately described by Margaret Atwood in the last verse of her poem "Girl Without Hands":

> Only a girl like this
> can know what's happened to you.
> If she were here she would
> reach out her arms towards
> you now, and touch you

with her absent hands
and you would feel nothing, but you would be
touched all the same.[18]

In our everyday life, most of us have experienced the touch Margaret Atwood is describing in her poem. Whether we know it or not, we experience at a cellular level the love or lack of love that is directed toward us. Unconsciously, children are very sensitive to the subtle body connection. A gorgeous doll will be laid aside in favor of an old pan if the doll is not given in love. The subtle body picks up the unconscious intention of the person with whom it is communicating. Acausal and nonrational factors in a field of relatedness are at work. This makes us aware of wider possibilities for prayer and healing through the subtle body.[19] In these areas, we are reconnecting at a new level with native cultures.

In workshops, we have learned that perceived and perceiver are one. Where two people are working as partners, what is going on in the heart and mind of the perceiver will be picked up in the body of the perceived. The more finely tuned the body becomes, the more subtle this process is. We have become increasingly aware of the power of imagery in the body, and between individuals, without a word being spoken. The level of consciousness of one person holding the concentration for the group can change the entire room.

The subtle body connection is quite clear in analytic work. The abandoned child, or the child who has not experienced acausal connection (love) with the mother does not trust that anything exists between mother and child if mother is absent. The sense of rejection quickly escalates into annihilation if mother's physical presence is not there. Nothing IS. This is one of the most difficult situations in analysis, because the abandoned child ceases to exist if the analyst is not present. (Think of the implications in relationships.) Once trust is built up through a feeling connection *in the subtle body*, the abandoned child can believe the analyst, who is not present, is still alive and does care. The Presence holds.

Acausal, nonrational, relatedness are words associated with the feminine. These words are not yet quite respectable in the West. But the scientific discoveries of the past several decades are forcing us to take seriously the ideas they embody. Scientists have begun to acknowledge that certain phenomena in the quantum world imply acausality,[20] and they have even constructed cosmological theories that *require* it.[21] These manifestations of the Feminine in the scientific world are yet another indication of the quiet transformation that is taking place as the paradigm shifts—a transformation that is enacting, globally, the transformation that has been taking place in selected individuals for millennia, a transformation that is the work of the Feminine.

Recall Jung's image of the two cones with apexes that meet and do not meet. This is the point where the transformation takes place, the location of the metaphor machine I saw in my dream. The findings of psychoneuroimmunology mentioned earlier in this chapter suggest that we are close to understanding how this transformation takes place. The work of the Virgin continually transforming—even transmuting—energies from instinct to psyche and from psyche to instinct, is mirrored by the work of the neuropeptides and their receptors continually transmuting chemistry into emotions and emotions into chemistry.[22] The images we assimilate (at the ultraviolet end) are as important to our well-being as the food we eat (at the infrared end). In the chakra system (discussed in chapter 2), a similar transformation takes place in the heart chakra where the energies from the three lower chakras mingle with the energies of the three upper ones. It is in this place of transformation that we can expect to encounter the Feminine.

And when she is encountered, she is not to be taken lightly. One young woman dreamed that a perfect replica of herself was lying on a couch in her living room. The replica was a plastic, made-up doll. A dark, ten-foot-tall woman knocked at her door and was welcomed. When the dark woman saw the doll, she opened her hand, thrust her raised palm toward the doll, and zapped her. Nothing remained.

The accidental circumstances in which she appears should not be taken as the only forms in which she manifests herself. As an archetype, she is always present, in different images, sometimes at more conscious levels. She has gone underground in some centuries, but she has never been absent. The tragedy is that she is present and we do not take the time to see her or to learn her basic laws.

She is compassionate. She does understand our human stupidity to a point. She honors our suffering. She seems to know that our place of wounding is where she will come in, where we will meet others in love, where we will celebrate our planet in love.

She is Mother, Virgin, and Crone. In her maturing, the Virgin becomes the Crone. True to her process, she comes to know her ever-transforming self in the bedrock of her being. Kali, with her fierce energy, sometimes appears as a beautiful young maiden. Her masculinity has honed his discernment, and he sees the Virgin in the Hag. Together, they have moved beyond duality. The Virgin is moving toward a consciousness that has never before been possible on the planet. In her embodiment, she is known. She is recognized by her Beloved. She receives the penetration of the Spirit that will change consciousness forever.

Her coming is heralded in the following dream:

I am standing by the sea. A great tidal wave is steadily rolling in. I am terrified. Gradually, I discern a large, chocolate-colored woman riding majestic on the crest of the wave. She is triumphant, her body poised, her arm uplifted like Delacroix's *Liberty.* She rides her inevitable way.

Suddenly, I am a molecule of energy in the wave. My friends and I are all molecules in the wave, each molecule dancing with every other molecule in love. We are all dancing with the momentum of the wave that will bring Sophia to land.

For we are in the deepest sense the victims and instruments of cosmogonic "love." I put the word in quotation marks to indicate that I do not use it in its connotations of desiring, preferring, favoring, wishing, and similar feelings, but as something superior to the individual, a unified and undivided whole. Being a part, man cannot grasp the whole. He is at its mercy. He may assent to it, or rebel against it; but he is always caught up by it and enclosed within it. He is dependent upon it and is sustained by it. Love is his light and his darkness, whose end he cannot see. "Love ceases not"—whether he speaks with the tongues of angels, or with scientific exactitude traces the life of the cell down to its uttermost source.

—C. G. JUNG

A human being is a part of the whole, called by us "Universe," a part limited in time and space. He experiences himself, his thoughts and feelings as something separated from the rest, a kind of optical delusion of his consciousness. This delusion is a kind of prison for us, restricting us to our personal desires and to affection for a few persons nearest to us. Our task must be to free ourselves from this prison by widening our circle of compassion to embrace all living creatures and the whole of nature in its beauty.

—ALBERT EINSTEIN

WE ARE ABOUT TO ENTER the new millennium. Our children and grand children will be the first generation to inhabit the planet as citizens of one world. Already, we are feeling the impact of global restructuring of trade and economic policies; we stand amazed before computers that can connect us to the Internet and open our way into the Louvre and the British Museum; world leaders are desperately attempting to create a system of laws that all countries will accept; already, world health plans are being recognized.

The quiet revolution that had its roots in the Sixties was more than a fad of the flower children. Within their protests were the seeds, at a culturally recognized level, of a movement based upon hope for a more meaningful existence. Fads come and go because they merely touch the periphery of our lives; the seeds of the "humane" revolution are still growing because they touch the core of our lives. The seeds grow in response to the growing realization of the collective threat to our survival. Our seas are being fished to the point of depletion; our lakes and rivers are polluted to the point of destruction; rain forests are being stripped; in many situations, technology is posing a direct threat to our physical health; always, there is the threat of overpopulation and nuclear weapons in the hands of irresponsible bullies. A few greedy monsters manipulate the imbalance and profit in the short term. Many other people around the globe, however, are facing the issues, attempting to find a resolution in a deeper, more lasting foundation. What began as a protest has become a challenge, a challenge that will involve not only technology, but a new understanding of human mythology.

Underneath the obvious chaos is an even deeper chaos. Most thinking people realize that we have come to the end of a paradigm that is not only not serving us, but is destroying us. The familial, tribal, and national loyalties that were so circumscribed in the past

are no longer sufficient. Indeed, isolated from a larger global loyalty,
they are a threat to human survival. Hierarchical structures are collapsing; religious wars based on archaic hatreds are endangering
global peace. "Who will have the most?" and "Who will sit on top
of the power pile?" are no longer relevant questions. The prospect of
becoming puppet kings in an overpopulated, poisoned desert makes
no sense.

The paradigm of power has forever been questioned. One
thinks of Shelley's Ozymandias, the Egyptian pharaoh with whom
Moses contended during the Exodus. In him we see the mold of
those twentieth-century dictators with whom many must still contend in their continuing exodus from the last round of global empire
building. "Two vast and trunkless legs of stone/Stand in the desert,"
Shelley's imagined "traveler from an antique land" tells the poet,

> . . . Near them, on the sand,
> Half sunk a shattered visage lies, whose frown,
> And wrinkled lip, and sneer of cold command,
> Tell that its sculptor well those passions read
> Which yet survive, stamped on these lifeless things,
> The hand that mocked them, and the heart that fed;
> And on the pedestal, these words appear:
> "My name is Ozymandias, King of Kings,
> Look on my Works, ye Mighty, and despair!"
> Nothing beside remains. Round the decay
> Of that colossal Wreck, boundless and bare
> The lone and level sands stretch far away.[1]

What began as protests in the Sixties has now become a challenge not only to world leaders but to thinking individuals around
the globe. These thinking people care about children and grandchil-
dren and generations to come. They know that men and women are
equal and must have equal rights; they know that spirit and nature
are equal and must be honored equally. They know they are the
offspring of an information revolution, a global communications network. They know that with a single electronic beep, they can be,
already are, in contact with events in every part of this global village.
And they take responsibility for that gift and individually search for

the new images, keep attuned to the global vision, and meanwhile honor ecology in their own kitchen sinks.

In the first chapters of this book, we discussed the paradigms within which most early tribes flourished. Here we will summarize briefly the essential aspects of those paradigms because new possibilities grow out of old roots.

Given the dependent, concrete, magical thinking of our early ancestors, given their symbiotic relationship with nature, it was natural that their primary mythology should center around nature as a Great Mother who gave life and took it away. Matriarchy was a natural state in which both men and women lived. The major religious structures were polytheistic, regarding everything in nature as imbued with a spirit-life related to the source, the Great Mother. In this *participation mystique*, the structures that gave expression to the bonds between people were inevitably tribal. Nature was seen as the final arbitrator of power, and therefore power could be assimilated from nature. Feathers, bones, amulets were worn to give the wearer something of the power that nature possessed. Rituals were performed to ward off that power, to appease the spirit, or to gain its beneficence. Often within the tribal structures, power was exercised as gift, in that the most powerful person was the one who had the most to give. This was seen as exercising the role of the Great Mother.

Starting with the end of the Paleolithic Age, however, a major shift in paradigms occurred. Of course, this shift took several hundred years, with the old paradigm greatly overlapping the emerging one. Indeed, traces of the early paradigm still linger.

With the emergence of ego consciousness, human beings began to separate out from the Great Mother. During this period, matriarchy evolved into a more conscious form of Goddess worship, flowering in Egypt and Crete. However, the predominant mythology began to look heavenward and away from the earth. All power became centralized in the Sun God. From this centralized source of power, a male God of the sky became the dominant symbol of divinity. The projection of power onto this solar God had to be represented on earth, hence the rise of kingship. The resultant need to transfer power downward set the stage for the evolution of hierarchical structures in society. The amount of power one wielded depended on how close one was to the Light—the figure that represented the divine will. Hierarchical ranking was largely based on strength. The most powerful person in the hierarchy was the one with the biggest army, the most wealth, the best access to privileged information, or the greatest cunning. The hierarchical structures that developed are familiar to us all: men, women, children, animals, insects, plants; pope, cardinals, bishops, clergy, laity; king, lords, freemen, serfs.

The establishment of hierarchies was paralleled by the emergence of a sense of individuality and independence. The significance of this emergence was twofold. First, under the influence of individualism, the collective thinking that had hitherto held societies together began to lose ground. Tribal identities gave way to individual identities; cooperation gave way to competition. Second, notions of independence ran counter to the underlying principle of hierarchal structures, which sought to exercise control rather than grant freedom. Growing tension between the two opposing forces would eventually lead to open conflict.

The abuse of power and the selfish, narcissistic, pursuit of wealth and land on the part of the upper tiers of the hierarchy led to revolt, rebellion, revolution—and the birth of modern democracy. Only after countless blood baths was individuality (and independence) accorded to members of the lower levels of the hierarchy. Even so, men were the chief beneficiaries of these advances. Until recently, women were not considered individuals in their own right.

As women are slowly achieving equality they are challenged with an interesting dilemma. Now that the structures are more open to women, do we want to take our place in the patriarchal power paradigm? Many women today say no. Then the questions become, "How do we transform the hierarchal structures without entering them? If we do enter them, how do we resist becoming patriarchal?" Men and women need a very conscious Mother, Virgin, Crone within to sail in these waters.

Throughout this book, we have shown through case studies how individuals follow a similar pattern through matriarchy and patriarchy in their attempts to find their own lives. Their first need is to free themselves from the inertia of the old crocodile and from the judgmental voice of the patriarchs. Their biggest task is to find their own path, their own paradigm. Both genders are without role models because the world we live in never existed until now, and every day a terrorist attack, a decision in a courtroom, an experiment in a laboratory changes the meaning of "NOW." That is one reason the patriarchal paradigm no longer works. It is static. Its standards of perfection depend on the unchanging stability of photographs and compact discs. Dreams eventually mock dreamers who never give up the old family car and continually play old tapes and old records in the old family house. And patriarchy is no longer feasible because it flies in mind and spirit, ungrounded. The unconscious compensation is already at work, releasing the repressed instincts in the body. The rejected instincts can be as vicious as the laws that attempt to repress them. The new paradigm envisions a balance of equals—body and mind, feminine and masculine, immanent and transcendent. Many men and women who are working toward the new paradigm are finding an image of that balance of equals through the Goddess, who comes out of the unconscious to guide them.

There are other guides, of course. This book happens to focus on the Goddess. Another book, a natural follow-up to this one, may someday be written about the Son, who is now beginning to appear as a small child in dreams. He carries the energy that will one day balance hers in the dance of mature masculine and mature feminine. That image belongs to a totally new consciousness. We have intuitions that point to it, but it is far from being lived in individuals, and it is almost unknown in the collective consciousness.

While a great deal of research has been done in the past twenty years on the matriarchal and patriarchal paradigms, only the briefest summary has been given here. Both individually and collectively, the energy is ready to move to a new sacred dream.

The paradigms shown in the table are born of sacred mythologies. Only in the depths of the unconscious can any new global mythology find roots that will survive. We, in the closing years of this millennium, are still in the unsettled transitional stage. For many of us, the strongest roots we can find are in the dark earth of our own bodies—not that we would go there of our own choice, but we are forced there through the guidance of the Dark Goddess in an addiction or an illness. Like our Paleolithic ancestors, who buried their dead with accouterments for the afterlife, we need to relate our reality to a greater Reality. Sometimes, the sacred bond has strange origins. The flames of passion in which we dance with food, alcohol, sex, drugs, death are flames in which we may dimly discern the other Reality as through a glass darkly.

Matriarchal	Patriarchal	Androgynous
instinctual self	ego self	soul/spirit self
tribal	hierarchical	ecological
polytheistic	monotheistic	inner marriage (interiorized spirituality)
power *from* nature	power *against* nature	power *with* nature
Cultural Expression		
power as gift	power as strength	power as love
Psychological State		
dependence	independence	interdependence
Approximate Time Span		
30,000 years	4500 years	?

In the Seventies, people discussed the first two paradigms and tried to imagine what the next one would be like. Generally, they agreed that the new paradigm would be neither matriarchal nor patriarchal; it would be *androgynous*. Rather than tribal or hierarchical, the structures of such a society would be *ecological*. Ecology would be an expression of *interdependence*, in which everything would be recognized in relationship to everything else. Power would no longer be from nature or against nature; it would be *with nature*. It would not be exercised as a gift or as strength, but as *love*. Little did we neophytes know the dangers of trying to differentiate the new feminine and the new masculine, or the difficulties we would face in allowing them to dance freely in the flames.

The most difficult transformation, as we move into this new paradigm, is the realization of an interiorized spirituality. Polytheism and monotheism as we have known them involve a projection "out there" onto Mother (Nature) or Father (Sun) or their surrogates. The Divine has relied, and continues to rely, on the evolution of human consciousness for continuing revelation. The most important step in the evolution of our consciousness is the pulling back of the projections so that we can begin the process of looking for the Divine within. Christ specifically warned that the kingdom of God does not come "with observation," by looking here and there, for, he said, "the kingdom of God is within you."[2] Mystics and saints, and others who have achieved a high level of consciousness, have sought and found that realm of inner spirituality. The great Spanish mystic, Saint Teresa of Avila, wrote of the Interior Castle. Far more than in the West, the religions and esoteric traditions of the East have been concerned with attaining higher levels of consciousness. Today, we are collectively moving to a higher plane as we are ushered into the new paradigm and the new millennium. We are being impelled to find our Interior Castle. The dislocations of the outer sphere of public policies, attitudes, and behavior are making it imperative for us to turn inward to locate ourselves in the "ground of our being."[3] Within the center of every living thing dwells the soul of the world, the *anima mundi.*

Moving into the "third sacred dream" requires us to live from this center, the place of paradox, where the tension of the opposites is held in balance, the "both/and" world of mind/body, masculine/ feminine, sexuality/spirituality, life/death. To live from the center is to transcend the dualities and achieve wholeness.

The following dream suggests that a tremendous leap of consciousness is required if we are to accomplish the shift into the third paradigm.

> I am in a broad-jump class. I am very anxious, because I am no jumper. The teacher is very tall, with very dark curly hair. She disregards my anxiety. She takes us up a cliff and tells us this is what we have been practicing for. I'm terrified. We are going to jump across a very wide, very deep gorge. It is a matter of life and death. I look at my classmates. I see a tall, very simple, very concentrated man with eyes like fire. I think, "That is Christ." He, too, will have to leap across the gorge.

This dream suggests that the kingdom that Christ came to inaugurate has not yet been ushered in (the Christ figure has not yet leaped across the gorge). It became fashionable in the post-War years to say that we were living in a post-Christian era. However, it could equally be argued that we are living in a *pre*-Christian era, in that the revolutionary message of Christ, though preserved over the years among a few, has never been widely put into practice under the power-as-strength mindset of the patriarchal paradigm. The basic principles of Christianity—compassion, forgiveness, repentance, love for one's enemies, tolerance, meekness—are a leap beyond what patriarchy stands for. In requiring the Christ figure to make the leap across the gorge, the dream highlights the folly of repeating old mistakes. The new paradigm must not repress the existing one as it emerges, but rather, integrate it, establishing a continuity with the past. At the same time, Christ as a symbol of the Divine will make the leap of consciousness, will be understood in a totally new way.

To the casual observer there seems to be little hope that such an integration is possible. Few signs of a creative transition present themselves. In our times, the lack of a guiding mythology, the fragmentation of the world, politically, economically, philosophically, have led to widespread despair. William Butler Yeats's poem, *The Second Coming*, expresses this condition most poignantly.

> Turning and turning in the widening gyre
> The falcon cannot hear the falconer;
> Things fall apart; the centre cannot hold;
> Mere anarchy is loosed upon the world,
> The blood-dimmed tide is loosed, and everywhere
> The ceremony of innocence is drowned;
> The best lack all conviction, while the worst
> Are full of passionate intensity.[4]

Two world wars and the horrors of a nuclear holocaust have drowned "the ceremony of innocence." Many have had their belief systems shaken to the core. These people, Yeats says, are "the best." The "passionate intensity" of "the worst" was the subject of a recent article in a national newspaper; the article suggested that "the spread of fundamentalism, cults and hatred may lead us to a new Dark Age."[5]

When the center does not hold, we regress. On a personal level, we may find ourselves being moody or demanding—like a two-year-old. When the crumbling center involves a paradigm that we have been immersed in for over 4500 years, we regress collectively to the infancy of our race. In regression, we return to the crux of an earlier unresolved conflict—in this case, the transition from matriarchy to patriarchy. This collective regression is manifesting itself today in the resurgence of fundamentalism and the proliferation of cults. Both rise in the face of fear. Both attempt to hold onto the old identity through a forced collective mentality. Individuality is forfeited. Thinking becomes rigid, concrete, dualistic, in an attempt to set boundaries against what is perceived as threatening. Personal security and meaning are preserved through a restricted world view. "Tribal warfare" ensues, verbally or physically, against the "enemy" out there.

When the center does not hold, enormous archetypal energies are released from the unconscious. Cults and fundamentalism emerge as an antidote to the potential anarchy contained in these energies. The "New Age" movement draws upon the more positive aspects of these energies, but its understanding of their true power tends to be somewhat superficial, and playing with powerful forces that one does not fully understand can be dangerous.

However, as Morris Berman suggests in *Coming to Our Senses*, the greatest danger lies in the fact that the established paradigm (patriarchy) has taken over the language and trappings of the New Age movement, thereby nullifying the somatic energy behind it. "[T]he somatic energy of holistic thinking," he writes, "becomes the conceptual structure of cybernetics, or systems theory. . . . And *that*, not a new Christianity or fascism, is the real threat facing us today. . . . Lived experience is not the same thing as conceptual formulations— dogmas and slogans—of lived experience, and given the Western ascent structure, there is an inevitable pull toward safety, crystallization."[6]

Although Berman does not equate "somatic energy" with the feminine, as we do, he does equate body with soul. He warns that if our experience is not grounded, "relational holism" will be deftly eliminated yet again in history. As we would say it, if our experience is not embodied, the feminine will once again be forced underground.

On a different front, the unfolding research of modern physics is providing a core for a new mythology. Science has made a "quantum leap" that is forcing us to rethink our notions about the nature of reality itself. No longer can we live in the rational and orderly world of Newtonian physics. In the universe of today's physicists, uncertainty and paradox abound. What is more, we have discovered that "[w]e are, in our essential makeup, composed of the same stuff and held together by the same dynamics as those which account for everything else in the universe."[7] That is, we inhabit within ourselves, as in the universe, a realm of uncertainty and paradox in which the absolutes of good and evil, truth and falsehood, no longer hold.

Contemplating the uncertainty in the state of matter[8] (including the matter that makes up our bodies), we realize that the paradox

and lack of coherence in our psychic lives is, in fact, mirrored in the
material world. We contain within ourselves apparently irreconcilable
modes of behavior not unlike the apparently contradictory wave/
particle behavior of light. The discoveries of quantum physics suggest that these seemingly irreconcilable modes of behavior, once considered a contradiction to be resolved, are not mutually exclusive and
therefore do not demand resolution. Seeing ourselves in this way
allows us to act both within ourselves and within the universe in a
manner impossible or inconceivable to earlier generations. A higher
level of consciousness is required for such a world view.

To rise to this new consciousness is to experience the unknowable in the opposites working together without ceasing to be opposites. Differing world views, once thought irreconcilable, are now in
collision as they confront one another in the global village, bent, it
seems, upon destroying one another. In the new paradigm, however,
they are not seen to be in conflict, though seemingly opposed. They
serve as a counterpoint to one another, and their discordant interaction at one level produces an overarching harmony at another, much
as the indeterminacy at the quantum level produces apparent stability
at the level of our sense experience.

The opposites are complementary, not contradictory. They are
partners in the dance of life—partners, that is, in the ongoing interplay between the observer and the observed.[9] This dance, this interplay cannot take place in a world of absolutes, for such a world has
no room for differing modes of perception—only for a patriarchal
God who is himself the observer and the observed. The world of
opposites is a world of relativity, a world in which the observer creates his or her own reality and engages it with the reality created by
others, a world in which *all* things are possible and all things coexist.
As science has had to embrace the complementarity[10] of wave/parti-
cle duality to absorb the revolution of the new physics, so will we all
one day embrace the complementarity of the opposites of everyday
life as we participate in the revolution of the new paradigm. Learning
to live the paradigm of the opposites is our present-day challenge,
our modern mystery.

Contemplating this mystery, Jung, in his memoirs, written at
the end of his life ("Late Thoughts"), used the expression "cosmogonic 'love'"—a love that transcends our human experience of love
and opens us to an unknowable reality that we cannot embrace,

though it embraces us. Seeing becomes a matter of perceptually seeing through, until at last we know only that we are seen. Knowing that we are seen, "if we possess a grain of wisdom," Jung writes, "we will completely surrender to this unknowable who embraces in love all the opposites."[11] He then continues:

> Whatever the learned interpretation may be of the sentence "God is love," the words affirm the *complexio oppositorum* of the Godhead. In my medical experience as well as in my own life I have again and again been faced with the mystery of love, and have never been able to explain what it is. Like Job, I had to "lay my hand on my mouth. I have spoken once, and I will not answer." (Job 40:4f)[12]

The intentionality of an Ultimate Observer is finitely repeated in every human act of unconditional love. Love is the dynamic of the opposites, holding them together in their opposition, free of the bondage of contractual union that may gratify the ego's demand for a reconciling synthesis, a demand that places the ego's restrictions or conditions upon the act of observation. This binding of the other to the demands of the ego is precisely what unconditional love rejects. There is what Jung calls the surrender of the ego to the Self—a Self that, far from being known, remains forever unknown. The surrender that Jung reaches at the end of his memoirs is the surrender of the unknown to the more unknown, a surrender that is now becoming the animating spirit of the new physics, a spirit that we call the conscious feminine.

At this point, some comment on the pages that follow may be of value. Otherwise, you may find yourself reading and wondering if you picked up the wrong book. You may have already found, and certainly will find, words put together in ways that are, perhaps, unfamiliar to you. We do not ordinarily speak of quantum physics and the feminine in the same breath, nor do we put neurotransmitters, Virgin, and metaphor machine into the same sentence. However, if we are ever going to see the world as a whole—interdependent, ecologically conscious, androgynous, embodied in the inner marriage, the realization of the third dream—then we are going to have to make some effort to understand each other's metaphors. Even in a partial exploration—and that is all this book intends to be—we can begin to see through other glasses, and recognize that the revolution

taking place in our own field of specialization is being mirrored in
many other fields. We all have an important contribution to make in
bringing the Feminine to consciousness. And with that consciousness
will come a totally new understanding of the Masculine.

Traditionally, words such as *irrational, illogical, uncertain, unfocused,*
subjective, have been associated with the Feminine, usually accompanied by a condescending smile or a dismissive wave of the hand.
Sometimes a thoughtless label was slapped on with a silencing judgment: *histrionic, hysterical, melodramatic, disorganized, naive, stupid.* In setting
boundaries that attempted to dispose of everything these words
stood for, patriarchy lost touch with half of life.

Now, however, from quantum physics come words and phrases
like *acausality, indeterminacy, chaos, nonlocality, complementarity,* "perceived
and perceiver are one." Modern science has now released these feminine concepts from their repressed condition. Even the uninitiated,
who mock body awareness with phrases like "touchy-feely," are
proud to talk about "somatic wholeness" or "relational wisdom," so
long, of course, as they don't attempt to bring a ray of consciousness
into their big toe. Let us by all means rejoice that these words are
honored, as are words like *relational* and *resonating* in the corporate
business world. At the same time, let us not forget that the words
hold the energy of the Feminine, that they speak for the half of life
that, outside of modern science, is still virtually repressed. These are
the very words that carry the potential for creative transformation.
We dare not allow the potential of the emerging feminine to fall
back into unconsciousness again.

Words *do* matter. Throughout history, abstract concepts have
co-opted personalized, feeling-toned words, thus driving the Feminine underground. As we move into the new millennium on this blue
planet whose survival is at stake, surely we will be conscious enough
to honor her Presence with words that carry the passion, the magne-
tism, the fire that is hers. In honoring her, we are also honoring the
Masculine that knows her. So long as we fail to acknowledge the
two complementary energies within, we cannot acknowledge them
without. Their conscious differentiation both within and without is
essential in order for their integration to take place. Dream images
often provide the precision that makes both differentiation and connection possible. Honoring the words we allow to resonate in our
bodies is crucial to that integration.

Science has been largely perceived as the domain of the masculine, theoretical science as the offspring of pure thought. Its practical applications have been closely associated with ideas of progress and perfectability, a kind of Utopian vision based upon the subjugation of nature to human reason. This understanding culminated in Newtonian physics, in which the whole of nature was understood in rational terms. The cosmos was seen as a vast mechanism, somewhat like a giant clock, governed by immutable laws that were discoverable by the intellect.

That view of science has been radically altered by a new recognition of the role of the observer in the process of scientific observation, or, more accurately, of who the observer is. The new physics has shown that the workings of the cosmos (especially at the subatomic level) are far more elusive than Newton had imagined, that intellect can actually interfere with what is perceived and can alter the way it is perceived.

Living in the seventeenth century, Isaac Newton did not have the benefit of our present-day understanding of the unconscious, as developed by Freud and Jung. The qualities we now associate with the unconscious—the instinctual, the acausal, the irrational—were traditionally associated with the feminine. These qualities, when encountered in nature, were to be disciplined, controlled, made answerable to reason, which was traditionally associated with the masculine.

One of the seventeenth century's guiding metaphors was the Great Chain of Being, structured very much along the lines of the hierarchically ordered social institutions of the day. The Chain stretched all the way from the mineral realm at the lowest end, through plants, animals, humans, and angels, to God at the highest end. The interaction of the members in this Chain was governed by the law that whatever was closer to God in the Chain must rule, by natural right, over what was more distant: men over women, humans over nature, and so on.

Accordingly, John Milton, also a seventeenth-century figure, and author of the great Christian epic *Paradise Lost*, defined the relationship between Adam and Eve in a single line: "He for God only; she for God in him." Man's fall from paradise was the result of woman's rejecting man's higher authority and following her own

foolish feminine desires. These desires were closely connected with
the serpent, who tempted Eve to eat the forbidden fruit of the Tree
of the Knowledge of Good and Evil. She, in turn, tempted Adam to
do the same.

Being a man of his times, Milton simply could not deal with
the feminine. In his epic, he presents Eve as the betrayer, even though
it was she who opened the way to a knowledge that would otherwise
have remained sealed. This was the knowledge of good and evil—
intuitive knowledge, not rational knowledge. This was knowledge of
the opposites, a knowledge necessary for higher consciousness. Good
can be known only by confronting its opposite, evil. This applies not
just to good and evil but to other opposites as well. In opening
herself to a knowledge of good and evil, Eve was opening up a new
way of knowing. By the end of the epic, almost against Milton's own
wishes, Eve, who was initially responsible for the Fall, is identified
with the Redemption. From her womb, the womb of nature itself,
will come the Savior whose Crone qualities transcend the opposites.

The plan of redemption is revealed to Eve in a dream. Adam is
surprised by her knowledge, unable to fathom where it came from.
Eve tells him that God does not communicate by man's faculty of
reason alone, "For God is also in sleep, and Dreams advise, . . ."[13]

Believed by many to be the most patriarchal of all English
poets, Milton was guided by a female muse, Urania, who came to
him nightly in his sleep to dictate his poem to him. In the opening
lines of Book VII, he invokes her to inspire him:

> Before the Hills appear'd, or Fountain flow'd,
> Thou with Eternal Wisdom didst converse,
> Wisdom thy Sister, and with her didst play
> In presence of th' Almighty Father, pleas'd
> With thy Celestial Song.[14]

She guides him to an understanding of the feminine, which only
now, with the advent of the new physics, is fully entering our consciousness as it informs our understanding of the operations of the
cosmos.

While Adam learns rationally, Eve receives the information in
her sleep. Similarly, while John Milton thought rationally during the
day, his muse dictated to him by night a poem that was beyond the

scope of his rational mind. It took Milton twelve books of *Paradise Lost* to discover that Eve is as much a participant in God's plan as Adam. He closes his epic with the following lines:

> They, hand in hand, with wand'ring steps and slow,
> Through *Eden* took their solitary way.[15]

Like his contemporaries, John Milton was immersed in the Judeo-Christian mythology that dominated the seventeenth century. Nevertheless, he had glimmerings of the power of the unconscious. He knew that he relied on his Celestial Patroness to write his poem. Jung, too, realized that an encounter with reality requires the presence of the whole psyche—including feeling, thinking, instinct, and intuition. For him, pure reason was a pure abstraction from reality rather than an encounter with it. Not only is objectivity, as it has been traditionally defined, not attainable, but it gives us a false picture of reality by virtue of what it excludes. Jung's friendships with people such as Richard Wilhelm, translator of *The Secret of the Golden Flower*, and Laurens van der Post, that man of soul, especially the soul of Africa, opened him to immediate experience in the acausal world. These men, like the Romantic poets whom we have mentioned throughout this book, were visionaries, essentially rejected in their own time.

The vertical orientation of seventeenth-century thinking and the unshakable belief in the existence of absolutes gave rise to the heady optimism of the Enlightenment of the eighteenth century, to unquestioning faith in the power of Reason not just to understand the universe but to solve the riddle of the human condition as well. The Enlightenment spawned modern science and the so-called "scientific method" with its emphasis on verifiability and objectivity. Scientific conclusions could not be considered valid if the scientist had a personal stake in the outcome of his experiments. He must put his personal feelings aside and approach his subject with complete detachment if he was to arrive at Absolute Truth.

It was in a climate such as this, in the early twentieth century, that discoveries were made that would change forever the way scientists would relate to their subject. The work of Albert Einstein, Max Planck, Niels Bohr and others uncovered a world that was very different from the one Newton and his successors had seen. Einstein showed that, on a cosmic scale, one's point of observation determined what one saw, that two observers observing the same event from different locations could have widely differing perceptions of what had happened. As if this was not enough to shake the belief in the existence of Absolute Truth, the work of Planck and Bohr opened up the infinitesimal world of subatomic particles, in which the very act of measuring something changed the state of that thing and thereby nullified the measurement, making it impossible to determine anything with even a modicum of accuracy.

Science today cannot but acknowledge that objectivity, the most cherished of its ideals, is unattainable. The experimenter *cannot* detach herself from her experiment; the thinker cannot separate himself from his thoughts. The observer is as much a participant in an event as the observed. As physicist John Wheeler states it: ". . . the particular *way* in which we choose to observe quantum reality partly determines what we shall see."[16] If quantum physics tells us anything, it is that reality is indeed in the eye of the beholder.

Once viewed as the bedrock upon which science founded its claim to legitimacy, objectivity now seems more like quicksand. The undermining of the credibility of objectivity poses a vexing problem for psychology and philosophy as well. If objectivity as we have conceived it is a mirage, then we are left with only the old subjectivity. In psychological terms, subjectivity results from projection. The subject unconsciously projects his or her own feelings, attitudes, motives, expectations onto the object, and is therefore unable to see the object as it may actually be. We seem to be left with no way of getting a "true" picture of the object—and the elusive question as to whether such a view is at all possible.

Attempts to find a solution to this quandary have led to a renewed interest in consciousness. Once the province of philosophers, consciousness is now the hunting ground of scientists of every persuasion. Each approaches the problem from the perspective of his or her own scientific discipline. Chaos theorists suggest that consciousness is an "emergent property" of matter. Neuroscientists seek it in the delicate structures within the neurons in the brain.[17] Psychoneuroimmunologists track down chemicals in the body in search of it.[18] Quantum physicists try to understand it in terms of quantum-mechanical principles.

In a recently published book, the mathematician and physicist

Roger Penrose suggests that consciousness has a quantum-mechanical nature.[19] The implications of this are enormous. If consciousness operates in a quantum-mechanical way, then every shift in consciousness has the potential for creating a new reality. In any situation, the level of consciousness of the participants is of immense importance. In the healing process, for example, the level of consciousness of the healer is crucial, as is the relationship between healer and patient. As observer of our own healing process, our own level of consciousness is equally important. Who we are and what we are observing, consciously and unconsciously, influence what is happening in our body.

In the first half of the twentieth century, physicist and Nobel laureate Wolfgang Pauli recognized the participatory awareness that quantum mechanics calls for and concerned himself greatly with the "split-off" aspects of his own consciousness as a scientist. He recognized, as many of us do, that the unconscious drives—perhaps more than our conscious ego—govern much of our interaction with the world and our interpretation of it. The deeper he delved into the subject, writes Fred Alan Wolf, a theoretical physicist, the more convinced he became "that the unconscious was far more instrumental in making theories about matter than most physicists would have ever contemplated."[20] He looked in his dreams for the resolution between spirit and matter, hoping to find in that resolution answers to the riddles of the quantum world.

Pauli's quest brought him into contact with Jung, whose own quest was the mirror image of Pauli's. Aware that natural science had replaced religion as the source of authority in the modern world, Jung sought to link his investigations into the unconscious with the discoveries of modern physics. He saw that if he did not do this, the gap between soul and matter, between psyche and soma, would widen. He was looking for a "scientific" basis for his theories about the workings of the psyche.

Jung and Pauli were a perfect match, for they complemented each other, each supplying what the other lacked and sought. Pauli was fascinated with Jung's theories about the interaction between consciousness and the unconscious, and saw in this interaction an analog of the complementarity principle of quantum physics. "It is undeniable," he wrote,

> that the development of "microphysics" has brought the way in which nature is described in this science very much closer to that of the

newer psychology: but whereas the former ["microphysics"—i.e. quantum physics], on account of the basic "complementarity" situation, is faced with the impossibility of eliminating the effects of the observer by determinable correctives, and has therefore to *abandon in principle any objective understanding of physical phenomena* [italics mine], the latter [the "newer" or Jungian psychology] can supplement the purely subjective psychology of consciousness by postulating the existence of an unconscious that possesses a large measure of objective reality.[21]

Pauli was intrigued by the parallel between the way nature was unfolding in the new physics and the unconscious was unfolding in Jungian psychology. He saw, however, that while the new physics had no hope of arriving at an *objective* understanding of nature, Jungian psychology offered the possibility of achieving objectivity by focusing on the unconscious, which he saw as possessing "a larger measure of objective reality."

Pauli's interest in Jung's psychology led him to come to grips with his role as a physicist in the new physics, as the observer who modifies and therefore partially determines what is observed. He realized that in order to fill this role adequately he would have to deal with his own unconscious and become intimately acquainted with it. He also came to realize, through a series of dreams, that the path to the unconscious lay in analysis.

These dreams, which Pauli analyzed with the help of Marie Louise von Franz, the foremost analyst of Jung's "newer psychology," led him to the realization that he needed to open himself to his own inner feminine, his *anima,* to access his unconscious. In the movement of the feminine in his dreams, he came to see an analog of the movement of the feminine in physics. He began to understand that the feminine (the new physics) was not in opposition to the masculine (Newtonian physics), that they were, as it were, partners in a cosmic dance.

In the dreams most concerned with the role of the observer in the new physics, three figures dominate.[22] The first figure is a dark-skinned young Persian who wants Pauli to help him get admitted to the Polytechnic Institute in Zurich. Presumably, his task would be to carry on the work of Einstein and Bohr by relocating it in the archetypal unconscious, which has the power to structure not only mental images but matter itself (the ultraviolet and infrared ends of the spectrum).

The second dominant figure, related to the first, is a light-skinned blond man who attempts, by means of a fire, to drive Pauli out of the upper rooms of a house where a local conference on mathematics and physics is being held. Once out of the burning house, Pauli encounters a light-dark stranger (a fusion of the Persian and the blond man) who tells him that he will take Pauli to the place where he belongs so that he can perform the task assigned to him. That task is a course on cookery, a well-known image for transformation.

The third dominant figure is a dark woman who works with the master whom she shares with Pauli. She is giving Pauli a music lesson. His task is to move beyond reading the notes to hearing the music. The woman sometimes looks like Marie Louise von Franz (with whom Pauli was working at the time), but more often like a Chinese woman. When the piano lesson ends, Pauli, about to leave the room, bows to the lady, but the master says to him, "Wait. Transformation of the center of evolution." The woman slips a ring "i" from her finger. The ring floats in the air. The woman tells him that the ring "i" symbolizes the union of the opposites, a union that makes the instinctive, the rational, and the spiritual into a unified whole that numbers without the "i" cannot represent. Pauli, in turn, explains to the woman that the ring "i" is the unity beyond particle and wave, and at the same time the operation that generates them both.

In 1951, Pauli realized that he could no longer "follow the abstract dictates of the modern logos" if he wished to penetrate the movement in the depths of his unconscious. He realized that personal feeling was the missing link in the rationality that governed the work of Einstein and Bohr. The key to that missing link lay in the feeling tone of his anima as it was projected onto von Franz in their working relationship. Though in his relationship to the male figures in his dreams he was "still driven by the male-like logos," in his relationship to the female figure (the piano teacher, associated to von Franz) he was driven by something far less rational. This irrational force was symbolized in the ring "i" carried within what Jung, at the end of his life, called "cosmogonic 'love.'" It is a love that we cannot know intellectually. Rather, it knows *us*, and if we possess "a grain of wisdom" we will finally surrender to it. "And She, who is one, can do all things and renews everything while herself perduring."[23]

Pauli died in 1958 without completing his work in "microphysics." What his journey was demanding of him in his work with Jung and von Franz was not merely the masculine advancement of new hypotheses about the nature of matter, but a life lived "beyond reading the notes to hearing the music." The unconscious seemed to be asking him to bring into life the balance of the opposites that he saw modeled in the new hypotheses. Wolf speculates that Pauli's death "may mean that now he really knows the truth about existence."[24] In this world, however, Pauli remains one of those giant male visionaries, along with Milton, Blake, Keats, and Shelley, who, despite their vision of the Feminine that inspired their best work, were at least partially bound to an oppressive patriarchy. As a result, their unconscious projections onto the women they "loved" made genuine relationship almost impossible.

Pauli's dreams echo other dreams presented in this book. Dreams point toward the center, the point where matter and spirit meet, and do not meet. This is the point of the judgment of Maat. For men, the dark eternal woman in her many guises is the bridge to the Self. For women, she is the feminine part of the Self. In both genders, she is the creative matrix that gives birth to the new order. Here is the meeting of soul and spirit (feminine and masculine) in a new *conjunctio*. From this center point, we can perceive the world in its complementarity and indivisibility, the opposites no longer in opposition. We hold the opposites—the mystery within which the unknown is operating.

This is the point where love becomes possible. We see the other with the eye of the heart, an eye not clouded by fear manifesting as need, jealousy, possessiveness, or manipulation. With the unclouded eye of the heart, we can see the other as other. We can rejoice in the other, challenge the other, and embrace the other without losing our own center or taking anything away from the other. We are always other to each other—soul meeting soul, the body awakened with joy. To love unconditionally requires no contracts, bargains, or agreements. Love exists in the moment-to-moment flux of life. Here is no lack of commitment to the other but a far deeper commitment to oneself. Making a commitment to another is really an illusion, a way of holding. In the end, it is to no avail. Making a commitment to our deepest Self, however, pulls us into life and opens the door to others. Love carries a great responsibility to go where life leads, to be where life resonates. If we have no passion for our own life, we will constantly seek it vicariously in others. Seeking a greater realization of the Self is the only commitment we can really make.

Within the "magical" thinking of our ancestors, intuitions and symbolic communication were the forces that drove human evolution. The reductionism and literalness of our recent patriarchal past, however, has been a hindrance to our further evolution. Nevertheless, with the emergence of the new physics, we are beginning to discover a new "magic."

Many people today are rediscovering wisdom in tribal cultures, in ancient techniques of healing, and in their relationship to the earth. This rediscovery is not surprising. "Body consciousness" has an innate wisdom of its own. It is a world view rooted in the natural wisdom of our own embodied nature. We can never go back to the earlier state of matriarchy, but the natural wisdom of that state, when it is transformed, will form the basis of a third sacred dream. The world is a spiritual unity, a dance between soul and spirit—the same dance that scientists find under their microscopes and in their mathematical formulas. Our ancestors were correct in recognizing the world as spiritual, but, at their stage of development, were able to express this recognition only concretely. Patriarchy, in its turn, has been no more able to go beyond the concrete.

The more we recognize the nonmateriality of the body, of nature, the more conscious it becomes. This consciousness is what we call *soul,* a soul no longer forced into exile. William Blake depicts this in his drawing *The Reunion of the Soul and the Body.* This reanimation of the body allows us to enter consciously into the flow of life. We can dance in the flames, dying and being reborn in every moment, because the fear that cuts us off from life has been eliminated. The soul knows its immortality, and does not fear death as the ego does. Living from the point of soul consciousness allows us to live fully in the NOW.

There is, today, a gradual shift away from the patriarchal logos of decisions based on statistics and administered from above to decisions made cooperatively that include the feelings of the people involved. Corporations are beginning to look at their own history as part of their planning, to realize that people on the "front line" often have a better idea of what will work in their own sphere of competence than those in the executive suite. People have an investment in their own lives and when their feeling is evoked in a constructive way, creative solutions become possible.

True interdependence, however, is possible only if other factors come into harmony. Conscious perception, seeing with the heart—and the interdependence this leads to—gives rise to creative possibilities, because it opens us to what Jung called *synchronicity.*

Synchronicity, as Jung understood it, is not ordinary chance or meaningless coincidence, but is closely allied to the archetypes. "In Jung's thinking, the activation or awakening of an archetype re-

The Reunion of Body and Soul
by William Blake.

leases a great deal of power, analogous to splitting the atom. This power, in the immediate vicinity of the psychoid process from which the archetype takes its origin, is the catalyst for the synchronistic event. . . . The activation of an archetype releases patterning forces that can restructure events both in the psyche and in the external world. The restructuring proceeds in an acausal fashion, operating outside the laws of causality."[25]

The release of energy from the archetypal source leaves a person with a feeling of numinosity or authenticity. Because the archetype, as a psychoid energy, rises from both body and spirit, its effects will be felt in the external and internal world. To understand how this works in our lives, we could draw some columns on a page and label them with such headings as important dreams, events, books that resonated, meetings with significant people, and so on. Down the left-hand side, we could put a period of time we want to look at, for example, 1 to 10 years. By looking over time at the events, books, dreams, or significant people we have met, it is possible to see the pattern that gave rise to our present position. In doing this, most people begin to realize that much of what has happened to them is the result of synchronicity. We went to the wrong place, but met the right person. We were wondering about something, and the right book fell into our hands. The happening was acausal. Who, we may ask, is the observer in this process? Whose consciousness makes it happen?

Jung developed this notion of acausality or synchronicity along with Wolfgang Pauli. "Indeed, Pauli and Jung proposed that the traditional triad of classical physics, space, time, and causality be supplemented by a fourth element, synchronicity, producing a tetrad. This fourth element operates in an acausal fashion, representing the polar opposite of causality."[26]

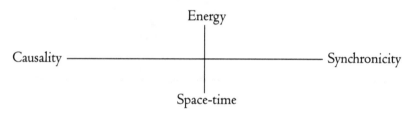

Here is a simple version of Wolf's diagram of this tetrad. Explaining it, Wolf writes, "To the extent that we know where and when events occur, we cannot say with what energy these events take place. So much is said by the uncertainty principle."[27]

> Thus space-time and energy are complementary descriptors of events, and in a similar manner synchronicity and causality are complementary to each other. They deal, just as energy and space-time do, with events. These events are marked by their psychic component as well as their physical component. Here is the crux of the matter: our Western consciousness has taken as meaningful only those events that are labeled causal. By losing track of or dismissing this other dimension of meaningfulness, we actually become unconscious of much of the universe.[28]

This "other dimension" is often revealed to us in dreams, active imagination, and the creative process in any art form. Our failure to understand nonlocal causality in physics and synchronicity can take the power of the archetypal energy into very negative implications for the world.

At a cultural level, the horrendous consequences of ignoring what the Black Madonna symbolizes became all too clear in Nazi Germany. In his sobering study of the Third Reich, Morris Berman writes, "All evil was dark and animalistic, all good was blond and spiritual. The dark forces worked to promote chaos; the light, to promote order."[29] Berman points out that in periods of overpowering transition, anxiety, economic depression, times that produce weak ego structures, a charismatic man like Hitler can fill yearning people with a dream of becoming gods, and if he supports that dream with ritual and images that evoke somatic response, masses of people will become captured by the light and blindly obey their leader.

We live in fearful transitional times. Archetypal energies are exploding all around us, energies strong enough to collide with our sense of personal responsibility. If we have dreams of Hitler or S.S. troops, we need to ask ourselves where these brutal and barbarous men surfaced in our thoughts and actions during the past twenty-four hours. We need also to remember that cults are forming at our own back door. Where energy has no link with a cherishing connection, it quickly bonds with evil. Where energy is surrounded by a free flow of trust, it perceives life through the eyes of love. Where opposites are polarized instead of held in balance, trouble erupts. What manifests depends on the eyes that are perceiving. Intentionality determines the outcome of most of the situations in our lives.

My own interest in synchronicity was awakened about fourteen years ago in connection with a friend, whom I will call Jane, who was in the last stages of Alzheimer's disease. She had been a vibrant, intelligent, caring woman who, at sixty-four, was reduced to an empty shell, staring vacantly into space, unable to recognize anyone or do anything for herself. On two successive nights, I had significant dreams in which Jane appeared, giving me very salient messages about my future path. On the second morning, her nurse phoned me and suggested that, perhaps, I should visit her. Apparently, two days earlier, Jane had found an old photograph of the two of us. She had put it on the dresser and had sat staring at it. Even in the absence of mental capacities, the soul can communicate in ways we know nothing about in our current models of reality.

Three or four months after this event, I was traveling for two weeks in the States. Being relatively young, Jane was in quite good physical health and I thought little of going away. Toward the end of my travels, I was in a hotel and went out to get some papers I had left in the car. It was about 8 PM and I looked up to see the "first star." I remembered rather playfully the old wish "star light, star bright." Then I became more centered and reflective, thinking, "What would I really wish for above all else?" At that moment I was seized with enormous love and gratitude. I thought of Jane and prayed that she might be released from the indignity of her terrible suffering.

I continued my trip, and two days later went to Virginia Beach to spend a couple of days at the ocean before flying home. Friends who knew my plans tracked me down and left a message there asking me to call Toronto. I called, and was told that Jane had suddenly and unexpectedly fallen into a coma and had died three hours later. I was a little startled when the nurse said that this had happened two nights earlier. I asked when she had fallen into the coma. "Oh, about 8 PM," she said. The funeral was the next morning, and I could not get back in time. Somehow it seemed unnecessary. The connection was present, had always been present. I went out and swam in the ocean, merging my tears with the waves. The ego grieves but the soul knows that death is only a ripple in the ocean of time.

The reason that the notion of synchronicity has been so difficult for us to grasp is that it is linked to the feminine principle. "The left-hand side [of the diagram, that is, causality] corresponds to what we would call memory—the linking up of events that are not occurring now with events that are. This process necessarily takes us out of the here and now and into our heads—our intellect so to speak."[30] Unlike causality, synchronicity is affective rather than intellectual. "It is a realization of a deep connection that can immediately be broken by logical dictate. . . . To the extent that we say left-hand-side events become deathlike as a result of analysis, right-hand-side events become alive as a result of experience—coming to our senses."[31] Synchronicity and acausality are the Goddess in action. Synchronicity rises out of the collective unconscious or the world soul, which contains all possibilities, the proliferating womb of Sophia.

In Europe, during the Middle Ages, this proliferating womb of Sophia was known by the Latin word *Sapientia*. In *Psyche and Matter*, von Franz, discussing the relationship between synchronicity and *Sapientia*, writes:

The *Sapientia Dei* is a kind of primordial unity, a single-formed image that proliferates itself into numberless primordial forms, which at the same time nonetheless remain within the primordial unity. (Today we would call these the archetypes.) The *Sapientia* contains higher mysteries than mere belief. As a feminine figure, it has more to do with feeling, a factor that we must also take into account in connection with Jung's idea of synchronicity, because the experience of meaning is not only a result of thought but also something connected with feeling.[32]

The medieval philosophers saw this unity as love. Marsilio Ficinio, for example, writes, "All the parts of the world, like the limbs of a living being, are dependent upon the *one* love, and are bound to one another by natural affinity . . . and that is the real magic."[33] Giordano Bruno "compares this love that runs like a current through everything with a lightning bolt (fulgur) or a light and also calls it 'the world soul' in the 'spirit of the universe.'"[34] Von Franz affirms that *Sapientia* represents "the psychic total interconnectedness of the universe through a spirit of love."[35]

The purpose of a myth is to locate human experience in the largest possible community, the community of life in relation to the Divine. Without a genuine mythology, human experience remains imprisoned within boundaries that are exclusive rather than inclusive, boundaries that may shrink to solitary confinement. Now that the planet has become, in essence, one country, the necessity of finding a way to relate human experience at the personal level to the entire community of life becomes critical. The role of the Dark Goddess at this moment of mutation is crucial. Her Presence is essential to the emergence of a global community that includes not only human relationships but the relationship of human beings to every form of life on the planet and to the planet itself in relation to the Divine.

In quietly bringing our thoughts and feelings about the Feminine together, let us return to some of our original questions: Who is the Goddess? What are her attributes? Who is she as Mother, Virgin, Crone? How does she relate to the Masculine? If we throw ourselves into the flames and dance in the refining fire, how will our everyday lives be changed? If we really do believe she holds the whole world in her love, how do we live that sacramental truth at our center?

If we concentrate on Edvard Munch's painting entitled *Madonna*, we may find within ourselves new questions, new answers. The image is both electrifying and disquieting. It leaves us pondering the mystery of the contemporary Virgin.

Munch has captured a fleeting NOW. Her body vibrates with sexual passion and not sexual only, but with the hidden Wisdom that is released in the rites of lovemaking.

Munch has written about this moment:

> The pause as all the world stops in its path. Moonlight glides over your face filled with all the earth's beauty and pain. . . . Thus, new life reaches out its hand to death. The chain is forged that binds the thousands of generations that have died to the thousands of generations to come.[36]

Madonna by Edvard Munch

She has entered into Wisdom, and is poised in that moment of
total fulfillment and total self-containment before she moves back
into life. Sophia shines through the transparent body, precarious, as
it holds the balance with spirit and matter. The subtle body of the
observer resonates—soul to soul.

Her body rests in the swirls of life around it. The scarlet halo
that crowns her flowing dark hair, and the bits of scarlet around her
suggest the flames of passion in which she is still burning. Here is the
reality of matter, the reality of the body, the reality of the rhythms of
nature and shimmering light. Here is Mary Magdalene purified
through her earlier excesses, coming through the flames of lust and
purified in those flames. And here is the Virgin Mary within whose
womb lies the sacred power to transform seed into fruit. This is a
moment of birth, death, physical and spiritual ecstasy. Here is soul
in body—feminine Being in its naked vulnerability.

And here is the anguish of the feminine. Her veiled lids suggest
inner rememberings and inner imaginings, as does her rounded belly.
Does she in this moment feel herself transformed—forever transformed, transformed by the new consciousness that will take shape
within her and come forth in the fullness of time? Can she bear the
fruit?

This Madonna has a vision of her child, or of herself, in the
deep left-hand corner of the painting—a tiny skeletal child like the
one who appears in dreams in a garbage bin into which it has thrown
itself. When the dreamer asks, "Why are you there?" the child replies, "Because you would have killed me." And most of us can pin-
point exactly when our child went into hiding, and the driven times
in our lives when we have left the waif to die. That is the soul child
that yearns to connect with us in our dreams.

Equally disturbing is the sperm, floating on its ectoplasmic way
around her periphery. Some strength is not in the phallus. Some
conflict with the masculine is unresolved. Some terror fills the embry-
onic child. The opposites are not yet joined without opposition. Will
the fetus reach maturity? Will the new consciousness be born? Will
the creative phallus within herself be strong enough to release the
child into life?

And if we turn the picture upside down, the eyes look into ours
with unspeakable wisdom, unspeakable beauty, unspeakable horror.
We feel we have lifted a veil we ought not to have touched, and turn

the picture right side up. But infinity still rolls through us because the truth that is in our cells is in her cells. They resonate true, too true.

This is a paradoxical Madonna, much more an expression of soul because she is so utterly grounded. This body carries the Black Madonna's energy. It is not concretized matter, body without feeling. In her, metaphor lives, energy transforms. Soul is in every cell, beauty in its naked essence.

Somehow this painting captures the Feminine in time, a Now in eternity. The angle of her body and her upturned head, the bare outline of her raised arms suggest a figure on a cross, an inner cross. Filled with the rapture of her love, her body still vibrating in ecstasy, she at this moment may be filled with new life—the moment of surrender that opens her to an unknown future. She echoes something of Botticelli's Venus rising up out of the sea, something of Bernini's Saint Teresa transcendent in religious rapture, something of da Vinci's Madonna veiled in her female depths. Each of these icons captures a moment when the Divine intersects the human. Each holds the tension between saint and whore, and the yearning of the lonely soul. What makes Munch's Madonna modern is the immediacy of the body—the boldness, the sweetness, the vulnerability, the divine fire, the knowing in every cell. Wisdom embodied. Sexuality and spirituality seem to be one in this picture. And yet, the tiny soul cowers in the corner wondering whether it is safe to come in. This is a painting in which the elements—womb, sperm, child—interrogate rather than affirm each other. Though they belong together, they are not yet one. In their separation, they speak directly to our unconscious. They disturb in order to illumine. This Madonna is not a victim. She embodies a new configuration. That configuration accepts death as a friend, knowing that nothing can change until the universal shifting is firmly grounded in somatic reality.

The Goddess is the unspeakable wisdom that grows into the very cells of the body. She lives with this sacramental truth at her center: the beauty and the horror of the whole of life are blazing in Her love. She is dancing in the flames.

Notes

Introduction

1. Fred Alan Wolf, *The Dreaming Universe* (New York: Simon and Schuster, 1944), p. 16.
2. Carlos Suares, *The Qabala Trilogy* (Boston: Shambhala Publications, 1985), p. 285.
3. Robert Graves, *The Song of Songs* (New York: Clarkson N. Potter, 1973), p. 9.
4. Ibid., p. 15.
5. Susan Cady, Marian Ronan, and Hal Taussig, *Sophia: The Future of Feminine Spirituality* (San Francisco: Harper and Row, 1986), pp. 117–118. The authors point out that many of the biblical references to Sophia appear only in Roman Catholic editions of the Bible.
6. Proverbs 8:4–11.

Chapter 1. The Fierce and Loving Goddess

1. Vivekananda, cited in David Kingsley, *The Sword and the Flute* (Berkeley: University of California Press, 1975), p. 145.
2. Ibid., p. 110.
3. Ken Wilber, *Up From Eden* (Boulder: Shambhala Publications, 1983), p. 42.
4. Ibid., pp. 122–123.
5. Percy B. Shelley, *Prometheus Unbound*, in David Reisman and Sharon B. Powers (eds.), *Shelley's Poetry and Prose* (New York: W. W. Norton, 1971).
6. Wilber, *Up From Eden*, p. 123.
7. Ibid., p. 126.
8. Book of Wisdom, from Elizabeth Johnson, "Jesus the Wisdom of God," in *Ephemerides Theologicae Lovanienses* (December 1985): 266.
9. Cyme, from Ibid., p. 270.
10. Ibid., pp. 268–269.
11. Proverbs 8:11.
12. Proverbs 9:1–6.
13. Wilber, *Up From Eden*, p. 142.
14. Ibid., p. 184.

15. Robert Goldstein, *The Encyclopedia of Human Behavior* (New York: Doubleday, 1970), vol. I, p. 340.

16. Gloria Steinem, *Moving Beyond Words* (New York: Simon and Schuster, 1994), p. 23.

17. Wilber, *Up From Eden*, p. 238.

18. Carol Solomon, unpublished personal papers.

19. Barbara Tuchman, *A Distant Mirror: The Calamitous Fourteenth Century* (New York: Alfred Knopf, 1978), p. 123.

20. E. F. Schumacher, *A Guide for the Perplexed* (New York: Harper and Row, 1977), p. 54.

21. Thomas Berry, "Planetary Management," Riverdale Papers VI (New York, 1979), p. 6.

22. Today, however, the body is plagued by viruses that are so powerful that, doctors tell us, we are moving into a "postantibiotic age." The immune system is breaking down under the onslaught of pollutants, toxic [contaminated?] food and water, and the rigid control of an overtaxed body that needs to dance.

23. Philippe Aries, *Western Attitudes toward Death* (Baltimore: Johns Hopkins University Press, 1974), p. 57.

24. Julia O'Faolain and Lauro Martines (eds.), *Not in God's Image* (New York: Harper and Row, 1973), p. 209.

25. Saint John Chrysostom in ibid., p. 138.

26. Rosemary Ruether, "Sexism and Liberation: the Historical Experience," in Eugene C. Bianchi and Rosemary Ruether (eds.), *From Machismo to Mutuality: Essays on Sexism and Woman-Man Liberation* (New York: Paulist Press, 1976), p. 15.

27. *Gesta Trevirorum*, from O'Faolain and Martines, op. cit., p. 215.

28. Ibid., p. 209.

29. Peter Giovacchini in Christopher Lasch, *The Culture of Narcissism* (New York: Warner Books, 1979), p. 88.

30. Michael Beldock in ibid., p. 89.

31. Jacob Needleham, *A Sense of the Cosmos* (New York: E. P. Dutton, 1965), p. 47.

32. Tsultrim Allione, *Women of Wisdom* (London: Routledge and Kegan Paul, 1984), p. 29.

33. Ibid., p. 29.

34. John Briggs and F. David Peat, *Turbulent Mirror* (New York: Harper and Row, 1989), p. 22.

35. Allione, *Women of Wisdom*, pp. 29–31.

36. Ibid., p. 33.

37. Ibid., p. 34.

38. Ibid., p. 34.

39. Ibid., p. 35.

40. Ibid., p. 35.

41. Perera, *Descent to the Goddess* (Toronto: Inner City Books, 1981), p. 40.

42. *Baha'i Prayers* (Wilmette, Ill.: Baha'i Publishing Trust, 1885).

43. Enoch I:42.

1. Tsultrim Allione, *Women of Wisdom* (London: Routledge and Kegan Paul, 1984), p. 37.
2. Ibid., pp. 37–38.
3. Ibid., p. 38.
4. David Whyte, *Fire in the Earth* (Langley, Wash.: Many Rivers Press, 1992), p. 51.
5. Allione, *Women of Wisdom*, p. 41.
6. Ibid., p. 41.
7. Barbara Walker, *The Crone* (San Francisco: Harper and Row, 1985), p. 51.
8. Ibid., p. 51.
9. John A. Wilson, *The Burden of Egypt* (Chicago: University of Chicago Press, 1951), p. 48.
10. Joseph Campbell, *The Inner Reaches of Outer Space* (New York: Alfred Van Der Marck Editions, 1986), p. 65.
11. Wisdom 2:1–4, 6:10–11, the Confraternity–Douay version.
12. Ibid., 6:12–13, 17.
13. Ibid., 6:24.
14. Sir E. A. Wallis Budge, *The Dwellers on the Nile* (New York: Benjamin Blom, 1972), p. 147.
15. Wisdom 6:27.
16. Nathan Schwartz-Salant, *Narcissism and Character Transformation* (Toronto: Inner City Books, 1982), p. 121.
17. T. S. Eliot, *Four Quartets* (London: Faber and Faber, 1954), pp. 32–33.
18. Rollo May, *Love and Will* (New York: W. W. Norton, 1969), p. 223.
19. Ibid., p. 234.
20. Paul Tillich, in ibid., p. 244, from *The Courage to Be* (New Haven: Yale University Press, 1952), pp. 81–82.
21. Schwartz-Salant, op. cit. p. 80.
22. Ken Wilber, *Up From Eden* (Boulder: Shambhala Publications, 1983), p. 249.
23. Saint John of the Cross, *Dark Night of the Soul*, Book II, i. Peers I, p. 375. Quoted in P. Marie-Eugene, O.C.D., *I Am a Daughter of the Church* (Chicago: Fides Publishers Association, 1955).
24. Marie Louise von Franz, *On Dreams and Death* (Boston and London: Shambhala Publications, 1986), pp. 147–148.
25. Ibid., p. 144, from *Letters*, v. 2, p. 45.
26. Ibid., p. 144.
27. Ibid., p. 149, from *Letters*, v. 1, p. 117ff.
28. Ibid., p. 149.
29. Ibid., pp. 152–153, from David Bohm, *Wholeness and the Implicate Order* (London: Routledge and Kegan Paul, 1980), pp. 147ff.
30. Ibid., p. 153.
31. Sri Chinmoy, *Kundalini: The Mother Power* (Jamaica, N.Y.: Agni Press, 1974), p. ii.

32. Jalaja Bonheim, "Befriending the Serpent," *Yoga Journal* (January–February 1993): 56.
33. Ibid., p. 56.
34. Ibid., p. 56.
35. Chinmoy, *Kundalini*, p. iv.
36. Marion Woodman, *The Pregnant Virgin* (Toronto: Inner City Books, 1985), p. 109.
37. Arianna Stassinopoulos and Roloff Beny, *The Gods of Greece* (New York: Harry Abrams, 1983), p. 99, from Kazantzahis in *The Odyssey*.
38. Ibid., p. 100.
39. Ecclesiasticus 51:20.

Chapter 3. Telling It Like It Is

1. William Blake, *Proverbs of Hell*, in David Erdman (ed.), *The Complete Poetry and Prose of William Blake* (Berkeley: University of California Press, 1982), p. 37.
2. Carol Cohn, "Sex and Death in the Rational World of Defense Intellectuals," paper published by the Center for Psychological Studies in the Nuclear Age, Cambridge, Mass., 1987, p. 16.
3. Ibid., p. 33.
4. Ibid., p. 6.
5. Ibid., p. 8.
6. Ibid., p. 9.
7. John Rowan, *The Horned God* (London and New York: Routledge and Kegan Paul, 1987), p. 94.
8. Ibid., pp. 85–86.

Chapter 4. And a Crone Shall Lead Them

1. Marie Louise von Franz, *Projection and Re-Collection in Jungian Psychology: Reflections of the Soul* (LaSalle and London: Open Court, 1980), pp. 125–126.
2. Ibid., p. 128.
3. Ibid., p. 128.
4. Owing to limitations of space, important details must, unfortunately, be left out. For the complete story and an excellent analysis, see Marie Louise von Franz, *The Golden Ass of Apuleius* (Boston: Shambhala Publications, 1992).
5. Arianna Stassinopoulos and Roloff Beny, *The Gods of Greece* (New York: Harry Abrams, 1983), p. 80.
6. Ibid., p. 85.
7. Barbara Walker, *The Crone* (San Francisco: Harper and Row, 1985), p. 30.
8. Ibid., p. 29.
9. Ibid., p. 29.
10. Stassinopoulos and Beny, *The Gods of Greece*, p. 161.
11. Ibid., p. 164.
12. Ibid., p. 162.
13. Janice Turner, "Teenage girls crave respect, support, national poll shows," *The Toronto Star* (March 12, 1992): A1.

14. Marion Woodman, *The Pregnant Virgin* (Toronto: Inner City Books, 1985), p. 63.
15. J. C. Cooper, *An Illustrated Encyclopedia of Traditional Symbols* (London: Thames and Hudson, 1982), p. 188.
16. Shakespeare, *Antony and Cleopatra*, Act V, Sc ii, ll. 290–92.
17. C. G. Jung, *Alchemical Studies* (Princeton: Princeton University Press, 1976, Bollingen Series XX), *Collected Works* 13, para. 38.
18. For a complete analysis of *The Handless Maiden* see Marie Louise von Franz, *The Feminine in Fairytales* (Dallas: Spring Publications, 1988), pp. 70–78.
19. Clarissa Pinkola-Estés, *Women Who Run with the Wolves* (New York: Ballantine Books, 1992), p. 449.
20. David Whyte, *Fire in the Earth* (Langley, Wash.: Many Rivers Press, 1992), p. 35.
21. Woodman, *The Pregnant Virgin*, p. 63.
22. Ibid., p. 63.
23. See Daniel's wild man dream, p. 106, also James's dream p. 122. For a thorough exploration of the wild man, see Robert Bly, *Iron John* (New York: Addison-Wesley, 1990). For further discussion of the evolving masculine in women, see Marion Woodman, *The Ravaged Bridegroom* (Toronto: Inner City Books, 1990) and *Leaving My Father's House* (Boston: Shambhala, 1992).

Chapter 5. The Rose in the Fire

1. M. A. Shaaber (ed.), *Selected Poems of John Donne* (New York: Appleton Century Crofts, 1958), pp. 104–105.
2. Friedrich Nietzsche, "The Use and Abuse of History," in *Thoughts out of Season, Part II* (New York: Russell and Russell, 1964), p. 7.
3. Carl G. Jung, "On the Nature of the Psyche," *The Structure and Dynamics of the Psyche*, trans. R. F. C. Hull (London: Routledge and Kegan Paul, 1960), *Collected Works* 8, para. 418.
4. James Lynch, *The Language of the Heart* (New York: Basic Books, 1985), pp. 26–27.
5. For a full discussion of these conclusions, see ibid., "The Hidden Dialogue," pp. 202–240.
6. Carl G. Jung, "The Personal and the Collective Unconscious," *Two Essays on Analytical Psychology, Collected Works* 7, para. 105.
7. Thomas Merton, *Zen and the Birds of Appetite* (New York: New Directions, 1968), p. 1.

Chapter 6. Chaos and Creativity

1. Adapted from a Shaker melody by Sydney Carter, 1915.
2. Fritjof Capra, *The Tao of Physics* (Great Britain: Fontana/Collins, 1976), p. 236.
3. David Kingsley, *The Sword and the Flute* (Berkeley: University of California Press, 1975), p. 122.
4. Ibid., pp. 134–135.
5. Ibid., p. 135.

6. C. G. Jung, "On the Nature of the Psyche," *The Structure and Dynamics of the Psyche*, trans. R. F. C. Hull (London: Routledge and Kegan Paul, 1960), *Collected Works* 8, para. 418.

7. To quote Ms. Pert directly, "My basic speculation here is that neuropeptides provide the physiological basis for the emotions. As my colleagues and I argued in a recent paper in the *Journal of Immunology*: The striking pattern of neuropeptide receptor distribution in mood-regulating areas of the brain, as well as their role in mediating communication through the whole organism, makes neuropeptides the obvious candidates for the biochemical mediation of emotion. It may be too that each neuropeptide biases information processing uniquely when occupying receptors at nodal points with the brain and body. If so, then each neuropeptide may evoke a unique "tone" that is equivalent to a mood state.

   "In the beginning of my work, I matter-of-factly presumed that emotions were in the head or the brain. Now I would say they are really in the body as well. They are expressed in the body and are part of the body. I can no longer make a strong distinction between the brain and the body." Adapted for publication by Harris Dienstfrey and reproduced under the title, "The material basis of emotions: the binding tie between body and mind is a dialog of opiate chemicals," in *The Whole Earth Review* (Summer 1988) (no. 3): 110.

8. Ibid., p. 112.

9. Shakespeare, *Julius Caesar*, Act 5, sc. I, ll. 115–119.

10. Thomas N. Johnson (ed.), *The Complete Poems of Emily Dickinson* (Boston: Little, Brown, 1960), no. 1732.

11. This insightful paragraph was written by Julianna Switaj.

12. T. S. Eliot, *The Love Song of J. Alfred Prufrock*, in M. Mack, L. Dean, and W. Frost (eds.), *Modern Poetry* (New York: Prentice-Hall, 1955), lines 104–105.

13. I am grateful to our friend David Kemp for letting me use this journal entry and for sharing his experience with us that Sunday morning.

14. William Blake, *Auguries of Innocence*, in David Erdman (ed.), *The Complete Poetry and Prose of William Blake* (Berkeley: University of California Press, 1982), p. 490.

15. Ibid., p. 127.

16. For a detailed discussion of the building of the container, see Marion Woodman, *The Pregnant Virgin* (Toronto: Inner City Books, 1985).

17. See Woodman, *The Pregnant Virgin*.

18. Margaret Atwood, "Girl Without Hands," *Morning in the Burned House* (Toronto: McClelland & Stewart, 1995), p. 113.

19. See Larry Dossey, M.D., *Healing Words: The Power of Prayer and the Practice of Medicine* (San Francisco: HarperSanFrancisco, 1993).

20. See Paul Davies, *The Cosmic Blueprint* (New York: Simon and Schuster, 1989), pp. 176–177.

21. Ibid., pp. 152–153.

22. The following statement by Candace Pert implies the reversibility of the transformation between body chemistry and emotions that is suggested here:

"When we document the key role that the emotions, expressed through neuro-peptide molecules, play in affecting the body, it will become clear how emotions can be a key to the understanding of disease." See Pert and Dienstfrey, "The material basis of emotions," p. 112.

Chapter 7. *Where Three Dreams Cross*

1. Percy B. Shelley, *Ozymandias*, in David Reinman and Sharon B. Powers (eds.), *Shelley's Poetry and Prose* (New York: W. W. Norton, 1971), p. 103.
2. Luke 17:20, 21.
3. Paul Tillich, *Systematic Theology* (Chicago: University of Chicago Press, 1963), vol. I, p. 139.
4. William Butler Yeats, *The Second Coming*, in M. Mack, L. Dean, and W. Frost (eds.), *Modern Poetry* (New Jersey: Prentice Hall, 1961), vol. 7, p. 75.
5. *The Toronto Star* (July 29, 1994), Section E, p. 1.
6. Morris Berman, *Coming to Our Senses: Body and Spirit in the Hidden History of the West* (New York: Simon and Schuster, 1990), p. 305.
7. Danah Zohar, *The Quantum Self* (New York: William Morrow, 1990), p. 101.
8. See Heisenberg's Uncertainty Principle, enunciated by Werner Heisenberg in 1927, which states that at the quantum level there are absolute limits to the accuracy with which pairs of physical quantities can be measured, the implication being that initial data cannot be specified with sufficient precision to apply the laws of classical physics.
9. For further discussion of the implications of the interaction between the observer and the observed, see the following section in this chapter, "The Eye of the Beholder."
10. The concept of complementarity was introduced by Niels Bohr in 1928 to explain the apparently contradictory behavior of light. Depending on the experiment, light sometimes behaves like a wave and sometimes like a particle. The two differing sets of properties cannot be observed simultaneously. Bohr suggested that neither behavior by itself was sufficient to understand the nature of light at the subatomic level. The two complemented each other, and must both be taken into account.
11. C. G. Jung, *Memories, Dreams, Reflections* (New York: Pantheon Books, 1963), p. 354.
12. Ibid., p. 353.
13. John Milton, *Paradise Lost*, Book XII, line 611, from Merritt Y. Hughes (ed.), *John Milton: Complete Poems and Major Prose* (Indianapolis: Odyssey Books, Bobbs-Merrill, 1976).
14. Ibid., Book VII, lines 8–12.
15. Ibid., Book XII, lines 648–9.
16. Danah Zohar, op. cit., pp. 44–45.
17. Stuart Hameroff suggests that the microtubules within brain cells might be the seat of consciousness. The microtubules are long, thin, hollow tubes of protein within the neuron. He found that under the influence of an anesthetic gas, the microtubules stop functioning. He concludes that the stopping of

their activity is what brings about the state of unconsciousness in anesthesia. For a more detailed discussion, see David H. Freedman, "Quantum Consciousness," *Discover* (June 1994): 88–97.

18. Refer to the work of Candace Pert, discussed in chapter 6.

19. See Roger Penrose, *Shadows of the Mind: The Search for the Missing Science of Consciousness* (Oxford: Oxford University Press, 1994).

20. Fred Alan Wolf, *The Dreaming Universe* (New York: Simon and Schuster, 1994), p. 285.

21. Wolfgang Pauli, *Collected Works* 8, para. 439, note 130.

22. We are indebted to Fred Alan Wolf for transcribing these dreams from the archives of Aniela Jaffe in Zurich, Switzerland, drawing as well on unpublished material including Pauli's letters to von Franz and Emma Jung.

23. Wisdom 6:27.

24. Fred Alan Wolf, op. cit., p. 297.

25. Allan Combs and Mark Holland, *Synchronicity, Science, Myth, and the Trickster* (New York: Paragon House), p. 74.

26. Ibid., p. 75.

27. Wolf, op. cit., p. 57.

28. Ibid., p. 57.

29. Berman, op. cit., p. 261.

30. Wolf, op. cit., p. 58.

31. Ibid., p. 58.

32. Von Franz, *Psyche and Matter*, p. 194–195.

33. Marsilio Ficino, in ibid., pp. 196–197, from *Giordano Bruno and the Hermetic Tradition* (London, 1964).

34. Giordano Bruno, in ibid., p. 197, from *Giordano Bruno and the Hermetic Tradition* (London, 1964).

35. Ibid., p. 193.

36. Noel Cobb with Eva Loewe (eds.), "Sphinx I." *Journal for Archetypal Psychology and the Arts* (London, 1988), p. 55.

Credits

The authors thank the following publishers and rights holders for permission to reprint material copyrighted or controlled by them:

Harcourt Brace & Company and Faber and Faber Limited for the extracts from "The Dry Salvages," and from "Burnt Norton" and "East Coker" from "Four Quartets," by T. S. Eliot, from *Collected Poems 1909–1962* by T. S. Eliot. Copyright 1943 by T. S. Eliot and renewed 1971 by Esme Valerie Eliot, reprinted by permission of Harcourt Brace & Company.

Harvard University Press for extracts from the poems of Emily Dickinson. Reprinted by permission of the publishers and the Trustees of Amherst College from *The Poems of Emily Dickinson*, Thomas H. Johnson, ed., Cambridge, Mass.: The Belknap Press of Harvard University Press, copyright © 1951, 1955, 1979, 1983 by the President and Fellows of Harvard College.

University of California Press for "The Cry of Innana," from Samuel Kramer, *From the Poetry of Sumer: Creation, Glorification, Adoration.* © 1979 The Regents of the University of California.

W. W. Norton & Company for the extract from *A Grain of Mustard Seed* by May Sarton. Copyright © 1971 by May Sarton. Reprinted by permission of W. W. Norton & Company, Inc.

New Directions Publishing Corporation for the extract from "The Goddess" from *Collected Earlier Poems 1940–1960* by Denise Levertov. Copyright © 1957 by Denise Levertov. Reprinted by Permission of New Directions Publishing Corporation.

Many Rivers Press for the excerpt from *Fire in the Earth* by David Whyte.

HarperCollins Publishers for "Passing an Orchard by Train"